ANFN

CANBY PUBLIC LIBRARY
292 N. HOLLY
CANBY, OR 97013

780.23
DES

P9-DUB-216

Creative Careers in MUSIC

Josquin des Pres and Mark Landsman

Second Edition

**ALLWORTH
PRESS**
NEW YORK

© 2000, 2004 Josquin des Pres and Mark Landsman

All rights reserved. Copyright under Berne Copyright Convention, Universal
Copyright Convention, and Pan-American Copyright Convention. No part of this
book may be reproduced, stored in a retrieval system, or transmitted in any form,
or by any means, electronic, mechanical, photocopying, recording, or otherwise,
without prior permission of the publisher.

05   04   03   02   01   00   5   4   3   2

Published by Allworth Press
An imprint of Allworth Communications
10 East 23rd Street, New York, NY 10010

Cover design by Derek Bacchus

Page composition/typography by SR Desktop Services, Ridge, NY

ISBN: 1-58115-382-1

Library of Congress Cataloging-in-Publication Data
des Pres, Josquin.
      Creative careers in music/by Josquin des Pres and Mark Landsman.—2nd ed.
          p.   cm.
      Includes bibliographical references and index.
      ISBN 1-58115-382-1 (pbk.)
      1. Music—Vocational guidance.   I. Landsman, Mark.   II. Title.

   ML3795.D356   2004
   780'.23'73—dc22

                                                            2004015077

Printed in Canada

CONTENTS

Preface to the Second Edition v
Introduction—A Career in the Music Industry vii

PART I   THE PUBLISHING BUSINESS
Chapter 1   Copyrights and Royalties—Your Property Rights 3
Chapter 2   Publishing Deals—Earning a Living from Your Songs 15

PART II   THE RECORD BUSINESS
Chapter 3   Major Labels—Bigger Is (Sometimes) Better 29
Chapter 4   Independent Record Labels—"Indies" 43
Chapter 5   The Do-It-Yourself (DIY) Approach—A Career on
             Your Own Label 57
Chapter 6   Touring—Road Rigor 77

PART III   THE VARIED CAREERS IN THE MUSIC INDUSTRY
             AND WHAT THEY ENTAIL
Chapter 7   Songwriter 91
Chapter 8   Solo Artist—On Your Own 103
Chapter 9   Group Member—It's a Team Effort 117
Chapter 10   Studio Musician—In the Studio and Elsewhere 131
Chapter 11   Producer or Engineer 143

PART IV   CAREER DEVELOPMENT
Chapter 12   Making a Name for Yourself—Earning a Reputation 159
Chapter 13   Professional Help—Lawyers, Managers, Agents,
             and Others 173

PART V   CHANGES IN THE MUSIC BUSINESS
Chapter 14   The Music Industry in Transition—The Future Is Now 191

Notes 213
Index 221

PREFACE TO THE SECOND EDITION

In the four years since the publication of the first edition of *Creative Careers in Music*, the music industry has seen vast change. Other industries can claim that this is also true for them: consumers demand more choice than ever before; competition drives technological and business-model innovation; globalization expands markets while offering new challenges. Sure, industries like cars, computers, telecommunications, and medicine look different than just a few years ago. But they're still recognizable.

Not so for the music industry, which has changed far more, and more rapidly, than any other business whose product is an everyday presence in our lives. Its arc of transformation extends far beyond the boldest predictions made just a few years back—one of those rare cases in which the reality exceeds the hype. Better described as upheaval, the pace is not just faster, but exponentially faster. Due principally, but not entirely, to maturing digital technologies, music is now created, marketed, distributed, sold, and enjoyed differently than it was four years ago.

The direction and nature of these differences were foreseeable when we wrote the first edition of *Creative Careers in Music*. We discussed trends and even made a few predictions. What has prompted a revised edition in four short years is that the sheer magnitude of change—initiated more by artists and consumers than by the industry itself—has been so great.

Revolution is always a threat to established ways. For instance, in the case of persons seeking musical careers, studio musician and staff songwriter are not growth industries the way they were in 1955. Yet, in the big picture, opportunities to create will be more plentiful than ever. Musicians must recognize that their prospects are much different they were twenty years ago, or even four years ago. We believe this revised edition will provide a clear take to help musicians stay in the game.

Introduction—A Career in the Music Industry

Firefighters, doctors, soldiers, and others have to follow a fairly set track to move into their occupations—rules, regulations, tests, and licenses don't leave much choice. By contrast, the path to a music career, which is no less specialized or demanding, can be much more circuitous. As we began researching this book, we noticed that people we talked to on the creative side of the music industry often didn't set out to have careers in music. Of course, there were exceptions to this generalization, but a basic pattern emerged.

The love of music, the desire to create it, is what drives people to make it the main priority in their lives. And, at a certain point, they find themselves expending so much of their time, energy, and emotional resources in music that it becomes their calling. Often, the conscious decision to pursue specific career goals follows some time after a person's actions have begun to define him. The artist is having too much fun making music to think about "a music career" in the traditional sense of apprenticeship, promotion, seniority, benefits, retirement plans, and the like.

The lack of attentiveness to the "career" side of a music career is legendary for performing artists. Routinely, they have been cheated out of their fair share of earnings, not only in arm's-length business dealings but by the very managers, agents, and companies whose income depends on their talent. Fortunately, in the last twenty-five years or so, excellent books and other resources have become available to help artists understand this complex business and find competent professionals to guide their careers.

This book is written to provide knowledge to help musicians make better informed choices, not only between various careers in the music business but also within their careers. For instance, Part I, "The Publishing Business," explains how songwriters earn money from the songs they write. It's surprising how many songwriters don't fully understand the concept of publishing royalties!

In addition, readers of this book will better understand how to survive in the continually evolving music industry by growing and changing.

THE MUSIC INDUSTRY DEFINED

For our purposes, principally to keep the topics from being too numerous and far-flung, it is necessary to limit the definition of what we mean when we speak of "the music industry." Broadly speaking, we mean the mainstream commercial popular music industry. It follows, then, that we're not going to discuss the career of a music teacher or professor at a school or college. Symphony musician, opera singer, and other classical music careers are not within the main focus of this book, although many of the same principles apply.

Therefore, our discussion of popular music concentrates on the activities by creative people within what are commonly known as the recording industry, the broadcast industry, the music publishing business, and the concert business. The end product of these activities—music you hear on commercial radio or television stations, enjoy at concerts, and find for sale as recordings at retail stores and Web sites—is popular music.

Other types of music, such as classical music and jazz, also enjoy noticeable popularity. Are they within the scope of this book? Yes, but to a lesser extent, because they constitute a much smaller amount of the market—a lot fewer careers are available. That having been said, some of the boundaries between categories are becoming blurred. For instance, "new age" music incorporates elements of jazz, pop, and classical for ever-larger numbers of listeners. General concepts of this book will apply no matter what kind of music is involved. For instance, the same copyright laws apply to jazz compositions as to pop compositions.

Undoubtedly, some musical activities fall between the cracks or slip into gray areas. For example, does this book intend to address Top 40 musicians who play at hotels or conventions, covering other people's music? That part of the music industry, like private lessons or playing in the army band, is tangential to our main scope. By the same token, musicians aren't static. It's easy to find people in the music industry, such as producers and songwriters, who started out playing in Top 40 bands. Many songwriters and musicians in originals groups also play Top 40 until they generate enough income through their own music. The subjects in this book address the interests of someone moving toward mainstream commercial popular music through other avenues.

CREATIVE CAREERS DEFINED

No matter what our jobs, creativity can enhance the product or service we provide and make work more enjoyable. Even seemingly humdrum and repetitive tasks, which don't seem to lend themselves to creativity, have room for it in subtle but meaningful ways. So, in a sense, all careers are creative.

For the purposes of this book, however, not all careers in the music industry qualify. For instance, we are not including luthiers, piano technicians, or engineers who design amplifier circuits. They help create the tools, but they don't actually create music directly. Nor do we discuss careers of record company presidents, promotion managers, or marketing specialists, even though all of these benefit from (and, to a degree, require) creativity. But, they're more within the realm of "industry" than "music."

Simply stated, the music industry careers that are the topic of this book are those in which the participants have a *direct and active* hand in creating music. Most obviously, this includes players, singers, composers, and songwriters, but it also includes producers and engineers.

Other music industry participants, such as concert lighting directors, clothing designers, album cover artists, and directors of videos, don't really participate in creating music but, rather, in its multimedia presentation and, on that basis, are excluded. (If we tried to discuss every possible career in the industry, this book would be too fat to lug around.)

There are some gray areas. For instance, thirty years ago, disc jockeys (DJs) were people who simply played records on the radio or at clubs. They would have been classified as being on the business side, not the creative side. Today, however, some disc jockeys actually "play" the record turntable as a rhythm instrument in live and recording situations, and their voice-overs are considered part of the performance. Those who do present themselves this way have come over to the creative side.

For the most part, though, the creative careers we discuss are limited to those contained in Part III (chapters 7–11)—people who sing, play, write, produce, or engineer recordings or who otherwise determine, in a hands-on manner, how music sounds when performed and recorded. When we started this book, we intended to cover career paths of arrangers and conductors, but we discovered that, although they're still around in the commercial pop music industry, they're nearly extinct. According to the information we got from industry professionals, the call for these professions will be even less in the future. Consequently, these endangered careers are not covered.

CAREER PATHS

The overwhelming majority of people we talked to on the creative side of the music industry started out in music simply as music fans or as players and singers at the "fun" level of garage band, church choir, or high school orchestra and chorus. This is as true for engineers and songwriters as it is for performing artists. They may have attempted careers as performers; they may even have enjoyed some success. Eventually, their lives' trajectories sent their talents down other avenues.

What drives this trajectory? Three things, mainly: the specific nature of talent, a personal inclination or lifestyle choice, and the marketplace. Let's examine the career of a hypothetical musician who plays keyboards. At some point, he realizes that his ears are much better than his technique ever will be. His shortcomings of talent lead him away from performance to a place where his natural tunefulness won't be limited by what he can play. He also learns that he hates being in bands anyway, because of the politics, and enjoys working by himself, writing songs. In the meantime, the market for country music has an inherent and constant need for songs.

This musician doesn't wake up one day and say, "Gee, after analyzing my talent, preferences, and the market for what I can do, I've decided to write country songs." Instead, through a series of small, incremental steps (probably while he's still doing other things, like playing in an original rock band and giving music lessons), he embarks down the road to a career. Perhaps a friend who likes one of his songs suggests he submit it to a publisher or an artist.

At some point, most people specialize—although the tendency now is to wear more hats than even five years ago. A guitarist with a bent for mixing and mastering becomes an engineer, an oboe player becomes a producer (like George Martin, who produced most of the Beatles albums), a piano player becomes a songwriter. Once these choices become paths rather than blind alleys, it behooves the musician to understand everything possible about the everyday reality of a career—what skills are required, how to develop or enhance those skills, how the industry works, what the working conditions are, how a professional is compensated and obtains jobs or contracts, and so on. The purpose of this book is to provide down-to-earth information about music careers.

It is possible (and in some cases, important) to wear several hats at once, of course: Singer-songwriter, producer-engineer, and band member-session musician are a few common examples that spring to mind. This busy role requires knowledge pertaining to each hat you wear. This also applies to musicians who change hats over time.

ORGANIZATION OF THIS BOOK

We feel it's necessary to have a strong foundation in the basic structure of the popular music industry and how it functions (anatomy and physiology, if you will) to get full measure from the descriptions and firsthand accounts of the professions, activities, and planning strategies for a career in the commercial popular music business. So, we've ordered this book so that the first two parts cover the publishing business (Part I) and the record business (Part II). Unless you have a strong background in these areas, we recommend that you read these sections first, rather than skipping directly to chapters that may seem more specifically related to your interests.

If you want to know how and why people in an industry do what they do, you need to comprehend how the industry works, where the sources of revenue are, and so on. Once this big picture begins to make sense, it's easier to focus on specific roles and functions within the industry. If, after reading Parts I and II, you want to skip around, you'll be reasonably well prepared for any chapter. So, do yourself a favor and begin at the beginning.

A NOTE ON LANGUAGE

In describing various careers, relating anecdotes, or giving examples, we typically use masculine pronouns, as in "When your manager gives you advice, you should at least listen to *him*." Please bear in mind that our doing so is merely a convention and a convenience. It shouldn't be construed to mean that women aren't present in the music industry, because that simply isn't true. Of course, wherever the stories of women musicians appear in these pages, the feminine pronouns are used.

WHAT YOU WILL FIND IN THIS BOOK

A thorough reading of this book will reinforce basic concepts and introduce to you others that are less familiar. The descriptions of various careers will help you become aware of the major issues you will face, or already face, in the music business. This book should answer many of your questions, and you may have questions we don't address; in either case, the first step to knowledge is to understand which questions need to be asked.

—JOSQUIN DES PRES AND MARK LANDSMAN

i

THE PUBLISHING BUSINESS

CHAPTER 1

Copyrights and Royalties—Your Property Rights

I f you're talented, hardworking, cunning, and lucky (the proportions may differ), you can make money in the commercial popular music business. Everyone knows that those at the top earn staggering amounts. Often, however, musicians who aspire to get there have little understanding of how the income is generated.

In the publishing business, the songs earn the money. The income earned by a song is called a "royalty." A hit song is the goose that lays the golden eggs—if it is popular over a long period, it will continue to generate royalties, even though the work of writing the song was finished years earlier. A catalog of hit songs may become very valuable.

Royalties on a song are paid to the owner of its *copyright*. The copyright is the legal ownership of the song; it creates a bundle of rights in the owner. Most important is the right to receive royalties. A useful analogy is to compare the copyright to a piece of rental property: Whoever has legal title possesses the right to receive the rents from the tenants. As with rental property, the owner of a copyright may enter into a contract to sell all or part of these rights.

The analogy to real estate goes only so far. The obvious difference is that real estate is tangible; it is property in the most basic sense. You can stand on it, you can build on it, you can photograph it. A copyright, on the other hand, is intangible—you can't build a house on it and live there. Lawyers refer to copyright as a kind of *intellectual property* (trademarks, for instance, are another kind). In essence, the "property" is a set of ideas that can be conveyed in a tangible form (for example, sheet music) whose uniqueness the law recognizes as being worthy of protection for the copyright holder. In reality, because ideas themselves are intangible, no one "owns" them, but the copyright law grants the right to profit from them.

THE ORIGINS OF COPYRIGHT

Protection for the copyright holder originates in the U.S. Constitution. The writers of the Constitution were aware that intellectual property can be an important source of commerce and economic advancement. To encourage citizens to be productive, rights to such property (now known as patents and copyrights) are specifically provided for.

The Constitution grants to Congress the power to pass laws to "promote the progress of science and the useful arts" by securing to composers and songwriters (and others including inventors and authors) the *exclusive rights* to profit from their creations for *a limited time*. When this time expires, the exclusivity terminates and the rights become universal; for instance, anyone can record a song whose copyright is expired without paying royalties to the writer. Such material is said to have entered the *public domain*.

There is a reason why this monopoly expires. The intent of the copyright portion of the Constitution is to encourage the useful arts for the benefit of the *whole country*, not just to help individual composers, authors, and inventors get rich. The time limits as enacted by Congress in the Copyright Act reflect Congress's best compromise—they're long enough to provide the individual incentive but not so long that the monopoly limits the nation's access to the invention, song, or book.

THE NATURE OF COPYRIGHT

If you're a songwriter or spend time with someone who is, how many times have you heard someone ask, "Have you copyrighted your song yet?" What the person is asking is whether you've *registered* its copyright with the U.S. Copyright Office. Contrary to a commonly held belief, registration does not create your copyright in the song—the copyright belongs to you *as soon as the song is created*. There are reasons why registration may be desirable and important, but registration is not necessary for your copyright to exist.

So, it is not true that, without registration, a copyright doesn't exist or somehow is invalid. However, registration of your copyright gives rise to certain legal protections that may make your life easier in the future. For instance, it creates a presumption of ownership in the registrant—anyone who challenges your ownership in court has the burden of proving that he is the rightful owner, as opposed to you having to prove that you are.

Copyright Ownership

Technically, the law provides the copyright owner with five *exclusive* rights:

1. The right to reproduce the work in copies or phonorecords.[1]
2. The right to create derivative works based on the original copyrighted work (for example, a parody of the original).
3. The right to distribute copies or phonorecords of the work to the general public.
4. The right to perform the work in public.
5. The right to display the work in public.

As we will see later, these rules have limits and exceptions—in practice, exclusive rights aren't *absolutely* exclusive. And, obviously, number 5 has little applicability to music. It applies to paintings, sculpture, photographs, and other visual arts.

Some Common Limits to Exclusive Rights

One common limit is the "fair use" exemption. An example would be a review that quotes lyrics of a song, poem, or book appearing in a newspaper or a snippet of a tune played on a radio broadcast as a review. In these cases, the fair use is limited to just enough of the song to convey its spirit and flavor. On the other hand, playing the whole song (without permission) in the course of a purported review might be viewed by the law as an unfair use.

Fair use, then, is use for criticism, journalism, education, and the like, use that does not diminish the commercial value of the work to its author. This sounds simple, but the applications can be tricky. For instance, a teacher may play a CD of a song in his class to stimulate a discussion about the music or lyrics, and that's fair use. On the other hand, if he makes photocopies of the sheet music and distributes them to the class, it's copyright infringement, because making copies cuts into sales of sheet music.

Even though the right to reproduce the work (i.e., record it) and distribute copies (phonorecords) is said to be exclusive, such exclusivity expires once the work is recorded. That is, a songwriter has the right to choose never to allow a song to be recorded and the right to choose who *first* records it. Once it is first recorded, any other artist may record it without obtaining permission. Quite simply, under a *compulsory license*, one who controls a copyright must grant the license whether he wants to or not—quite a big exception to exclusivity! See the discussion in chapter 2 of mechanical royalties and compulsory licenses.

Copyright Eligibility

For a writer's work to be eligible for copyright, it must be *original*. For these purposes, "original" may include a work that is similar to a previous work, as long as the previous work *originated with* the same writer. This is more easily illustrated than explained. Suppose you write a song, and register it for copyright with yourself as the author. Then, after living with it for awhile, you decide it's repetitive and needs a bridge. You write a bridge, then reregister the copyright to the new, longer song. The new registration is eligible because you were the person who wrote the song in the first place. If someone else tried to do the same thing with your song, that person's work would *not* be original.

To be original, the work also must have originated with the author copyrighting it. Stolen songs are not eligible for copyright. "Stealing" the original essence of someone else's copyright and passing it off as your own is called "copyright infringement." On occasion, pop musicians steal existing melodies, then try to call them their own work. The deception is usually camouflaged with a different song name and slight differences in production. This is analogous to someone pretending to be the landlord and collecting rent from a tenant—he has no right to the royalties. It's blatantly dishonest and unfair. If the victim of infringement discovers it, he may file suit to recover the royalties that got paid to the thief (as well as other damages provided by law).

Becoming generally available in the 1980s, sampling technology has enabled would-be songwriters to assemble songs (or what pass for songs) using sampled portions of someone else's recorded music. In the early days of this practice, it was common for the sampler to do so without permission from the samplee. A spate of copyright infringement controversies and lawsuits followed. Now the prevailing practice is to inform the copyright holder and negotiate a percentage split *before* the "new" song earns any royalties. This eliminates the potential dispute over who owns the copyright.

Infringement lawsuits can get ugly. Unfortunately, it is not always evident whether a person claiming infringement is the actual writer of a song or just an opportunist trying to cheat the true writer out of his fair share of the royalties. Sometimes, no paper trail or other evidence easily proves the facts one way or the other. This can result in expensive, drawn-out litigation that doesn't always provide a just result. Although copyright registration is no guarantee that this will not occur, it is a big step in the right direction.

Musical Works and Sound Recordings

The copyright laws establish various categories of works that are eligible for copyright. Readers of this book are interested primarily in two categories: *musical works* (songs or other compositions) and *sound recordings* (the finished product that documents a performance).

The law treats musical works and sound recordings differently for the simple reason that their creators may not be the same. For instance, many songwriters are not performers; their copyrights would be for *musical works*. Similarly, many performers may not be writers, but actively release many recordings. When a song is "covered" by a new artist, royalties that accrue to the *writer* are for the *musical work*, but royalties that accrue to the *recording artist* for his CD sales are for the *sound recording*.

Obviously, in the case of the singer-songwriter and self-contained groups, the musical work and a sound recording of it are created by the same person(s). The copyright owner of each is the same. However, another artist who records a cover version of the song has rights with respect to that sound recording only, not the song itself. Thus, an appealing song has only one copyright as a musical work, but there may be hundreds of copyrights to sound recordings performing it. There's some serious money to be made by the writer.

Since lyrics are words but not music, are they considered to be a *musical work*? Or, are they categorized as a *literary work* under the law, the way poetry would be? The answer is straightforward: If the lyrics are integrated with music, then they are considered to be part of a musical work. If, on the other hand, they are "freestanding"—that is, not connected to music—then they are considered to be a literary work and may be copyright registered as such.

It is not unheard of that lyrics copyrighted as a literary work are later adapted to music. However, in most cases, song lyrics begin their artistic lives intended as such and are not offered for copyright registration until they are joined at the hip with music, at which point they are considered to be a musical work.

DOCUMENTING THE INTANGIBLE

A song or other musical composition is intangible and fleeting. If you sing it and play it on an instrument, it disappears into thin air as you perform it. You might know it well and be able to repeat it in its exact form, but it's not yet eligible for copyright registration. In order to qualify, a musical work must be capable of being put in, and in fact be put in, what the law calls "a fixed and tangible form." As a practical matter, this means that it must be transcribed as sheet music or recorded in an audio medium such as magnetic tape, CD, or phonograph record.

A song is in fact intangible and exists only during its performance. Although sheet music (or an audio recording) is not the song itself, it is a representation or embodiment of the content of the song. It's a way of *unquestionably* and *objectively* demonstrating what the song consists of. By way of counterexample, an application to register a song for copyright would be rejected if it said, "The melody represents human hope and longing and sounds like the creaking of the floor at an old country church." This is correctable; the application would be acceptable if the melody was represented in musical notation, with treble clef, notes, rests, accents, and so on.

A copyright of a musical work itself consists of a bundle of legal rights. As a practical matter, the most significant is the right to receive royalty payments when someone else uses the copyrighted work. A registration will not be valid unless it allows a determination to be made regarding these rights. This makes sense: You have to be able to demonstrate what you wrote before you can prove you own the rights to it.

COPYRIGHT REGISTRATION

Earlier in this chapter, we touched on copyright registration. Now let's talk about what it consists of and how it's done. First of all, remember that registration is not required to obtain copyright—it's merely advisable as a way to protect yourself. It was not always so; under the old copyright law, "you snooze, you lose" was the rule. Without registration, you had no copyright.

Although current law does not require registration, it does encourage it. If you register your copyright and give proper notice (more on this later), you gain significant protection. Most notably, in the case of an infringement lawsuit, it's easier for you to prove your ownership than if you had not registered. In addition, if you prevail in the lawsuit, you are entitled to recover larger costs and damages than if you had not registered. Not insignificantly, you also may be the type of person who sleeps better knowing you've done everything you can to protect your interests.

Dealing with the Copyright Office to register a copyright might sound like a bureaucratic nightmare, but it isn't difficult. For most musicians, we're talking about Form PA (for registering a work of performing arts, that is, a song or other musical composition) or Form SR (for a sound recording). Basically, you fill out the form, attach a copy of the work in fixed, tangible form, pay the fee called for on the form (as of the time of this writing, the fee is $30), and mail the whole package to the U.S. Copyright Office. It isn't within the scope of this book to lead you through the forms, but the information on how to fill them out can be obtained from the U.S. Copyright Office itself, as well as many other sources.

The work in fixed, tangible form typically is a CD, cassette tape, DAT, lead sheet, phonograph record, transcription, or the work on some other medium. For Form SR, you must send in the *specific sound recording* you're trying to register (not the rough mix with the now-deleted backup vocals). For Form PA, any medium works, as long as it adequately conveys the song. For instance, it can be sheet music or a recording of a performance of the song in the sheet music. If you send a cassette tape or a CD (common media), it need not be studio quality, but it must be intelligible. When the copyright application is approved, you will receive back your original form with the official seal of the U.S. Copyright Office. Even though this process may take months (be patient), the "official date" of the copyright registration is the date your application was *received*.

If you want to register a copyright but feel uncomfortable dealing with legal forms and procedures, by all means get it done by a professional. In addition, if more complex circumstances are involved (such as multiple authors or reregistration), you should seek help from someone more experienced. It's always better to spend a little money to do it right than it is to live with the nagging feeling that you left some loose ends.

Though registration isn't a prerequisite to ownership of a copyright, it is a prerequisite to maintaining a lawsuit for copyright infringement. So, even if you didn't file Form PA when you first finished a song, you will have to file it before going to court to protect your rights.

COPYRIGHT NOTICE

We mentioned copyright registration and that it affords some protection. Now let's talk about its sister, copyright *notice*. Like registration, under the old law, notice was a prerequisite to the existence of a copyright. That's no longer true, but notice is still a good idea, and it's easy. Simply stated, notice means identifying yourself as the copyright owner in the manner required by law. We've all seen it, as in (most commonly) "Copyright 2000 John Green" or "©2000 John Green." Because the symbol © has more significance beyond U.S. borders, it is advisable to use it exclusively. In addition, more international protection is afforded when you add the phrase "All Rights Reserved." Therefore, the preferred version of the example would be "©2000 John Green. All rights reserved."

The year you put next to the symbol is the first year of publication of the work. (More on publishing in the next chapter.) If the work is unpublished, use the year the work was created. If you're shopping a demo around, use the current year. That way, it won't seem that the song is old, failed, or otherwise unworthy of consideration.

For copyright notice of sound recordings, the international copyright is symbol is ℗, a "P" instead of a "C" inside the circle. So, an album cover should state, "℗2000 Heartthrob Records. All rights reserved." If lyrics to songs appear on the cover, then both the © and the ℗ symbol would appear as notices of copyright (of the musical work and the sound recording, respectively).

Notice is a way of saying, "OK, everybody, I own this copyright. Because I'm telling you in no uncertain terms, you can't later pretend you thought there was no copyright." Why is this important? Because a person who *wasn't* put on notice that a work was copyrighted can claim he *innocently* infringed the copyright (that is, claimed it as his own without the intent to deny anyone else's rights). In a lawsuit for copyright infringement, an innocent infringer will not have to pay as much in damages to the true owner as a guilty infringer. It's pretty easy to protect yourself if you're the copyright owner—just give notice.

Giving notice involves nothing more than writing (or printing, or stamping, etc.) the notice on *all* of your work product that has a chance of falling into someone else's hands. That means lead sheets, demo tapes, rough mixes, CDs, lyric sheets—everything. Put it where it can't be separated from what you're trying to copyright. For instance, if your demo is on a CD, include the notice on the shell of the CD itself, as well as the CD sleeve. That way, an infringer won't be able to claim innocence by saying, "Gee, I didn't know it was a copyrighted song. I must have lost the sleeve, and the CD itself said nothing about copyright."

Does giving notice mean your copyright won't be infringed? Unfortunately, no; no more than having a car alarm means your car won't be broken into or engraving your valuables with identifying numbers means they won't be stolen. However, by analogy, prominently displayed notice may lessen the chance of theft or increase your chance of recovering the maximum payable under the law.

OWNERSHIP OF COPYRIGHTS—WORKS "MADE FOR HIRE"

The general rule is that the "author" (this broad category includes novelists, poets, composers, songwriters, lyricists, and so on)—that is, *the person who creates or publishes the work*—is the owner of the copyright. Like all rules, this one has a few exceptions.

The major exception is works "made for hire." In this scenario, the owner of a work may, in essence, bargain away the copyright for a fee or a salary. For instance, in past years some staff songwriters were employees of a publishing company. When they wrote songs, the copyright of those songs belonged to the employer, in return for which the writer received a salary or other compensation. Today, film scorers, jingle writers, and writers of music to accompany video games and CD-ROMs are examples of authors whose compositions may be "works made for hire."

In order for the ownership of an author's work to belong to the employer under this rule, the work must be created *within the scope of the author's employment*. For example, not every composition written by a jingle writer belongs to the employer, only those written for the job. So, songs written on the side are *not* works made for hire—the copyrights belong to the writer.

Every industry has its prevailing customs, and the music industry is no exception. Yet, change in the industry occurs very rapidly. What is a work for hire in one era or in one company may no longer be just a year or two later. The examples that appear here are for illustration only and do not necessarily reflect business arrangements that prevail or that you should feel compelled to accept. In general, the trend is away from work for hire and toward creator-maintained ownership of copyrights.

DURATION OF COPYRIGHT

The law grants a bundle of rights to the holder of a copyright, but they don't go on forever. Remember, the law doesn't exist just to enrich you and your family but to encourage your creativity for the good of the whole nation. Still, you are granted the opportunity to get rich. Under current copyright law (the 1976 Copyright Act, as amended by the Sonny Bono Copyright Term Extension Act of 1998), a copyright endures for the life of the author of the work, plus seventy years. If the work is a joint work (such as a lyricist-composer effort of two or more people), the seventy-year clock starts ticking upon the death of the last surviving author.

Current law is more generous in copyright duration than the previous (1909) act. Copyrights originating under the 1909 act are eligible for renewal, which extends their total duration to a maximum of ninety-five years (versus a maximum of fifty-six under the 1909 law before it was amended). This renewal does not occur automatically; the copyright owner is obliged to file a renewal form to extend the protection.

ADVISABILITY OF COPYRIGHT REGISTRATION

If you are a songwriter and your career hasn't yet blossomed, you may wonder whether you should file a Form PA to register the copyrights for all your songs (at least, all the good ones). After all, it's not inherently fun, and it's not free ($30 per application). Even though this expense can be mitigated somewhat (the Copyright Office allows recordings of up to six songs to be submitted within one application), the fees can add up.

Especially if the songs you write are performed in public (either by yourself or someone else), there's always a concern that the songs will be "stolen" by a person who tries to pass off the work as his own. And if the songs are not protected by registration, what happens when you discover someone did steal them? Let's say you unexpectedly hear them, or one of them, on commercial radio a year or two down the line.

There are two schools of thought about this scenario. One school of thought is, don't worry. You can probably prove that you are the original writer, through various means such as your original home demos, affidavits from fans, or band members who heard you perform it years before, and so on. The rationale is that someone else is getting your song heard, and now it's up to you to go to court to get both the money and credit due to you. Your own hard work of trying to "break" as a songwriter wasn't working, so now you are in a *better* position—even though it is, ironically, the result of someone else's illegal, unethical act.

The other school of thought is that this approach is too risky. After all, you could lose, even if you're in the right. Anything can go wrong in litigation: Most of all, your documentation that the song originated with you may be spotty. Clearly, this would not be as much of an issue if you have registered the song with the Copyright Office. An audacious song thief may make you out to be a gold digger trying to muscle into his new-found success. If you've properly registered, he may still claim *you* stole the song from *him* and shamelessly registered it first, but he's the one fighting the uphill battle, not you.

Both approaches to this issue have valid points. If you are serious about a songwriting career and expect to be successful, then you should register at the point your songs are sufficiently exposed to others that it's feasible they could be lifted by an unethical person. Whether or not you register them before your career takes off, it is *always* advisable to plaster the proper © copyright notice (including your name) on everything that contains your original work—song lyric sheets, demo CDs, and so on. The greater likelihood is that a theft of your work would occur from one of these "fixed, tangible forms" than from a live performance.

The "Poor Man's Copyright"

Perhaps you've heard of the "poor man's copyright," but you aren't sure what it is, or whether you should use it. It's nothing more than a cheap, unofficial way to create a trail of evidence that you are the author of a work (most relevantly, writer of a song). It does cost less than proper copyright registration.

The way it works is to mail to yourself (preferably by certified mail) a demo and lyric sheet (or a lead sheet). Then, you don't open it—you just put it away and save it. The theory is that the song is now preserved in a sealed envelope containing the official date stamp of the U.S. Post Office. The poor man's copyright does leave a trail of evidence, including a date.

Does it help? Well, not really—whatever you've heard, don't rely on it. Because you are handling the logistics yourself (rather than leaving them to an impartial government agency), the evidence is subject to skepticism: that, after the fact, you may have tampered with the seal or otherwise rigged the mailing envelope to include self-serving evidence. If you're going to document your copyright, use formal registration with the Copyright Office.

Cheap as it is, the poor man's copyright isn't worth it. You're taking too much of a chance with your intellectual property.

Keeping Copyright Law Current with New Realities

Internet applications of digital music have challenged Congress to keep up with the times. For instance, is online transmission of music a performance, or is it a phonorecord (because it can be downloaded and replayed)? This is not merely a philosophical inquiry—the accepted answer will have tangible economic consequences. Not every online transmission is necessarily a performance, and not every performance is downloaded. Internet technology itself is not yet mature enough to provide an answer to each potential question.

Urged on by the music and film industries, as well as by software companies and book publishers, Congress has, since the mid-1990s, amended copyright laws to try to address needs brought about by the evolving nature of the media in which protected materials are stored. Because the reach of the Internet is global, more than ever, the United States must try to coordinate its copyright laws with those of the rest of the world.

Since the changes in the law affect publishing rights rather than the nature of copyright itself, further discussion appears in chapter 2.

Summary

Copyright is the legal means of recognizing ownership of intellectual property, and it is a fundamental of our law based in the U.S. Constitution. In the commercial popular music business, such property consists primarily of songs (*musical works*) and musical performances (*sound recordings*).

The principal benefit conferred by copyright ownership is the right to receive royalties in return for licensing one's work. Licensing results from the law's grant of certain *exclusive rights* to the author to use the work he created. Since he controls the rights, he may grant to others a license to use the work, in return for the payment of royalties. There are certain exceptions and limitations to the exclusivity of rights, including "fair use" and *compulsory* licenses.

Although under former law, a copyright did not exist until registered with the U.S. Copyright Office, current law recognizes the existence of a copyright as soon as it is represented in a "fixed, tangible form"—typically, a recording and written sheets of music or lyrics. Copyright notice consists of putting the © symbol, the author's name, and the relevant date on versions of the work.

Like registration, notice is not required for a copyright to exist. However, it is advisable (as well as cheap and easy) to place notice on all demo recordings, lyric sheets, and music. Registration, by contrast, is not as easy and costs money. Opinions differ about the importance of copyright registration for unpublished songwriters.

The "poor man's copyright" is sometimes used to avoid the expense and formality of copyright registration. However, it's a weak, unacceptable substitute.

CHAPTER 2

Publishing Deals— Earning a Living from Your Songs

There are two sides to the commercial popular song. First, there's the "art" side—the part that touches hearts and minds. The other side is business—getting the song recorded and released and generally doing anything involved with collecting royalties. The business side of songs is known as "publishing." The songwriter writes songs; the publisher helps the songwriter release the songs to the public; both make money from them.

The business of publishing is straightforward in principle but complex in its detail. This chapter is not intended to be a complete guide to the details. For instance, it doesn't refer to deal points you need to look out for when you negotiate a publishing contract. However, it will help you understand the basics. To use a sports analogy, you'll understand the objectives of the game and the playing field.

What Publishers Do

The publisher's job breaks down into several main components. First, the company finds artists to record your songs. Traditionally, this role has been called "song plugging." Song plugging evokes images of a fast-talking fat guy with a cigar making endless phone calls to try to get every manager, producer, artist, agent, record company, or whoever will talk to him, to listen to the song. The music industry has grown tremendously since those days, and a "shotgun" approach to placing songs is too unwieldy to be of much use anymore. However, placing songs still takes time and hard work—things the writer is better off leaving to the publisher in order to devote his own time and hard work to songwriting.

The publisher also handles copyright administration, a multifaceted and important task, which begins with copyright registration. Usually, writers leave it to publishers to file copyright registration forms (which themselves become far more relevant as the publisher places songs). Once users for songs are found, the publisher issues licenses, devices through which songs earn money. Then, the publisher collects money through the licenses, and pays the *writer's share* to the writer, keeping the *publisher's share* for itself.

By long-standing industry custom, the writer's share is 50 percent and the publisher's share is 50 percent. If you are a songwriter who writes for other people to perform and haven't yet become so successful that you self-publish, this 50-50 split is standard and nonnegotiable. The rationale for the 50 percent publisher's share is that administration is expensive, because the publisher handles all costs and overhead (salaries, phone calls, insurance, postage, fees, etc.). By the time these are accounted for, the profit left for the publisher represents a fair return for its work. Anyway, that's the prevailing theory.

In addition to finding licensees for authorized use, administration also includes defending the writer's copyright against unauthorized use (infringement), if need be. Once a song is placed, a hardworking publisher doesn't stop there—it tries to find other artists to cover the song, in order to maximize royalties. In appropriate cases, it tries to get the song published as sheet music. This is where the term "publishing" originated. Prior to the wide availability of recorded music, this was how writers earned most of their money.

Publishers can earn money both from their back catalogs (some high-earning songs may be decades old) and from new songs. In fact, some publishers have no new writers' songs under contract; all they do is administer their back catalogs. On the other side, publishers that are actively seeking to work with new writers have staffers whose roles are more creative than administrative. Their job is to locate and evaluate new writers and to work with them to develop their skills toward commercial ends.

THE MECHANICS OF PUBLISHING

As you recall from chapter 1, ownership of the copyright gives the writer the right to transfer it to someone else. A writer who enters into a publishing deal transfers the copyright to the publisher. In return for this transfer (called an *assignment*), the writer receives the 50 percent writer's share of royalties, and the balance of royalties goes to the publisher's share.

The assignment is more than just transferring away 50 percent of the royalties—the writer must also assign the rights to issue licenses and collect the money that flows to them. Without the assignment, the publisher would have no authorization to do these things. Of course, by virtue of his contract with the writer, it also has an *obligation* to do them.

COMPULSORY LICENSES

Publishers administer, among others, compulsory licenses and the mechanical royalties that follow. These are based on the exclusive right of the copyright holder to distribute copies or phonorecords of the work to the general public. The term "phonorecords" includes the audio media only. As of this writing, it means compact discs and less and less frequently, cassette tapes (whereas it once meant grooved wax cylinders, then grooved vinyl records). This exclusive right means that, if someone other than the copyright holder wants to record the song, he must license the song from the copyright holder and pay royalties on the "manufacture and distribution"[2] of the CDs and tapes.

For a song to be *first* recorded for commercial release, the artist must obtain the authorization (license) of the copyright holder, who has the absolute right to turn him down. After this, the copyright law places limits on exclusive rights of the copyright holder—once a phonorecord containing the song has been recorded and distributed (often called "first use"), any other artist may proceed to record it, and the right to refuse disappears. For this reason, the license that issues as a result is called a "compulsory" license.

An artist or the artist's producer is free to decide to cover the song as a single or part of an album, knowing that no permission is necessary. If a compulsory license is used (as we shall see, this is rare), it is necessary to notify the publisher and pay royalties for each CD or tape distributed.

MECHANICAL ROYALTIES

Mechanical royalties are the royalties paid to the copyright owner under a license (including compulsory license) issued for the use of his song on a tape or CD. For compulsory licenses, the copyright law contains a statutory rate. For each recording "made and distributed," this rate is currently 8.5 cents or 1.65 cents per minute of playing time or fraction thereof, whichever is greater. The rate adjusts with the Consumer Price Index and has been escalating over time. Effective January 1, 2006, those numbers will bump upwards to 9.1 cents and 1.75 cents, respectively.

The law provides mechanical royalties for phonorecords "made and *distributed*," not just to those actually *sold*. Therefore, promotional albums (known as "free goods") given away to promoters, radio stations, and others don't directly generate revenue with which to pay royalties but still give rise to royalties, just as if they were sold. Rest assured, if record companies distribute promotional albums, it's definitely with an eye to increasing sales—but even if these endeavors fail, the mechanical royalty still applies.

In practice, the compulsory *license* is rarely used, even where the compulsory *rate* is used. This is because the Copyright Act contains demanding provisions for accounting and payment that most record companies find impractical. For the publisher, a direct license is easier to administer (since otherwise administration would go through the Copyright Office itself). So, it's typical for the publisher and the record company to make a separate licensing agreement for a song that avoids the regulations set forth in the law.

In any licensing agreement, the statutory rate is the highest possible rate that can be paid. Think about it—it's the amount that the law requires if there's no agreement between the user and the copyright holder. Even a songwriter who hates an artist or record company and would prefer to price a song's royalty rate sky-high can never go higher than the statutory rate. Of course, royalties can be negotiated to a lower rate and often are.

In real-life deals, songwriters who are less well-established often have to accept less than the statutory rate to get their material on a particular record. It's very common that the major record companies (the players to whom licenses are actually issued) offer only 75 percent of the statutory rate. In such circumstances, the writer who holds out for the statutory rate almost certainly will lose—the record company will decide not to use the song. Obviously, depending on bargaining power, the writer (through the publisher) goes along.

Recognizing this reality, many publishing contracts allow the publisher to accept lower than the full rate on behalf of the writer or explicitly provide for 75 percent. The publishing contract of a well-established writer (whose songs are in great demand) may call for the writer to receive 100 percent of the statutory rate irrespective of what is paid by the record company. In this case, the difference comes out of the publisher's profits. Don't cry for the publisher, though—by working with an in-demand writer, it's still doing all right.

In summary, the most significant aspects of the compulsory license and the statutory mechanical royalty rate are the following:

- Once a song is "first used" for manufacture and distribution, the writer's monopoly on it ends; afterward, anyone may record and distribute phonorecords containing that song
- The statutory compulsory license rate represents a ceiling on the rate that a publisher can collect for sales of phonorecords

COLLECTING MECHANICAL ROYALTIES

Most record companies account for and pay royalties on a quarterly basis, that is, four times per year. In practice, many publishers don't directly collect mechanical royalties. It's a major accounting and administrative headache to account for each writer's royalties on each of the songs, match them against the payments, and pay the writer's share.

The "trench work" of mechanical royalties is largely administered by the Harry Fox Agency, Inc., based in New York City. In essence, it's a watchdog for mechanical rights. In return for a 5.75 percent commission, the agency issues mechanical licenses, collects license fees, and reconciles the fees against earnings statements. After deducting its fee, it pays the balance collected to the publisher. The agency also audits record companies to uncover unpaid royalties and often finds them.

Many publishers, especially smaller ones for whom the administrative expense of doing this work would be prohibitive, use Harry Fox's services. Larger publishers often do, because even for them, it's more efficient to farm out this work to a specialist. The agency is very well regarded in the industry for its diligence in protecting the rights of copyright holders.

The Harry Fox Agency is commonly referred to as a "mechanical rights organization." Although it is the dominant force among such organizations in the industry, several others perform similar services.

PERFORMANCE ROYALTIES

The copyright law grants the copyright holder the exclusive right to perform his song in public. It follows that someone else who wants to perform the song must obtain a license to do so and pay the appropriate royalty. Performance means not only live performance but broadcast on radio and TV, in music clubs, some restaurants and bars, and so on.

In practice, publishers are even less likely to directly license performance rights than they are to directly license mechanical rights. If you think about it, it would be impossible for a publisher to monitor all outlets playing its artists' songs in a recorded medium. It would have to keep track of every TV and radio station in the country and throughout the world—then it would have to obtain a license from each user. The task would be overwhelming.

This is the reason behind *performing rights organizations*. The dominant ones in the United States are called ASCAP, BMI, and SESAC. In essence, they act as agents for writers and publishers to license songs and to collect royalties *for performance*. Even for these large organizations, the administrative task of licensing and monitoring song by song, performance by performance, and user by user, is infeasible. In place of specific licenses, the user (a radio station, for instance) pays these organizations a single fee granting it a license to *all* the songs in their catalog.

Once the performing rights organizations collect the license fees, they pay royalties in proportion to how much their songs are performed. ASCAP, BMI, and SESAC are nonprofit organizations. After paying actual expenses, all proceeds are paid for the benefit of copyright owners. Because of the large number of songs and users, it is impossible even for ASCAP, BMI, and SESAC to specifically track every song in every publisher's catalog. The tool they use to measure how much of their total collections to pay each publisher and writer is called "sampling."

Sampling is a statistical technique of estimating the breakdown of a total by measuring only part of the total. It is used, for example, in national polling to determine the public's mood—and (when designed properly) can accurately represent the whole country from only about 1,500 participants. By careful, scientifically valid decisions on how to randomly sample parts of the big picture, sampling provides an accurate measurement of the big picture itself. Performing rights organizations sample radio station performances by collecting log sheets from selected stations and actually listening to stations and keeping their own records. TV stations provide copies of logs they keep.

Obviously, the choice of what is "representative" of the whole is crucial in sampling. ASCAP, SESAC, and BMI go to great lengths to refine their procedures to justify the results they obtain. Each uses a different method, and each feels its method is the best. Since each organization's method is backed up by sound assumptions, it seems unlikely that going with one can be said to provide an advantage versus the others.

Basically, the only way for a songwriter to keep track of and get paid performance royalties is to affiliate with a performance rights organization—the job is too big to do oneself. A songwriter may affiliate with only one performing rights organization at a time. However, the writer is not prevented from cowriting with someone who belongs to a different performing rights organization. ASCAP, BMI, and SESAC have individual Web sites that explain why each feels its services are the best for songwriters. The sites also contain valuable information for all copyright holders. Discussion of a choice among the three organizations is beyond the scope of this book.

Depending on the size and variety of their rosters, publishers (unlike songwriters) may (and may have to) affiliate with multiple performing rights societies. Since ASCAP, BMI, and SESAC pay the publisher's share directly to the publisher, and the writer's share directly to the writer, they require that a publisher belong if its songwriters belong. They want to pay royalties only to *affiliated* writers and publishers—members of the same club, as it were.

CHANGES—LIMITS ON PERFORMANCE ROYALTIES

In late 1998, the Copyright Act was amended by the Fairness in Music Licensing Act, which effectively disposed of an issue that had been brewing for some years. Under prior law, most bars, restaurants, and similar businesses that play radio and TV broadcasts of music for the pleasure of their patrons were required to obtain permission to do so. In practice, this meant that they paid annual license fees to the performing rights organizations.

Under the Fairness in Music Licensing Act, many restaurants and bars are exempt from having to obtain permission (that is, paying license fees to writers and publishers) to perform copyrighted material, provided that they meet certain requirements. Basically, the requirements are these:

- The music they perform is from licensed TV and radio stations and not rebroadcast outside the bar or restaurant
- The size of the establishment in square footage does not exceed a fixed amount (smaller means more exempt)
- No cover fee is charged (if so, the exemption is lost)

ASCAP, BMI, and SESAC were strongly opposed to the new law and (on behalf of writers and publishers) consider its title to be ironic. The legislative history behind the bill shows that it was pushed primarily by lobbying groups for the hospitality industry and by the senators and congressional representatives to whom they make contributions. By its supporters, it was touted as a victory for small business. Their rationale was that the TV and radio stations already pay license fees for performance, so all it does is prevent double-dipping by copyright holders.

By ASCAP's estimate, over 70 percent of restaurants and bars are now exempt from paying music license fees (performance royalties). From the perspective of songwriters and publishers, the bill is just a way to allow most restaurants and bars to get for free something they used to pay for and, by right, ought to pay for. To these copyright holders, the double-dipping argument is all wet, because the bars and restaurants that play broadcast music do so to enhance their profits—they're the ones taking the second dip. "We're also small businesspeople," argue the songwriters, "and it's unfair to give away our stock in trade."

The act became law at the same time as the Sonny Bono Copyright Term Extension Act, which increased the copyright term by twenty years (from life plus fifty years to life plus seventy years). This helps writers and publishers, by extending the duration of their limited monopoly over songs. Only a naïve songwriter would perceive the coupling of the two laws as coincidental. Increasing the copyright term while cutting into licensing rights was obviously Congress's attempt to make the latter seem more acceptable. Since the Fairness in Music Licensing Act is so new, it's too early to measure its effect on royalties paid to songwriters and publishers. But clearly, they can only go down.

SELF-PUBLISHING

Discussions of publishing often get confusing. In talk about the publishing "pie," sometimes it's unclear whether "your publishing" means just the total (100 percent) of the *writer's* 50 *percent* of the publishing (giving up part of this is discussed in more detail in chapter 7) or the "entire 100 percent" of the publishing, that is, *self-publishing*, which is the subject of this section.

Well-meaning musicians and industry advisors often say, "Keep your publishing." This is especially true in talking about self-contained groups, those writing material for themselves to perform. After all, if you can get to a recording contract, you don't need to find artists with whom to place your songs. In that case, why give away any rights?

Well-meaning advice to keep "100 percent of everything" does not represent the way that most writers can operate. Achieving that level requires that the writer go into the publishing business—take on the tasks of placing songs, administration of copyrights and royalties, and so on. This is time consuming, expensive, distracting, and not necessarily the kind of thing songwriters have the expertise and inclination to do. In other words, most writers need a publisher, and it's worth bargaining away 50 percent for the services they receive in return.

Particularly successful writers whose songs are in great demand or those in a self-contained group that need no publisher to place songs are good candidates to keep 100 percent of everything, that is, to self-publish. They form their own publishing companies and directly hire a manager to deal with artists, producers, and record companies—this cuts out the slice of profit that would have gone to an independent publisher. Even so, they are likely to contract with a publisher to administer their catalogs, for which they pay a fee. (This is known, sensibly, as an administration deal.) However, it's understandably much lower than the 50 percent the publisher would charge for full service.

Of course, many writers begin as self-publishers by default. They publish themselves because initially they can't find a publisher to take them on. In today's competitive market, many publishers are reluctant to sign a writer who doesn't already have (by some measure) at least one hit song. Once writers become successful, it's easier to affiliate with a publishing company, and they usually do so. It's more profitable in the long run for writers to devote time to writing songs, which are the income generators. This increases the size of the pie, and we all know it's better to have 50 percent of a large pie than 100 percent of a tiny one.

Self-publishing is not for everybody; but if you are adamant about retaining control over your copyrighted material, it's the way to go. Just be prepared to wear a business hat, not an artist hat, much of the time. And, if it isn't working, then consider working with a publisher.

COPUBLISHING

The meaning of "copublishing" is broad. It refers to a number of different situations in which more than one publisher is involved for a song or catalog of songs. Here, we look just at the writer copublishing with a publishing company.

It's not uncommon for a writer to copublish with a publisher. Under this arrangement, he retains not only his writer's share but also gets half of the publisher's share. Thus, the writer ends up with 50 percent plus half of the other 50 percent, for a total of 75 percent. This differs from the general

50-50 split discussed earlier—and in favor of the songwriter. It arises because the publisher wants the writer badly enough to offer him the extra enticement—supply-demand factors run in the writer's favor (because of expectations for his songs, the health of the market in general, etc.).

Controlling an "extra" 25 percent of the publishing pie can come in handy when a writer needs to bargain, as later chapters will discuss.

OTHER SOURCES OF INCOME

Another source of income is foreign rights. The mechanism by which songwriters earn income when their songs are played outside the United States is called "subpublishing" or "foreign licensing." In subpublishing, the domestic publisher enters into agreements with foreign publishing companies. These publishers collect mechanical royalties and pay them to the U.S. publishers (for which they naturally receive their percentage). Performance rights societies in the foreign countries collect performance royalties; they pay the publisher's share to the U.S. publisher and remit the writer's share to ASCAP, BMI, or SESAC, which pays it directly to the writer, as it does for domestically earned royalties.

Synchronization ("synch") rights are the rights to use a musical composition in a film or TV show. We've all heard popular music as incorporated in these other media; at this point it's par for the course. These rights are typically purchased for flat fees; a percentage is more likely for music that is commissioned for a film or show. Naturally, famous songs by famous writers (especially if prominently featured in the movie or show) command the highest fees. Even for writers not yet in this category, more income is always welcome. In addition, for less well-established writers and artists, getting a song into a popular movie or TV show is a great way to get exposure—and ultimately to increase income from "the usual" mechanical and performance royalties. In recent years, albums containing songs associated with movies have been big sellers.

If a song is popular enough (meaning it produces substantial mechanical or performance royalties), a publisher might be able to strike a deal to publish it as sheet music. Royalties from sheet music are no longer a big chunk of the income generated by a song, but there is money to be made in this older but still viable medium. Sheet music is published stand-alone for popular songs, as well as contained in collections ("Biggest Hits of the Nineties").

For foreign rights, synch rights, and sheet music, the royalties payable to the writer by the publisher are contained in the publishing agreement.

PUBLISHING RIGHTS EVOLVE WITH NEW TECHNOLOGIES

For many years, the publishing compensation model was straightforward: if sheet music, records, tapes, or CDs were sold, the artist got mechanical royalties. If a song was played on the air, a performance royalty was paid via a performing rights organization. But the Internet has changed matters drastically—not because the above is no longer true, but rather, because online music delivery is, in most cases, instantaneous, anonymous, and unbilled. These factors vastly increase the difficulty of collecting royalties, even as Internet downloading of music files has to some degree taken the place of traditional "brick-and-mortar" retailing.

The film, software, and music industries lobbied (and continue to lobby) Congress to amend the copyright law in order to eliminate or minimize the feared loss of revenue from unauthorized downloading of copyright-protected material. Although a complete discussion is beyond the scope of this book, the most significant piece of legislation passed so far is the Digital Millennium Copyright Act (DMCA).[3] Among other provisions, the DMCA requires that webcasters pay licensing fees to record companies (in the same manner as ordinary radio); makes it a crime to circumvent anti-piracy codes built into software; outlaws devices which can be used to illegally copy software; and generally attempts to protect rights of copyright holders without hindering the legitimate flow of information on the Internet.

For the music industry, the webcasting portion has been the most significant aspect of the DMCA. Its licensing fees have effectively made webcasting of licensed music prohibitively expensive for most independent operators. The effect has been to perpetuate the primacy of on-air broadcasting as the way most consumers find music—exactly the situation sought by the record labels, publishers, and established artists.

Despite changes in the law, cheating (primarily in the form of royalty-free file sharing) abounds. One solution, already in effect in Canada, is to build licensing fees into the devices and media consumers use to store digital music files (commonly called MP3s). Thus, the retail price of blank CDs and MP3 players includes a surcharge that is used to reimburse copyright holders. Until this practice extends to larger markets, the (potential) loss of revenues remains.

The DMCA is far from comprehensive, and it certainly is not the last word. For now, technology's illegitimate offspring—file sharing, bootlegging, piracy—continue. In 2003 and 2004, the RIAA, official lobbying group for the major record labels, went so far as to file copyright infringement lawsuits against small fry, in an attempt to use financial intimidation to stem the tide of unauthorized downloading. Though the legal action probably deterred some individuals, it didn't work out as a public-relations ploy, and so-called "peer-to-peer" (PTP) file sharing continues.

The development of Internet music sales sites (such as Apple's iTunes) as a replacement for brick-and-mortar stores suggest a possible solution to this problem, but some consumers (broadly defined) will continue to refuse to buy something they can get for free. Eventually, the law will catch up, but for the time being, enforcement will remain a difficult issue.

SUMMARY

Publishing is the business side of a song; it's what happens when the creative process of writing has finished. Publishers place songs with artists, administer copyrights, and collect royalties. For this, the standard rate is a 50-50 split with the writer, which divides total royalties into the *writer's share* and the *publisher's share*.

The right to receive a royalty arises out of the copyright owner's right to issue a license for someone else to use the song. Under copyright law, *mechanical* royalties are payable on the "manufacture and distribution" of phonorecords (CDs, tapes, vinyl, etc.). Once a song is first recorded, any other person may record it, but the artist must have a license and pay a royalty to the writer. If no specific license agreement is made, the license issued is called a *compulsory* license. The compulsory license carries with it a *statutory rate*, that is, how much the user must pay the writer if no agreement is reached.

Typically, compulsory licenses are not used, but the statutory rate serves as a ceiling on the amount of mechanical royalties that can be charged to the user. The statutory rate is set by Congress and adjusted periodically to reflect the changes (rises) in consumer prices. After collecting mechanical royalties from record companies, the publisher pays the writer his share.

Performance royalties (which also arise out of copyright law) are the royalties paid to a writer who licenses his song to be performed by someone else. Typically, these reflect airplay on radio and television. ASCAP, BMI, and SESAC are the major *performing rights organizations* that monitor performances and collect license fees from broadcast outlets, live performances, restaurants, bars, and other users of music. These organizations collect a single annual fee from each user, then apportion it to their affiliated writers based on the relative number of performances.

A writer can affiliate with just one of ASCAP, BMI, and SESAC at any given time. These organizations pay the writer's share directly, not through the publisher. Although, technically, membership is voluntary, there's no feasible way for a songwriter to monitor the performance of songs, issue licenses, and collect royalties—so if he wants to collect royalties, he must choose to affiliate. Recent changes in the law have limited performance royalties payable by establishments such as bars and restaurants for using broadcast music in their environments.

Self-publishing is nothing more than the writer retaining 100 percent of the publishing pie, rather than splitting 50-50 with a publisher. For most songwriters, it's not practical, and they're better off going with a reputable publisher. Only the most successful, well-established writers can afford to self-publish, because they don't really need a publisher's services to shop material. Often, they still use the administrative services of a publisher, for a reduced fee.

In *copublishing*, the writer retains the writer's share and splits the publisher's share with the publisher, in effect retaining 75 percent of the pie. Such deals are common where the writer's songs are potentially profitable. Songwriters also stand to earn money from the self-explanatory *foreign licensing* (also called *subpublishing*) and *synchronization* (or "synch") *rights*. Synch rights are sold to film and TV producers who wish to use songs in their movies and shows; typically, a flat fee is used. Sheet music, once the basis for all publishing but now of far less importance, is yet another source of income where songs gain substantial popularity.

U.S. copyright law lags behind the use of Internet to download music without paying royalties. Trying to balance the interests of copyright holders against the need for free flow of information, Congress has passed some remedial legislation. However, its effect on the problems has been minimal. Artists, publishers, and record companies continue to oppose file sharing, but the public does not. Until a global solution is reached, some royalties will go unpaid.

ii

THE RECORD BUSINESS

CHAPTER 3

MAJOR RECORD LABELS— BIGGER IS (SOMETIMES) BETTER

I f you're a performer, you've heard, "The only way to get anywhere in the music business is to go with a major record label." This statement is repeated so often, by so many people, that it's easy to think it must be true, like the law of gravity. But, unlike gravity, the music business sometimes presents us with alternatives.

If you want to begin a career as a recording artist, the most basic level is to produce, manufacture, and sell your own recordings. These days, it's often called "DIY," for "do-it-yourself." At the next level are independent labels ("indies"), generally mom-and-pop companies that do the same things, in most cases on a much greater scale than artists can accomplish themselves. At the top of the heap are the major record companies ("majors"), owned or operated by huge, publicly traded multinational corporate conglomerates.[4]

Our discussion of the record business begins with the majors. If at first this seems backward, it isn't; the majors are the model by which the advantages and disadvantages of DIY and indies are evaluated. A basic understanding of the majors is helpful, at the very least, for an artist to make the most informed decision about his career path.

HOW THE MAJORS ARE SET UP
At one time, the majors did everything in-house. They owned and operated their own studios, with engineers, producers, and arrangers on staff. They designed jacket covers in-house and manufactured records in their own plants. Decision making was an inside job all the way. Beginning

in the mid-1960s, however, these functions began to be farmed out to contractors, leading to the present-day system, in which very little true music production is done by the major record label.

These days, the major record companies are really just investors (and lenders) of money. To be sure, they choose the acts in which they invest and try to control the major decisions regarding their investment. However, the producers, engineers, arrangers, session musicians, and others involved in creating a recording are all "hired guns," not employees of the labels. Contracting out the mass manufacture of CDs and tapes is now more the rule than the exception.

The talent scouts of record companies are called "A&R representatives" (reps). A&R stands for "artist and repertoire." Back when the majors did everything themselves, the A&R reps were more than talent scouts—they were a lot like producers, shaping the artists' sound, finding material to record, and generally nurturing artists' careers on behalf of their employers.

In addition to the administrative aspects of any large company, two major functions are *distribution* and *marketing and promotion*.

The majors have large distribution companies for their products.[5] Distribution is surpassingly important in the record business. No matter what kind of buzz there is about an act, no matter how much airplay is received, no matter how many people see the live shows, no matter how terrific the record is—a consumer who can't find the record in a retail store can't buy it.[6] The majors have four megasized distribution companies to get their products to stores. There's only so much shelf space, and the company that gets it has the chance to sell. This is one huge advantage majors enjoy over their smaller competitors.

Marketing and promotion are the other keys to selling records. A lot of "product" is released each year, of which records by majors are a small proportion. Yet, something like 90 percent of all sales racked up are for major label releases. This, in large part, is because people hear major label recordings (and hear them often) on commercial radio stations and music television such as MTV. They see advertisements for the records in newspapers and magazines—outlets where you need big bucks to buy space. The economic power of the majors enables them to out-market and out-promote smaller competitors—and they can afford to pay specialized staff members to do these jobs.

WHAT MAJORS OFFER

Simply stated, the majors have more resources than any other companies. This means that they can afford the best of everything—the best producers, the best studios and engineers, the best session musicians and arrangers, the best album cover photographers and video directors, and so on. They can promote their products more effectively than their smaller competitors by being in position to dominate commercial airplay. They can market their product more effectively through target advertising and market research. And, they're in the best position to sell product because they control the distribution network.

The flip side of what the majors offer is what they don't offer. They are large, impersonal, bureaucratic business entities. Even if they were founded out of a love of music, they've long since evolved into the "finance company" model, in which the bottom line is profits, not music. By virtue of their organization and size, they have to keep the cash flowing to pay their overhead, feed the mouths of those who work there, and (Warner now excepted to some degree) satisfy investors in the stock market.

Even though music is a risky business for the majors, it is a high-return business. A big act can make an enormous amount of money for a label, compensating for money lost on the many unsuccessful ones. And, because big business by nature tries to minimize its risks, the major's first concern is its own money, not the financial or artistic well-being of the artist. This is not to stand in judgment of the major labels—they're driven by market forces.

Because artists are viewed as investments by the major labels, every effort is made to have them bring a financial return. The sooner and better this is understood, the more prepared will be any musician who deals with them. In the balance of this chapter, we will explain the major label deal from its inception.

GETTING SIGNED

"My objective is to get signed." "I'm going to get a big advance." "All I have to do is make the record and I can start cashing in." We hear a lot of proclamations like these. They speak of a major label deal as the finish line of a process. More realistically, though, it's a starting line. If you remember this, you're doing yourself a favor.

Yes, if you don't have a deal with a major label, you won't record for one. But, just because you have a deal, you shouldn't necessarily count on making a ton of money and having a great career. This may be the case even if you sell what seems to be a lot of records. Many factors enter into this situation, but the first one you should know about is *recoupment*.

Artists who sign major label deals usually receive advances. If these are large dollar amounts, say, $500,000 and up, the news makes the trade and business papers. Rumors swirl around the act's old circle that "they've hit it big." But, what is an advance? It's merely an advance against future royalties, and it's *recoupable*—this means that it's subject to being *paid back to the label*. Therefore, even if the act's first release sells well and earns them $500,000 in royalties, the artists won't receive any of the money until the advance they received is paid back. The label will pay *itself* the first $500,000.

Does this still sound like a pretty good deal, a loan to the artists to tide them over until the sales pile up? Think again. The advance is to be used for production of the first album—in other words, the artists pay for it, *not the record company*. After paying for the studio time, the engineer, the session musicians, the producer's advance, and 20 percent off the top to the manager, very little of the advance is left for the artists to live on. If the act is, say, a four-member band, the amount for each person is cut still further. Most of the money is gone, not into the artists' pockets but, rather, invested in producing a master recording.

On top of this, consider the scenario if the record fails to sell well enough for the label to recoup the full advance. The sales cycle now is over, and at the end of it the artist *may well owe the record company money*, if recording and other expenses exceed the advance. If they're thinking about recording a second album, they are going to start in the hole[7] even before they get another recording advance, which will put them further in the hole—well, you get the picture.

There may be no second album, if the label doesn't pick up its option—this, known as "getting dropped," is not uncommon.[8] A new label looking to sign an artist who has been dropped probably will have to pay off at least part of the artist's debt to the old label. The artist then starts his life at the new label in debt by this amount. An artist and his company must really believe in the long-term sales potential to take a breath and dive in again.

Why do the major labels insist on recoupment? Because they have the bargaining power to do so. If they've got what you want, you have to make their deal, not yours. Their deal is to shift costs from themselves to the artists whenever possible. Clearly, it's in the artists' best interests to try to control production costs as much as they can. Still, when a major producer is involved, usually at the insistence of the label, there's a constraint on the artists' ability (for instance) to limit studio time.

Artist Royalties, Real and Imagined

In the basic equation, the royalty payable to the artist is calculated as follows:

$$R = n \times P \times r$$

where R is the royalty in dollars, n is the number of units sold, P is the retail price per unit, and r is the artist's royalty percentage. Sounds pretty straightforward, right?

Well, it isn't. Even where the artist's royalty rate stays constant, the sales base on which the calculation is made is reduced in practice. First, there is a reduction for promotional CDs and tapes given away. This number is often estimated up front, and for a new artist, it's a large percentage. The theory is that no royalty is due where there is no sale. Then, the artist is charged for packaging costs, further reducing the base on which royalties are paid. This is a flat rate or percentage of the retail price and often exceeds the true cost. But a new artist lacks the bargaining power to reduce or eliminate it.

Another deduction of the base for artist earnings is the breakage allowance. This number is based on the historically high rate for vinyl records, a medium that has been supplanted by less fragile tapes and CDs. No matter, if you're a new artist, you have to live with it.

These are examples of the major reductions in the amount payable to the artist in major label contracts, but they're not intended as an exhaustive list of deal points (which is beyond the scope of this discussion). As oppressive as these reductions seem to be for the new or established artist, they represent the commercial realities of the deal.

OTHER POST-SIGNING REALITIES

If you're a musician who's never had a label deal, you probably still think in terms of art—making the best music you can make, believing that the public will like it, and giving a career your best shot. Sure, you recognize that not everyone likes what you do, but you have to hope enough people will, right?

It's admirable to think this way, but that isn't how the major label sees you. Instead, they see you as an investment. Therefore, they want to make sure that every penny spent on you goes into making you the most profitable asset you can be—even if this means disregarding what sets you apart from the pack. Instead, the company will play up how your sound fits into the latest trend or use whatever other strategy it thinks will work to "break" you. The whole approach might even be wrong. Majors often are—the proportion of new acts that get up to the breakeven point is less than 5 percent (yes, *five* percent), by many estimates. But since it's their money, the companies are the ones who get to make the decisions on how to spend it.

Before you think we're cynical, here are two points:

- There's a reason record companies call artist's records "product"
- When the artist begins to make money for the label, his bargaining position improves, and he's in a better position to stand up for his own artistic and business judgments

Suppose that you, a new artist, wish to control your destiny by self-producing your first album. In addition, this will cut out the amount that would be paid to an outside producer. You've never produced before. Will the record label agree with you? In all likelihood, no. Again, the company views this scenario through a lens of money at risk.

As much as anything can be guaranteed in the music business, a producer with a track record will deliver a record that "sounds marketable." This producer may cost more, but the extra money is spent to protect the company's major investment. If, on the other hand, you're allowed to self-produce and the company finds the product (in their estimation) unmarketable, then it faces the choice of scrapping the whole project or spending even more money starting over.

Even though individuality is a component of popular music, big business doesn't want to rock the boat by putting out something it's afraid the market isn't ready for. If it seems ironic that a major label markets the uniqueness of its product at the same time as it homogenizes it, the answer is yes. Consider laundry detergent, another kind of product—companies are always trying to put a new ("improved!") spin on it. But it's unlikely that they will market a new detergent, for instance, that consists of black or dark gray crystals, because people wouldn't be ready for it. Corporate America is not going to take too big a risk of rejection.

THE RECORDING PROCESS

After the contract is signed, production begins—but what does this mean? First, a producer is found. Within limits, the act's choice of producer will be honored by the label, as long as the producer has a good track record, a reputation for being on time and within budget, and seems appropriate for the act. The producer then submits a budget, showing how much money he thinks he needs and how he intends to spend it.

When a final budget[9] is approved, the act goes into the studio to record. If it's not a self-contained group, some of the budget is set aside for session musicians to play on the tracks. The other big expenses are the producer's fee, studio time, and the engineers for recording and *mixing*.[10] In addition, there are costs of materials (for example, recording tape), cartage (lugging instruments and gear to the studio), and other incidental expenses.

The producer oversees the recording process. Some producers are very hands-on, in some cases writing the artist's material. Other producers are less obviously involved, instead, finding ways to allow the act to sound "like itself." Where there is artistic disagreement between a newer artist and the producer, the producer usually wins. The major label would rather take the veteran's advice than rely on the judgment of the artist making a first commercial recording. The more established an act is, the more this balance of power shifts toward it.

Recording ("tracking") and mixing time varies, depending on the budget, the type of act, things that go wrong, and limitations on the availability of some of the key players. At a minimum, usually three to four weeks of tracking are required to make an album—but those weeks of work may cover as much as two to six months. In many respects, proper mixing of a major label album is as important as good songs, strong performances, and well-engineered tracking to capture them. Mixing can be the key to making a recording *radio-friendly*—the ultimate criterion, even in the Internet age, of whether it can be a big seller.

When the producer, the act, or the label isn't pleased with the initial mixes, mixing can take longer than tracking. In some cases, copies of the master tapes[11] are sent to an alternate mixing engineer to see if he can do better. Once the recording is mixed, it is then *mastered*. Mastering is the process that prepares the recording to be commercially duplicated and released: Songs are sequenced and spaced properly, end-of-song "fades" are determined, volume levels from song to song are adjusted for consistency, and so on. CDs will be reproduced from this master.

WHO'S THE BOSS?

The typical major label deal contains *options* after the first album. Which is to say, the company may exercise *its* option for the artist to make a second or third (or further?) album. The artist, however, has no options. It works like this: The company may choose to allow the artist to make more albums, or it may refuse. The artist has no say in it. If the label is making money off the artist from the get-go (or if it continues to believe in the artist's future despite slow initial sales), it's going to exercise those options, in which case the artist is obligated to honor the contract. If this sounds like a one-way street, it is.

Commonly, the company would like to bind the new artist with up to six or seven options. If the act is successful, then the last few albums of the contract are huge money makers for the company. For the act, this isn't nearly as favorable—it's locked into the lesser deal (lower royalties, etc.) of a baby act, even though it's no longer a baby act.[12] Again, the contract favors the major label's bargaining power and point of view—if it helps to create a cash cow, the major will want to milk it for all it's worth.

Major labels also will demand (and get) from a new artist more control over the recording(s) than most artists would prefer. It's not within the scope of this book to discuss and analyze the principal "deal points" of a major label contract, but here are a few examples:

- Choice of producer
- Choice of material
- Choice of single from album
- Right to insist artist deliver a "commercially satisfactory" recording (this determination is the company's alone)[13]

These are just some that appear in the ordinary contract. The manner in which an act is marketed (for instance, which song should be used for a video) and many other aspects of a new act's career effectively are controlled by the major label even without specific contract provisions. Since the label is the "money partner," the label calls the shots. If the company is wrong, it will survive, but the act probably won't recover for a long time (if at all).

Before you musicians out there think this is just too unfair, reflect on this: The company wants you to succeed, not fail. True, it defines success in its terms, not yours, but there's a good bit of crossover between your well-being and its. By many estimates, to break a new act in the marketplace costs a minimum of a half-million dollars (and closer to one million dollars) for a major label. To invest this much in an artist, the label must believe in the artist. After all, it has no way to be sure an act will deliver one "commercial" album, much less the option albums. Once an artist is a proven commodity, there will be a shift in bargaining power (and attitude).

TIMING IS EVERYTHING

Just as it may take many months for a major label to sign an artist after expressing initial interest, sometimes it takes as long as two years from that point before the first record is released. This is due primarily to the sheer size of the major label. Its chain of command is long. Not infrequently, the time to get budget approval is excruciatingly slow. Because a major has many acts on its roster, in some ways they're competing against each other for the attention and money of the company. The business offices have only so many people to do the work, and there's only so much time in the day (or week or month) to do it. So some acts get higher priority, which means others get put on a back burner.

A major label may have so many acts that (as ridiculous as this sounds) its products compete against each other in the marketplace. As a practical matter, there's a limit to how many records a given company can release at one time without spreading itself too thin. Even for the majors, money is not infinite.[14] Company executives like to see some sales dollars roll in before they approve more expenditures. The resources that can be marshaled to advertise, promote (think airplay), and otherwise generate sales for its acts need to be doled out. So, release dates are staggered to minimize the effect of the company's products thinning out each other's sales.

On top of this, there are seasonal factors that affect release decisions for big business. For instance, some albums, thought of as "Christmas" or "gift" albums, are going to be the ones that get the big push in the holiday season. Albums by well-established artists are more likely to be purchased as the result of this kind of promotion, so they'll be released while the newer acts wait their turn. Many factors enter into release decisions, including which competitors are releasing albums by their artists. Again, the major is going to make the decisions it feels are most favorable to its business. Suffice it to say that corporate executives are under a lot of pressure to produce in the short term.

For the new artist, there are several ironies in delay. First, because the music business is so trend driven and ephemeral, the initial "buzz" created by an artist wears off quickly. By the time the album is ready to make hay, the sun no longer will be shining on it. Second, if the artist is part of a "sound" or "movement," by the time he gets to market, a competing act might get there first, stealing most of his thunder (and sales).[15]

Perhaps the most critical timing issue for new artists (and for older, less successful acts) relates to turnover of personnel within the company. The "life span" of an A&R rep at a major label is eighteen to twenty-four months, by most estimates—and higher-ups, such as vice-presidents and label heads, also turn over rapidly. Almost invariably, when a new boss comes on board, he replaces most of the A&R staff with people of his own choosing. What this means for the artist is that the A&R department—which signed him, understood his music, and nurtured him—is gone. The A&R department now has a new staff, and that staff is interested in signing and developing *its own* new acts. Under these circumstances, it's pretty easy for a new artist (or an older one who hasn't "broken") to get lost in the shuffle.

This is a nice way to say that the act's career could be over before it got a chance, because most major label record deals do not obligate the company to actually release the records.[16]

MARKETING AND PROMOTION—WHERE MAJORS SHINE

Many listeners think records "break" this way:

- A record is introduced on radio (and, increasingly, MTV and similar outlets) in a free, open, competitive market
- Then listeners hear the song and like it
- Then listeners buy the single or album and demand (request) repeated airing
- Then radio responds by playing the record even more
- This then stimulates demand even more, and so on, until the record's a hit

Not so. Even in the "old days" of the 1950s, when popular music was in its infancy as a big business, it didn't work like this. The commercial radio market is about as open and free as a state prison. Access is nearly completely controlled by just a few players: the majors. Almost every record played on commercial radio stations and just about every song featured in a music video (check the credits) is the release of a major label.[17] Considering that major label releases constitute a small portion of each year's total, common sense would suggest that some independent-label or self-released records would find their way onto commercial radio—and eventually turn into hits. Yet, this almost never happens, and there is a reason.

Controlling access to markets in radio is simple in concept. In the 1950s, it was called "payola," a system of bribes to station managers and program directors to play certain records. Consider this: A station can broadcast only 168 hours in a week, and fewer than that are prime listening hours. Also, because the broadcast spectrum is limited by technology and federal law, just so many stations are on the dial. Every time a station plays a record, it diminishes the opportunity to play a different one.

If all the stations play the same record(s) many times a day, and it's not because of payola, how does it happen? The answer is, now there's a legal form of payola, a multilayered effort of

- A promotional barrage that can be afforded only by major companies
- Expensive advertising that is affordable only by the majors
- The incentive majors have of supplying brand-new product by established artists, with the proviso that the stations play their other products
- Everything else money can buy, including what used to be called "bribes" and now are known as in-kind marketing expenses and promotional tools

Is this bad? If you're affiliated with a major, no; if you're competing with the majors, yes. Marketing and promotion are where the majors shine. They give the majors the opportunity to produce *really big numbers*, in which case an artist can prosper as well.

Compare the pop music market to the market for cola drinks. If you visit a chain grocery, the chances are you're going to see *just* Coke and Pepsi (and maybe the chain's bargain brand). If you go to a fast-food restaurant, you're going to see Coke or Pepsi (but not both—the drink makers tie up the chains with exclusives and incentives). You don't know what other cola drinks are produced, and you probably don't think about it. You accept what these big corporations sell, at least in part, because they're the only game in town.

This is the way it is for recorded popular music. For most people, the only source of what's going on in music is the radio in their car and the few music video channels on their cable TV system. Since there's almost no material on these outlets other than what's offered by the majors, it's easy for the average listener to think that it's the best, newest, and freshest pop fare available. Unless people dig pretty deep, they think it's the *only* music available.

College radio, mom-and-pop record stores, and increasingly, the Internet, serve as sources of non-major label music and have made a dent in the majors' stranglehold over recorded music. Still, they serve a relatively small (if enthusiastic and knowledgeable) segment of the market. The growing impact of independent labels in the 1990s and how they operate are the subject of the next chapter.

THE MAJORS ADAPT—THE 'NEW PARTNERSHIP' MODEL

Unless you've been on another planet the last four or five years, you know the music industry has become less profitable and more risky for the majors. No one is sure whether unauthorized downloading and piracy in other forms is the reason, but what's significant is that the risk climate is shifting the way the majors operate. In some cases, the relationship with new artists is evolving in a way that may benefit both artists and labels.

In the ongoing model described above, the label acts as a financier; in the new version, the label becomes, in essence, a partner. The artist, of course, is the other partner. This newer version of the relationship gives the artist a better chance to succeed. It cuts down on recoupable expenses, allows a higher royalty rate, and provides incentives for the label to stick with the artist even if his early recordings don't pay off immediately.

This "new partnership" recognizes that the short-term/high-stakes model wasn't working well for the labels, much less most artists. It represents a shift of business structure, not generosity. In return for more favorable contractual treatment concerning the artist's releases on the label, the artist is required to share with the label his revenues from other sources, including merchandising (T-shirts, for example) and concerts.

The label is required to give up its windfall if the artist hits it big early on; the artist is required to share some of his gains that his recordings have helped to foster. Both sides give up something, but both reduce uncertainty and lower short-term risk. We believe such partnering arrangements, properly structured, may increase the success rate for both artists and labels. Labels will have the incentive to seek artists with long-term potential rather than just trying to jump on a hot trend.

SUMMARY

An understanding of the basic market and modus operandi of the major labels is primary, because they've dominated for so long—and continue to dominate. They're the models everything else is measured by and compared to.

Major labels no longer do everything in-house, as they once did. These days, for the most part, the labels don't have their own studios, producers, arrangers, session musicians, and manufacturing plants, as they did in the past. Instead, they contract for these services with independent service providers and companies. What the majors do today, in essence, is to finance the production, manufacture, and marketing of records. The labels find new artists through their A&R staff.

Majors, which are part of multinational entertainment conglomerates, have substantial capital available for every aspect of their operation. They have enormous competitive advantage over independent labels in marketing and distribution—only the majors have their own distribution companies. Their resources assure them virtual control over commercial pop radio and music television (the major promotional tools of music sales). For the artists, the majors' unwieldy size, impersonal bureaucratic nature, and emphasis on immediate profits are "the bad" they have to accept with "the good." The "good" is the chance to do very large numbers and earn a lot of money.

For a new artist, a major label record deal, even one with a sizable advance, is no guarantee of success. Advances are recoupable—they are withheld from earned royalties until the last dollar is paid back to the company. Since advances are to be used for production of a master recording, the company, in effect, makes the artists bear the cost of recording while loaning them money to pay for it. It's not uncommon for newer artists with substantial sales to still owe their company money when they enter the studio to record their second or third albums.

Once signed to a recording contract, the artist chooses a producer. After the producer's recording budget is approved by the company, recording begins. The producer is like a supervisor or a movie director—he doesn't do the work of making the music[18] himself, but makes sure that it gets done right. It's the producer's job to deliver a commercially viable master recording that the company can release. For unproven artists, most judgment calls in the studio are made by the producer, although the balance of power shifts toward the artist as he becomes more successful.

Major label deals contain a series of options. In essence, these give the company the freedom to continue its relationship with the artist by "picking up" the options for subsequent albums or to discontinue the relationship by opting not to. Such freedom does not extend to the artist. The label makes a major investment in an artist and seeks to protect it. As a result, most deals for new artists are structured to give the company extensive control over the artist's recording career.

Because of the size and complexity of a major label, it often takes many months (sometimes eighteen to twenty-four) for the company to release a new artist's first album. Internal budget issues, large amounts of the company's own product coming to market, competing products, time of year, general market conditions, and other factors all may contribute to a delay. In addition, it's not uncommon for an act to "lose" its A&R rep, even most of the A&R department, during its tenure at a major label. The new staffers may be less than enthusiastic about the old acts, which can get lost in the shuffle.

Despite the apparent difficulties for an artist on a major label, the majors do offer tremendous advantages of marketing and distribution. They pretty well have a lock on commercial radio and music television airplay, and through their distribution companies, they control the flow of most product to retailers. As a result, all the very biggest selling records appear on major labels (or their affiliates who reap the benefits of these advantages). So, while the major label deal for a new artist seems stacked in the label's favor, the artist does stand to profit heavily—if this is one of the acts generating big numbers.

Recent music industry downturns have forced the major labels to reconsider how they do business. Increasingly, the contract of the future may look more like a partnership than the one-sided major label deal that is still the staple.

CHAPTER 4

INDEPENDENT RECORD LABELS—"INDIES"

I n the 1990s, "indie rock" emerged as a new classification of commercial music. Although independent labels had been around for years, they finally came into their own as a force that made the major labels reexamine what they do on every level—artistic, A&R, production, marketing, and so on, down the line.

While independent labels release many types of music, the indie rock "sound" that shook up the industry came to be associated with stripped-down, post-punk guitar pop. This sound began in what was, in its beginning days, appropriately called "alternative" music. In the early 1990s, it *was* a real alternative to the highly produced, predictable heavy metal and dance music offered by the majors.

Indie records carried a cachet of integrity. Their "low-fi" production values emphasized attitude and passion more than production. The rebellious, antiauthority sentiment expressed by the music, while certainly not novel, seemed fresh to a new generation of listeners. More important, the production style and antivirtuosity stance of the acts matched the message of the music. The whole package was just right for the rock audience of what has been dubbed "Generation X." The indie rock sound gained a strong foothold on college radio.

When the majors caught on to the trend, they began to sign acts that either started out as indie rockers or, at least, sounded like they did. Within five or six years, the term "alternative rock" mutated into a description of "grungy" guitar and other sonic trademarks of much commercial rock sold by majors. In other words, "alternative rock" now means mainstream. As of this writing, there are more original acts that call themselves "alternative" than any other category—including plain old rock and roll or rock.

Indies represent a true alternative to major labels. There are business, cultural, demographic, and technological reasons for their surge.

MONEY MATTERS

The most immediately noticeable thing about independent labels compared to majors is that they are small businesses.[19] Most of them aren't even *large* small businesses, but rather, mom-and-pop operations that began as labors of love by the owners. Their offices aren't in downtown high-rise buildings or lush corporate office parks. Indies are more likely to be run out of a spare bedroom, garage, or borrowed office space. Often, there are very few employees—the owner, a spouse, an intern, a member of one of the label's bands, that's about it.

Majors are under constant pressure to minimize the risks they take with their acts and to maximize the profitability of the company. For the most part, they follow, rather than lead, the trends in popular music. They can't afford to sign only acts that the head of the label likes personally. Majors have high overhead and must answer to their shareholders. If the job done by the managers of the company is found wanting, they will be replaced. Small wonder that, in this environment, every decision is weighed gravely and only the risks judged to be suitably prudent will be taken.

By contrast, the independent label is a seat-of-the-pants operation, which typically gets started because the founder enjoys and wants to support the music of certain acts. Sure, he'd like to make enough profit to keep going and to quit his other job, but that's as far as it goes in most cases. In the beginning at least, the driving motivation is not financial but supporting the music and the music scene. By and large, the folks who start indies are young people (eighteen to thirty), contemporaries of the bands they support. They're not the "suits" of corporate business.

Because of the financial status of the indies, their business philosophy is different. In some ways it has to be; after all, they lack the resources to operate like a major label. In addition, they don't really have the same objectives as majors. Their market share is infinitesimally small, so they aren't concerned about maximizing it. Unlike the publicly held majors, they're risking nobody's money but their own. Indies, particularly in the rock genre, freely champion certain sounds and groups, if that's what the owner likes.

NECESSITY IS THE MOTHER OF LO-FI

Because independents are underfunded by comparison to the majors, their business philosophy is to make records cheaply—very cheaply. Majors often spend $200,000 or more to produce an album; to many independents, this figure is so out of reach it might as well be $200 billion. More commonly, an independent label spends somewhere between $1,500 and $10,000 to record an album. Needless to say, the advance to an act is commensurately smaller. No artist becomes flush by getting signed by an indie.

What lower costs mean to the independent label, though, is that fairly modest sales can recover those costs. Sales of 10,000 units, for example, usually result in a profit to the indie. However, for a major, 10,000 units would be abject failure, not just on a symbolic level but on a financial one. In industry jargon, the label would get killed, bringing in probably a few pennies for each dollar spent.

Ironically, the lo-fi production sound that came to be associated with indies was originally a result of their constrained budgets, more so than a planned sonic style. With only so many dollars, there's a limit to how much production the label can afford. For example, tracking and mixing time, engineers and producers, quickly eat up a recording budget of $2,500. That wouldn't be even one day's budget for a major-label recording slated to take weeks. The major-label producer and engineer probably will not have "gotten" the drum sound by that time, much less begun tracking. By contrast, the indie band might have to record their whole album in one session. It's synergistic, then, that the sound they want can be had for $2,500.

TECHNOLOGY, AFFORDABILITY, AND THE RISE OF INDEPENDENT LABELS

Prior to the 1990s, even a modest pro recording studio required gear so costly that not many people could afford to get into the business. This situation changed with the arrival of digital technology for recorders and signal processors. Gear that once cost as much as a nice house now can be had for the price of an ordinary new car. While that still isn't trivial, it does make entry into the recording studio business much easier.

The lower the cost of gear, the cheaper the rates a studio can afford to charge for recording. Moreover, cheaper gear means more studios go into business, and more studios mean more competition. Except at the high end, all studios have felt this effect. The increased competition has made recording more affordable for independent labels and encouraged their proliferation.

Recording has become so accessible that many acts pretty much produce their own records—they use the independent label for "pressing" (manufacturing), distribution, and whatever other support is available. Sometimes the band makes a recording strictly using gear that it owns or self-finances a recording at a studio. PC-based home recording gear has proliferated, enabling many musicians to make their own recordings. Either way, the independent label is in a position to acquire the master, or nearly finished master, with a minimal investment.

Because the time and money spent on production are minimal by major label standards, the production quality of some indie rock recordings is distinctly lo-fi. Since much alternative rock embraces a grassroots, populist ethos (rejecting professionalism, virtuosity, and slick production), this isn't negative at all. In fact, for the acts associated with indie rock, lo-fi is part of the sound they want. This makes for a perfect pairing of artistic and business objectives—labels and acts that can't afford full-blown production values don't really need them anyway.[20]

Within the sphere of indie rock, alternative music—call it what you will—limited production has worked fine. However, if your music is different, this may not be the case. Even if you start your career on an independent, you may later want to graduate to a major for the resources available to make the records you want. Of course, whether this option is available is another issue. If you're an artist whose music requires a lot of production expertise, studio time, and attendant expense, don't expect that it will be easy to make the records you want recording for most independent labels.

STAFF SUPPORT AT INDEPENDENT LABELS CONTRASTED TO MAJORS

Major labels are run like other big businesses. They have many departments, a chain of command between the departments, a pecking order within them, and internal politics. Majors typically have A&R, accounting, legal, promotions, marketing, publicity, and other departments. Each department may be divided into sections, such as Urban Promotions or Latin Promotions. Theoretically at least, there is a department for each important function, and responsibilities are clearly and narrowly defined. Major labels have hundreds of employees to do these jobs. The companies are so big that employees who need to work together may not even work out of the same city.

By contrast, independent labels typically have no distinct departments. Instead, they have a small number (usually single digits) of employees, most of whom do many, many jobs. In a typical day, an employee of an indie may

- Attend a meeting with the label head about whether an act should be signed
- Talk to an artist about something he needs done to finish his record
- Follow up on promotional CDs sent to radio stations and request airplay
- Call record stores to see whether they have an interest in carrying the label's product
- Arrange a photo shoot for cover art
- Listen to a rough mix of an upcoming album to check its progress

- Arrange an "in store" (promotional) performance by an act
- Coordinate local press coverage for a band on tour
- Do anything else that's required

At the major labels, one department "hands off the ball" to another department to do its separate job. The people in Marketing don't really get involved in A&R, for instance. By contrast, an indie employee who has responsibility for an act will tend to wear many hats for it. Moreover, because so few people do the work, the job each person does constantly shifts, based on the demands of the business. One executive with major label experience, who's currently working at an independent, sums it up this way:

> A major label is a man-powered machine. At most labels, you have 150 to 200 employees, each of whom has a specific job to do. You have specialized departments with a high level of concentration in specific areas. Resources are much greater [*than at an indie*], monetarily and manpower-wise. An indie label is a whole different ethic and a whole different approach to putting out records . . . I worked in publicity for a major label, and I dealt strictly with the print media . . . here everyone is multi-tasking, working retail, dealing with distributors, doing press, doing radio, bringing the bands in, negotiating contracts.

This is a matter of necessity, due to limited resources—but it is also a byproduct of design. The philosophy of the indie meshes with the market it serves, particularly in indie rock.

THE INDIE ETHOS—WHAT MAKES INDEPENDENTS "INDIES"

Though some independent labels release music whose sound is mainstream, the majority of product put out by indies is not. The typical indie act is one in which the major labels have no interest. Indie labels often feature artists who are relatively raw or undeveloped—artists the majors deem as lacking the radio-friendly sound it takes to get airplay on commercial stations. Many indie labels actively seek artists, styles, and genres that you just don't hear and that you likely never will hear, that is, on commercial radio.[21]

Since independent labels are started by people who want to put out music that they like, bands that they like, within a very constricted budget, little monetary investment is made in a given band or record. This may seem limiting, in terms of production values, marketing, and distribution, but there's an upside as well: Indies don't have a need for a large, immediate return on the investment, as would be the case with a major label. So, for an indie, sales of 30,000 units over the life of a record is usually considered a big success. As noted earlier, that number is a drop in the bucket for a major label, which ships 30,000 units of a new release in the first week. For majors, sales of even 300,000 units might not yield profits.

The small scale and personal nature of an indie means that the label is passionately committed to the artists and their records. By keeping things small, this situation allows indie acts to develop artistically over the course of two to four albums. This gradual growth, without an expectation of explosive profits, also allows the acts to build their fan base through live performances and increase sales on successive albums. According to Brian Spevak, an independent label executive:

> It's a way for an artist to get out there and grow without jumping into a major label situation. Even if a new act attracts major label interest, there's always a question about whether signing would be the right move. Being unproven, with no existing fan base, no following and no sales base to work off is just like spinning the roulette wheel.

Artists on independent labels should understand that they're not going to receive the monetary backing they would get on a major. However, if they work hard on their careers, they're probably going to receive continued support from their indie, even if their initial sales are disappointing. In the climate of today's major labels, they would probably get dropped.

THE UNDERGROUND NETWORK OF INDEPENDENT MUSIC

At the time the first edition was published, an Internet site called the Underground Railroad was the most visible contact list for indie rock acts, consisting of clubs, record stores, promoters, and friends of alternative music in different cities. Though Underground Railroad no longer exists, many other contact lists, on and off the Internet, are available to support such acts.[22] When these artists are on the road, they need not worry about having someplace to stay or having to spend a lot of money for something to eat. With the lists as a guide, and through word of mouth, they are considered friends of other indie rockers in whatever town they visit. According to an industry veteran:

> The life of an indie rocker is the antithesis of rock stardom. Instead of private jets, luxury hotels, limos, and tour buses, you've got the Ford Econoline van tour . . . eating spaghetti at someone's house if you're lucky, eating fast food if you're not. You sleep on someone's couch or in the van. The pay guarantee for a show is only $100 or $150 . . . The lifestyle involves selling T-shirts and CDs at your shows . . . on the road, you live off merchandising money. But it's a way to get out there and develop your career.

Compared to the structure and financial backing of a major label, this is bare bones stuff—but indie label artists are much more in control of their destiny than those artists at the majors. Because doing astronomical numbers isn't the name of the game at independent labels, the focus on the fan base is entirely different. It's very grassroots oriented: Rather than being promoted by commercial radio, music television, and other major media, indie rock is promoted by word of mouth through enthusiastic young fans—over the Internet, in proudly amateurish tabloid magazines known as "fanzines" (or "zines") published in garages and basements,[23] by live shows, and over college radio.

When an independent act rolls into a town where they're playing, they usually head straight for mom-and-pop record stores that they know sell CDs and tapes like theirs. If they've called ahead, they may do an "in store," that is, a short promotional show, after which they'll mingle with fans and sell some CDs and merchandise. They'll do an interview with the publishers of local fanzines, maybe one with the local college radio station. All this legwork can only help their draw at that night's show. This, in turn, may mean more pay and a bigger turnout the next time they play locally. Some independent label acts have been able to sell 50,000 CDs of one release this way—small potatoes by major label standards, but profitable for the indie label and the artists.

INDIE PROMOTION AND RADIO

All the industry people we talked to agreed that, for majors, commercial radio is almost everything in breaking a new act. The radio stations understand this and increasingly have tightened their formats to increase their own power. This, in turn, has encouraged the majors to allot even more of their mighty resources into dominating the medium. The independent labels lack the financial muscle to compete with the majors in this arena. As alternative music was breaking in the early 1990s, some independent labels thought they could segue their success into commercial radio, but they failed. The money just wasn't there. Occasionally, an indie record is added in light rotation, but the circumstances have to be just right. For instance, a group with a large, rabid local following might be added on one commercial station in that market, but the chances are few and far between.

Since commercial radio for independents is just about a nonentity, college radio is the major source of airplay for independent music. The free-form nature of college radio works in the indies' favor; that is, the students who are involved do so out of enthusiasm for music and often go out of their way to avoid playing mainstream records. Unlike the majors, who send singles to the commercial stations, independent labels don't service singles. An artist's entire CD is sent to the radio station, with suggested singles highlighted on the label with a bold pen. If the disc jockeys like it, they play it; if not, they don't. The indies have no economic hold over college radio, but they do have sympathetic ears. Labels work hard to develop contacts, which result in college radio airplay for independent releases.

That's the good news. The bad news is that, in the scheme of things, the impact of college radio is extremely limited. True, it's more helpful in breaking records for indies than commercial radio. However, in the entire United States, there are just a handful (six to ten, depending on who you ask) college radio stations whose signal is strong enough to be any kind of presence. This pales next to the hundreds of commercial stations with powerful signals. Typically, college radio is hard to receive outside of an extremely limited broadcast area, so coverage is poor. Sometimes it's available only on cable.

For indies, college radio is important, not so much because it can compete with commercial radio, but because it's all they've got. The balance of promotion is through the underground network of fanzines, one-on-one relationships with independent record store owners, Internet links with alternative music fans, and the bands themselves. Through ceaseless touring, interviews, and merchandise sales, bands can develop a fan base and a buzz. Unlike the mass merchandising available to the majors, it happens one fan at a time.

MAJOR LABEL MINDSET COMPARED

It's not untrue to state that, at a major label, you have a chance to "win the pop music lottery" and make a big splash right off the bat. "That may sound great in theory, but you've got to realize that in any given month there are five to ten records being released [at the majors]," says executive Brian Spevak. "If your record isn't the one the label gets behind, you're out of luck."

Long-time record executive Paul Fishkin says, "the current trend with major labels is very hit-oriented, everyone's looking to make a huge killing on the first record." He continues:

> Unfortunately for the artists, that means there's very little emphasis on careers. At one time the major labels could afford to develop an artist until he became profitable after three or four albums . . . no more. The industry's structure doesn't permit it. So the act gets only one shot, and if they don't hit, they're likely to get dropped. If your A&R person was fired or went to another label, you don't have anyone to champion your project . . . And once a band, in particular, gets dropped by a major, the perception is there that you're damaged goods, like the smashed loaf of bread on the bargain shelf. It might be the case even if you've made a great record.

By contrast, the standards of failure are much different on an indie. Because the records are less risky and the label head is often a personal fan of the acts signed, a record that is artistically successful is likely to be considered a success in any event. "Besides, if you fail on an indie, you may be able to stay with the indie or move to another indie," adds Spevak.

In a boom-bust cycle, many independent labels of the late 1990s have become victims of their own success. Earlier in the decade, lower and lower recording and manufacturing costs led to a proliferation of product by "underground" or "alternative" acts. The fan base was there, and sales of indie rock grew enormously. This increase occurred without the benefit of commercial airplay, music television, or recognition by mainstream print media. When some of the indie acts (particularly those with the "Seattle sound") became too successful to ignore, the majors got involved and signed the groups.

Initially, the majors were able to sell product by some of the alternative rock acts by the usual methods—commercial radio and music television. So, they kept digging deeper into the pool of bands and signing more of them. The majors tried to sell alternative music the way they sold everything else—more, more, more. "They capsulated it, plugged it into a formula and tried to make it work," says Spevak, adding:

> In a few years, the strategy backfired . . . much of the music was street level music. I don't want to call it "blue collar rock," but it's the antithesis of the major label world. They saw groups selling 40,000 records on indies, and figured they could easily do ten times that . . . but they didn't know how to sell it in a way that was true to its roots, and they weren't able to capture much of an audience . . . they even lost a lot of the core audience due to backlash . . . The major labels lack credibility in the alternative music world, which they didn't appreciate until it was too late. . . . [Unlike the independent labels] they spent way too much money to make records. The independent labels who are doing it right are either making records very cheaply or putting out records which were already recorded.

The independent label, by comparison, is very personal. The artists are perceived as being just like their fans. The notion of achieving big numbers seems so remote, and in most cases *is* so remote, that indie rock seemed to have an integrity the majors could not duplicate. The majors failed to account for the fact that this street-level, Everyman quality is a huge part of the appeal of indie rock. The consequences of the majors' miscalculation are still being felt by them—and by the independent labels.

The majors' incursion into alternative rock did bring formerly little-heard music and artists to mainstream consumers. Major labels bought into some of the more successful indies or purchased them outright. The smell of money also resulted in signing too many acts for the market to support. Inevitably, there was a glut of product of both major labels and indies. The expectations of new artists began to rise. "Bands that would never have been talked to in the early 1990s were now being courted," says Brian Spevak, "and came to independent labels looking for signing money, tour support, videos, and other goodies. They were completely unrealistic—independent labels can't compete on those terms."

Ultimately, the success of indie labels with alternative rock revolved around the ethos of the music and the bands—very word of mouth, very underground. The major labels didn't understand the mechanism. They saw a band selling 20,000 to 40,000 units on an independent label and thought they could do better with their usual methods, but they didn't realize where those sales really came from and who the buying public was. To majors, sales come from chain record stores (and increasingly, big-box retail stores like Wal-Mart). However, in the indie world, most sales come from the mom-and-pop record stores that cater to the specialized market, part of the underground network mentioned earlier. Since they misunderstood the buying public, simply turning up the heat didn't work. "It's a scene, that if you're not involved with it, is difficult to understand. It seems like it should be something you can take and just build on, but that was proved wrong," says Spevak.

The high-water mark for independent labels as a whole was tied into alternative music. With the passing of the alternative rock rush, both the majors and indies suffered. In the case of the majors, it was because they misread the market, spent millions of dollars, but failed to sell enough product to justify the investment. For the indies, the damage was done by the glut—there were too many acts, too many labels, competing for shelf space and the ears of listeners. Most indie rock labels have seen their sales drop; acts whose early albums sold well found that subsequent albums did not.

INDEPENDENT LABELS TODAY

Increasingly, independent labels survive by:

- Picking up records that are already done, then manufacturing and distributing them, which requires no cash advances.
- Releasing as many different, and extremely cheap to produce, records as they can. Sales are modest on any one release, but multiple small profits add up.
- Partnering with a major label in a "pressing and distribution" deal.[24]
- Partnering with a major label on a joint release. The record appears to be released by the major, which usually has little to do with its production or development of the artist. Here, the major has a greater investment than in the distribution deal and stands to make more money if the record is successful.
- Selling contracts of their more promising acts to major labels. This results in instant profits, but very little artistic satisfaction for the label owners. Usually, they don't like to think of themselves as mercenaries, but . . .

The effects on artists looking for major label deals are also noticeable. Increasingly, majors are unwilling to take a chance by signing an act off its music alone; they're looking for some kind of track record, whereas before, they were far more willing to develop acts after signing them. Having gotten burnt by overpromotion of alternative rock, the majors have become more conservative, more standoffish, in signing new acts.

An artist who signs with an independent label should realize what is expected. The act should be working already and playing shows. It should be prepared for touring and perhaps has been playing out-of-town shows already. There should be some fan base to build on. The artist should be ready to make records cheaply—maybe having a self-produced an EP or full-length release. The label is looking for motivation and a work ethic; the music alone isn't enough, not anymore. In a very real sense, independent artists must be prepared to sell their own records—which at this point includes being Internet savvy.

The passing of the first big wave of alternative music caused most independent labels to scale way back. Now that the majors are slower to sign artists, indies have a chance to pick up some more of the market.

Effect of Independent Labels on Artists Contemplating Contracts

Beginning with the rap labels of the 1980s and continuing into the alternative rock years of the 1990s, the major labels got a big scare from independents. Says Paul Fishkin, who began working in the music business around 1970,

> They proved you don't need a major label to sell records. You have to real-ize just how radical this really was . . . for the first time, they felt threatened. It took them awhile to figure out what indies did better than they did, which was picking up trends from the street . . . the reaction of the majors was to use their money and their clout to harness this power.

According to Fishkin, the sales charts of the 1990s contained "a dis-proportionate amount of artists who are going through some independent entity. Now that the big companies finally understand it, more acts are com-ing in by that route than through their home-grown A&R departments." Acts are coming to majors from outside, independent, or copartnered sources, which can only increase the importance of those sources.

The effect on artists is tremendous. Artists who have proven themselves on indies are then chased by the major labels, which is the reverse of how things often work. No longer does going with an independent label consign artists to toiling in obscurity—it may be their best route into the majors. By signing with an indie, the artist has the opportunity to develop artistically as well as commercially before going to a major. This provides both artist and label a greater likelihood of success (or at least the perception of it).

For the majors, signing an act by making a joint venture with the indie label cuts down on the per-unit profit, because they have to share it. However, they risk less because they're embracing acts that are, in Paul Fishkin's words, "somewhat proven at the local level. Even though [the major label is] paying a middleman, the greater proportion of success makes it profitable for them."

An incentive for an act to continue the indie route is that, in the words of independent label executive Brian Spevak,

> The artist who sells 30–50,000 copies of a record on an independent label can make money, but on a major label, he wouldn't. There's less cost to recoup . . . Most independent labels offer either a fairer royalty rate or a flat royalty rate, where a band is guaranteed, say, two dollars or two dollars plus per CD sold (including mechanicals) . . . some companies even have a pure profit sharing arrangement, 50/50 between the act and the company. It's a fair situation for an artist who's done a lot of work and is starting to see the sales.

In the world of major labels, the stakes are so high that an artist might prefer to stay with the indie, even if doing so means sacrificing the opportunity to move product in the really big numbers—which could cost him a lot of money. But, he's also avoiding exposure to a situation in which, even if he doubles or triples his sales, he's not going to earn anything and is likely to get dropped. Not every artist has designs on a high-profile career with the attendant risks and pressures.

INDIE—SPRINGBOARD TO THE MAJORS?

There are advantages to being on a major, and most of them start with the word "more"—more advance, more promotion, more distribution, more radio, more tour support, and so on. The ultimate advantage, of course, is more income; but even with the other benefits, there's no guarantee. Still, the lure is there.

Eric Goodis, head of Cargo Records, a successful indie label, says that the time for an act to move to a major is, "Either when the money is so good that nothing else matters, or when their music is at the point when they have to make very little compromise to give the major what they are expecting." This is a concise and perfect summation, but how does an act know when the music is sufficiently developed? Eric Goodis continues:

> Starting with an indie has major advantages for a young act. On an indie you will have the time to develop not just your music, but your stage performance. If and when your music begins to click, and you get a chance to switch to a major, no one is going care how many indie CDs you released that did not sell big numbers. Major label failures, by contrast, tend to stick with you . . .

> But most important is the artistic freedom an indie allows you. Most indies do not care if your music does not attempt to attract the widest possible audience. Most of them prefer niche appeal. This allows you time to develop viable original music.

In essence, then, although not all indie acts move to majors (or even *want* to move), the independent label experience serves as both a grooming period and a testing ground for those who do make the move.

In contrast to earlier eras, the 1990s saw a number of high-profile acts whose indie recording careers were well established before they moved to majors. The most notable of these was Nirvana, one of the two or three most influential groups of the decade. In addition to the phenomenon of artists moving up, several of the more successful indie labels sold all or part of their business to majors. All things considered, the 1990s were the heyday of the indie label. Nevertheless, some observers predict even bigger things for indies in coming years, largely due to changes in the major label structure.[25]

As more and more music is purchased online, and if conventional radio is supplanted by other types of exposure to new music,[26] the playing field will level and independent labels will rise in importance. To the extent that the major label model breaks down in the future (if only because majors react slowly to ever-faster-moving trends), indies will assume a greater role in the marketplace. However, as of mid-2004, the field is still tilted heavily in favor of majors and their power to control consumer access.

CHAPTER 5

THE DO-IT-YOURSELF (DIY) APPROACH—A CAREER ON YOUR OWN LABEL

I n most cities and towns, you can go to a club and hear bands or solo artists who are virtually unknown, outside of a small circle of friends. Plenty of these groups are hard-pressed to draw a dozen people to a show. This is the way music has been for decades. What changed in the 1990s is that now, there's a good chance that the performer you and eight other people are listening to has a self-released CD or tape or is in the process of making one. Groups that have been playing together for less than six months commonly release product. Sometimes an act performs just one or two live shows before going into the recording studio. In years past, this would not have been the case.

If you want to have a career as a recording artist, the most basic level is to produce, manufacture, and sell your own recordings. These days it's often called DIY, for "do-it-yourself." You don't need to convince a business-person to like your music or believe in you. You don't need to ask anyone else to risk the money. You don't have to worry about artistic control. If you have music, and some money, you can do it yourself. As with any other decision, the choice to DIY ought to be made for the right reasons and with a full understanding of its benefits and drawbacks.

THE DIGITAL REVOLUTION—SOUND FOR LESS MONEY

Although, to a degree, making and selling your own recordings has always been feasible, modern computer-driven digital technology has greatly reduced studio costs. These savings have been made possible by inexpensive digital recording machines and signal processors. The devices are not only affordable but relatively easy to use, and they are capable of making excellent recordings. In terms of operation, adjustment, and repair, they don't require the strong electronics background that previous gear demanded. Musicians can now choose to record using home PCs and the programs available for such recording. For those willing to self-engineer, this cuts the cost further and increases convenience.

In addition, an avalanche of information is available on how to use all the gear. Many community colleges offer courses in basic recording. Classes are filled with aspiring musicians as much as with engineering students. These days, a lot of people know how to use the studio well enough to make at least a serviceable recording. Many musicians have their own high-quality studio gear or have friends who do. Music and pro-sound stores rent out recording gear cheaply, making it available on an as-needed basis to musicians who might not have the desire or finances to buy it. The small studio business has grown as the cost of equipment has dropped, and rates are extremely competitive.

To an artist this means that making a studio-quality recording is far more feasible than it used to be, even in the early 1990s. The costs are much less, and a lot more people are around to help you do it. In real terms, you can make a pretty fair recording for the price of a good guitar and amp, whereas previously several times this amount was required.[27] If a four- or five-piece group is involved, expense-splitting cuts the outlay to each member even more.

Another boon for the DIYer is that the manufacture of quantities of CDs has become inexpensive. Advances in computer automation and laser technology have made replication equipment far cheaper, so getting into the manufacturing end of the business is easier. Starting up no longer requires a capital investment of hundreds of thousands of dollars, and many new companies have come into the industry. The sheer number of firms in the market has led to intense competition. Ever-lower prices and quick turn-arounds are advertised in trade magazines, on the Internet, and wherever else musicians commonly inquire. Because their business has expanded beyond wholesaling to record companies, manufacturers have become consumer savvy. For instance, most of them now have toll-free phone numbers and accept credit cards.[28]

The bottom line is this: For those who want to do it themselves, production and manufacturing no longer are daunting obstacles. However, this begs a question: Does the fact that you *can* make your own CDs necessarily mean that you *should*? Notwithstanding the factors that might indicate otherwise, more and more musicians are making their own product. That many new recording studios and manufacturing companies have come into the market is not merely a matter of lower entry costs. The trend also reflects an increasing demand for their services—a demand driven by factors independent of cost.

WHY DIY? WHY NOW?

Many local record stores and local affiliates of major chains now have a large section devoted to local recording artists, most of whom are unsigned by a label or whose product is on a local independent label. At least in terms of the size of the shelf space devoted to such releases, this a relatively new (1990s) development. Why has this happened, and why now?

The answer is that there are far more musicians than there were in the past and, especially, far more bands. Well into the 1980s, not that many young musicians were playing popular music. "Almost everyone you meet now, their brother or sister, their uncle or their kid, is in a band. Or, they are themselves! A few years ago, it wasn't like this—only weirdoes were musicians . . . a breed apart," says one guitar store owner, who adds, "I like it. It's good for my business!" Some commentators think that music television has brought participants into music by making it seem glamorous. Long-time music executive Paul Fishkin states:

> MTV has made music, being a musician, sexy and cool. Kids now want to do it as a career choice, like being a baseball star used to be. It's not necessarily because they're artistically driven . . . as a result we've got a lot of product, and not all of it is good. The more product you have, the more of everything you're going to get.

Regardless of the reason, sales figures for instruments (especially rock instruments) and equipment have continued to expand mightily, which is a pretty good indicator that there are more musicians than before.

Even though there are many more musicians than ever, there has been no proportionate increase in the number of opportunities to record on a major label. If anything, the opportunities are fewer. In this era in which the major record companies are run by Wall Street, the emphasis is on cost cutting as a way to beef up the short-term bottom line. This means, among other things, dropping acts making too little money. Even though they might sell many albums in a long career, an act that doesn't show profits right out of the gate has no chance. Increasingly, the majors concentrate their immense resources on proven winners, rather than in trying to create new winners.

After expanding strongly and steadily since the mid-1980s, sales of CDs on major labels began to fall in 2000. The decline accelerated in 2001 and 2002, then slowed somewhat in 2003. As we pointed out in the first edition, there were ominous trends beneath the seemingly healthy pre-2000 numbers.[29] For one thing, much of the momentum of sales was fueled by older catalog material—basically, people were replacing their vinyl records or first-generation CDs by purchasing great-sounding remastered albums. This backfilling has largely been exhausted, and even when it was robust, it didn't translate into signing new bands or solo artists.

Since now there's a glut, comparatively speaking, of new artists and not much opportunity (or perceived opportunity) at majors, the musicians who wish to record are turning to independent labels and DIY.

THE PUNK ETHOS AND DIY

In the late 1970s, the popular music business had its first brush with what, at the time, was called "the punk revolution." In large part, punk is responsible for the DIY ethos and the rise of indie labels. To understand this, let's review a little history.

The initial energy and popularity of 1950s rock and roll had been suppressed by the early 1960s. It was rekindled by the so-called British Invasion groups of the mid-1960s, which became the "classic rock" music boom of the 1960s and early 1970s.

By the mid- to late 1970s, rock music had gained artistic respectability and had made a huge commercial impact. In doing so, some of its visible stars had shed their formerly rebellious, anti-Establishment image and joined the respectable show-biz elite. Critics and many young fans viewed much of the music being produced by the major labels as self-important, overproduced, disposable kitsch. Punk music was the response. Even though its immediate commercial impact was moderate, its effects reverberate into the present.

The first-generation punk groups were consciously anti-Establishment, antislick, simplistic, juvenile, and fun. The instrumentation typically consisted of distorted, out-of-tune guitars and bass, crashing drums, and angry vocals that were not sung with attention to musical virtues of melody and pitch. The lyrical content was political, anarchic, and snide in one song, crude and personal in the next. Much of the music was played at breakneck tempos; the best of it made up in energy what it lacked in originality or musical substance. Its proponents saw it as a continuation of rock's youthful spirit; in their eyes, the major acts of the day had become bloated, irrelevant dinosaurs.

After its initial splash, punk disappeared from the commercial music horizon. It didn't really go away completely; the punk scene continued to percolate as an underground phenomenon throughout the 1980s. Finally, in the early 1990s, punk and punk-influenced groups emerged onto major labels, where they had a much greater commercial impact than in their original incarnation of the late 1970s.

In a fundamental way, this punk ethos changed the way musicians think about their music. In the days where there was no real alternative music and no viable alternative to the major labels, artists had little choice. They could go the show-biz route and become "entertainers," in which case their music and their message would be diluted and homogenized. Or, they could simply give up, defeated by the established music industry. But, punk and independent (or alternative) musicians, fueled by their own underground support system,[30] said, "Hold everything, we can do this ourselves!" And they were right; they were able to shun the major labels and everything the labels were perceived to stand for. The values of the music and its artists coalesced with their disdain for, and independence from, the music-business establishment. And, as discussed previously, it's no small benefit that the newer technologies supported the possibilities as never before.

Since much so-called alternative music has been co-opted by the major labels (which are always anxious to jump on trends that can turn a profit), it's easy to underestimate the impact of the punk ethos. You have to dig deeper than just listening to commercial music radio or perusing chain record stores, with their promo posters for middle-of-the-road pop divas. The punk ethos has not been co-opted. Listen to college radio. Go to a show. Surf to an independent music Web site. Visit your local independent record store. Pick up some of the fanzines you find there and read them. Many musicians you will read about have no desire to "make it" by watering down their music and message.

Even in nonpunk genres, there's a skepticism about whether "making it" on a major label is even beneficial. Zachary Najor, a member of the funk-jazz group The Greyboy Allstars (who release CDs exclusively on their own label, Greyboy Records), expresses this sentiment when he says: "The response of the major record companies introduced much more of a controlled approach to our project . . . Before you begin to build, count the cost. Many people have been down this [major label] road in search of mass appeal and when they get it they find themselves high and dry."

ARTISTIC CONTROL ISSUES

When an artist's album is released by a major label, an inherent filtering process has been at work. Majors are big business; big business is interested in generating big numbers. Generating big numbers means having a product that can be sold to a broad audience. Even where music is marketed as "new," it must have enough familiarity in form or sound that it holds mainstream appeal. Therefore, by their very nature, majors avoid artists whose music is extreme, experimental, and uncompromising.

In the words of former major label music executive Bruce Flohr, the implicit pact with the artist is this: "Bands who sign with us want to make money . . . they wouldn't be here otherwise. They understand that means being on the same team." This translates into making a "commercial record"—as that term is defined by the company. While this approach doesn't inherently compromise the sound of acts that already are commercial, other artists want no part of it.

Zachary Najor of The Greyboy Allstars explains artistic control in practical terms:

> After three or four years of work, we began to attract the interest of some major labels. By that time, however, we were fairly settled in our ways. The idea of another chef in the kitchen didn't appeal to us, so we didn't sign a deal . . . Once again, major labels enable astronomical sales but I don't believe our particular style of music has that sort of mass appeal. Having the big boys behind you really helps, but it's a trade-off because the record company may want to change your music.

So, releasing their own albums is a business decision based on artistic concerns. The group feels that the music they play doesn't have the potential to sell massive numbers of albums, and they aren't willing to change it for two reasons:

1. They derive fulfillment making music together in their own way. "We enjoy playing together and people enjoy listening to us," says Zachary Najor.
2. Earning enormous sums of money isn't a career objective. Najor summarizes it this way: "I think more practical goals should be set in professional music . . . this way of thinking offers the most realistic way to experience longevity and joy in this craft."

For The Greyboy Allstars and other groups, releasing CDs on their own label is a conscious decision on the career path, not a result of failure or default.

BUSINESS DECISION OR VANITY PRESS?

In the literary field, some novelists and poets do business with what's called a "vanity press." As the name implies, the publication of a vanity press book is not the result of a commercial or artistic commitment by the publisher. Rather, the author approaches the press and pays the company to have a small run of copies published. Because the resulting books are professionally bound and typeset, it's a step up from printing and binding your book at the local photocopy center.

Most of the time, the author gives copies of the book away to friends, family, and members of the local community, making no real effort to get reviewed or sell the book. He isn't really interested in a career as a writer, but in feeling good about himself—having an identity as a writer. In the trade, vanity press books are usually thought of rather condescendingly as the result of a large ego driving a small talent—a hobbyist or dilettante whose work has been rejected as unsuitable by the various publishers who pay their authors, rather than the other way around.

Because musicians, in effect, produce and manufacture their own recordings in much the same way, does that mean they're looked on condescendingly by the music industry? Not at all. In sharp contrast to the book business, such recordings definitely are seen in a positive light, the work of a striving and industrious artist. In the 1990s, and into the twenty-first century, many of the more successful major label acts started out with their own labels or small independent labels that had only a few acts on their roster.

Many fine musicians are hobbyists, rarely perform in public, and still produce and manufacture their own recordings. These are the business equivalent of the writers whose work is published by vanity presses. Unlike the book world, such recordings are not looked down on as amateurish but rather as the musicians' way of creating a tangible chronicle of the music they make. In many cases the musicianship is first-rate; the players just have no aspirations other than to enjoy making music and to have a record of what they do.

The bandwagon effect of the DIY movement has also swept up garage bands and other musicians with no clear-cut strategy; many acts make CDs and tapes with no real game plan. "They press 1,000, sell 60, and give away 90. It's pretty typical for one of these bands to break up, leaving 850 unsold CDs under someone's bed," relates a recording studio owner, shaking his head, "they record and manufacture without giving any thought to why they do it." Not surprisingly, a lot of the musicians who do this are young and inexperienced at business. Unless you understand the business of DIY, you won't make a profit or even recover your costs.

Can you make money making and selling your own records? Yes, unquestionably. The premier example is Ani DiFranco, a solo artist who has never been affiliated with a major label or independent label. She started her own label, Righteous Babe Records, out of her parents' garage when she was nineteen or twenty years old, and reportedly sells in excess of 20,000–30,000 copies per month. Righteous Babe now has its own office, Web site, fifteen employees, and a toll-free number for direct sales of albums and merchandise. Ani DiFranco and her label now are nationally known and have been featured and reviewed in major media outlets such as Rolling Stone, Time, the New York Times, and Musician magazine.

Anyone with a few dollars can make a record and have a few thousand CDs manufactured. In fact, many people are doing this. What is Ani DiFranco doing right, when the majority of other musicians fail to sell enough copies to cover their costs, much less make enough profit to pay their bills without having a day job? In addition to whatever talent and luck are on her side, the answer is that she treats it as a business and a career.

The Artist as Businessperson

To have a career going the DIY route, you have to make all the moves as an artist that you would make on a label—*and* you must pull double duty as a label. This means that you must arrange for the production of your CD, contract for artwork and labeling for the package, manufacture the CDs, and distribute them. You are responsible for marketing, sales, collection of money, accounting, and so on. In other words, you are all the departments of a major record label, rolled into one person (or a few, if this is a band).

In some respects, this isn't much different from being signed to a small independent label, because even though the label supports you, it has little support to give. A lot of what was said in the previous chapter about the underground network of independent music applies here. Still, production, manufacturing, and distribution are all wheels the DIY artist must reinvent. By contrast, on an indie label, these channels would be established and handled previously *for* you instead of *by* you.

To have a DIY career, the artist must be prepared to work extra hard—because (at least in the beginning) he's got no one else to do the work for him. In a 1999 *Guitar World* interview, Ani DiFranco says, "The downside is that it's a lot of work, and that it takes about ten years to do what a major label can do in six months . . . people hate to hear that they have to get out there, get gigs and do that every night. It's a much more attractive proposition to have someone from a record company say they're going to put a lot of money, publicity and marketing behind you." Even now that Ani DiFranco is a self-made success by any measure, she's on the road thirty to thirty-five weeks a year, doing the shows that go hand-in-hand with her product sales.

Making a Record

The first step in the DIY process is recording your music. Although this is the "fun part," business and technical considerations go into it as well. Capturing the essence of live music on tape is not easy, even for the big guys—and *they* enjoy the advantage of having large corporations, prominent producers, and high-powered advisors behind them. For the DIYer who has to wear most of the hats, including that of financier, making a record[31] that sounds the way you want and gets the job done is a major accomplishment.

To start, you should think about what kind of record you want to make. A serious consideration is whether it's your first record or a subsequent one. If you've already released product, you need to take heed of your audience. On the one hand, you want to continue in the vein that interested people enough to induce them to buy your earlier record(s). On the other hand, new product that sounds too much like the old can be a turn-off: Why should I buy this record when I already have one that sounds just like it? The goal is to broaden your audience to include new listeners, while not losing touch with core fans. This can be an artistically challenging task, even for established major label performers.

It's always tempting for artists to make the records *they* like, based on their current tastes, enthusiasms, and life situation. If this is done without regard to the marketability of the record, chances are the sales won't be as strong as if it's more carefully crafted to the audience.[32] One way artists play it safe is to include some tracks that are similar to earlier record(s) and others that represent a departure. The more unique and well-established the artist, the less likely he is to get burnt by demonstrating more artistic daring. This is a judgment call; there's no formula for striking the perfect balance. If there were, surely the major labels would've figured it out.

Choice of material is even more critical in making a first record. Artists who've been able to build a following from playing out are well advised to at least consider incorporating those songs that go over best live. If their essence can be captured successfully on a recording, the artist is justified in thinking he can sell some CDs and cassettes. This is not a hard-and-fast rule; the songs that live audiences respond to most positively might depend on particular visuals, set dynamics, and other factors (often including the inebriated state of a club crowd) that don't lend themselves to an audio recording.[33] But in general, the adage "go with what works" applies.

Once the material is chosen, you must figure out who's going to play it. If you are a self-accompanied solo artist or part of a complete band, the answer is simple: you and nobody else. No problem. However, those who need a full backup band or just one or two session players, will have to

- Locate and, if necessary, audition them
- Select the appropriate players and singers (these may be the best you can afford, not necessarily the best you can find)
- Come to an agreement with them to play on your recording
- Teach them the material or rehearse them as necessary
- Make sure they show up to the session(s) on time
- Pay them

This is a pretty tall order—you must be the musical director, contractor, bank, and cheerleader—all wrapped up in one. As to the practical matter of pay, many independent musicians network with other musicians and play on each other's recordings for little or no cash compensation. It's done as a favor out of a sense of community. Whatever amount is involved must be factored into the overall recording budget, or you might find yourself running out of money before you're done.

Now that you've got your material chosen and your players lined up, the next consideration is where and how you're going to record. You want to make the best-sounding, most impressive recording you can afford.

Remember, the record is not only a product to sell; by virtue of word-of-mouth, it's also its own best promotional tool for future sales. In addition, your CD plays a big part in your quest to obtain bookings for shows, attention from the media, and attention from major or independent labels (if you're so inclined).

A few independent records made at live shows have been artistically and commercially successful. However, most recordings are done in a studio, where (compared to a club or theater) it's easier to control the recording variables, fewer things can go wrong, and the acoustic environment is more favorable. The technical difficulties of making a good-sounding live recording are pretty daunting, and it's hard to find an engineer and club sound person who are up to the task. If that's the sound you want, it's generally better to go for a "live feel" in the studio. This can be accomplished by having all the musicians together in the same room, playing at the same time, for most of the tracking. This method won't automatically generate the adrenaline that playing before a live audience does, but if the players cooperate, relax, and enjoy performing together, they should be able to capture "the moment."

The studio easily affords the capability of multitracking and overdubbing, which (while feasible) is far more difficult to achieve in a live recording.[34] For instance, suppose your band has only one guitar player. Live on stage, he can play just one guitar at a time. In the studio, multitracking allows the same person to play several leads and rhythms, if that's what sounds right on the record. Studio recording also allows vocalists to do multiple takes (and even to use snippets of different takes) to get the best performance. Live, if you're not in good voice that night, you're just stuck with it.[35]

Choosing a recording studio is a major decision. While desiring to make the best-sounding record he can, the DIY artist usually won't have the budget to pay for the top-of-the-line studio and the expert engineer with major label credits. By the same token, if you strongly believe that presentation of your music on a CD requires this level of production, try to find a way to make it happen—even if you spend a lot more money than you originally planned. This is your music and your career we're talking about. You should look forward to earning back the added expense through increased sales and better paying gigs.

If you don't want to record at a deluxe studio, many serviceable, economical studios are available in most areas. As noted earlier, modern, lower-cost, high-quality gear has made this possible. Assuming a studio has the requisite equipment and space to record you, the most significant consideration is the engineer who will be doing the tracking. Does he know how to use his mikes, mixing board, signal processors, recorders, and so on to record your music? Does he know how to work with musicians generally and, in particular, with players of your style? Does he have "good ears" responsive to the sounds you're looking for? If the answers are yes, you'll get a fine recording in a modestly equipped studio; if no, you'll be unhappy with the recording even if the gear is the latest and the greatest.

You can search for a high-quality recording studio by simply doing your homework. Ask around for recommendations from other musicians. Look at the labels of CDs and cassettes produced in your area, particularly those whose sound you admire. Visit studios where you might record, and ask to hear samples of finished product recorded there. Take home the CDs and listen to them in your own environment—nearly everything sounds huge on studio monitors and you don't want to be misled by this and ultimately disappointed by your own recording. Compare several studios and narrow down your choices.

It's OK to shop price. Studios charge by the hour, and almost all offer discounts for buying large blocks of time. Some other factors may lower your costs:

- A willingness to record during less desirable hours
- Making an agreement to pay in advance, at least in part
- The sympathy of the studio operator toward your music
- A personal relationship with the studio operator
- "Slow time" for the studio (for instance, the week after New Year's Day)
- Your reputation: the studio will cut you a better deal if the owner thinks that your recording there will be a feather in its cap

It's OK to bargain, but don't grind such a hard bargain that the studio operator feels he's being taken advantage of. A dispirited or angry engineer won't help your record to sound better.

In effect, every record has a producer—someone who calls the shots in the studio. Most DIY artists self-produce, sometimes with help from the engineer. The question is this: Should you use an *outside* producer for your DIY studio recording? Here again, the issues are availability, cost, and benefit. Most big-name producers won't go near a project without substantial front money and a points guarantee; typically, the DIY artist can't afford them. Other producers commonly are musical friends of the artist, who participate on a reciprocal basis.

If you know someone whose expertise you believe will *significantly* benefit your record and can afford to pay for such services, by all means pay for them. Even so, remember this: While production values matter in presenting music well, the DIY record buyer is not the mainstream pop record buyer. Buyers are less likely to be moved by, or may even be suspicious of, high-gloss production. They are likely to be much more into the songs, the performances, and the overall message (or vibe) of the music. If your record captures these elements, you're doing everything right. It doesn't matter whether you use an outside producer and a fancy studio or not. There's no point in paying for something that won't help you (and in extreme cases, may hurt).[36]

Once your record is tracked, mixed, and mastered, you're ready to go into manufacturing. Most local, regional, and national music publications are full of advertising for CD and cassette reproduction companies. Some publish guides to these services, usually on an annual basis. A dizzying array of choices and packages are available; the lowest prices are for the bare-bones manufacture of bulk CDs and cassettes. As you purchase more packaging (jewel boxes, printed inserts) and services (graphic design and consulting), the prices go up. As you buy more copies, the unit price goes down—pressing 5,000 CDs is a better deal than 1,500. This is because the most expensive part of the replication process is the setup, which is labor intensive. After this, running off copies and packaging them is relatively cheap, because it's automated. Reorders are cheaper than the original run, because the setup does not have to be repeated.

Get a number of bids from different companies for your replication order, and make sure they're "apples and apples," so your price comparisons are meaningful. Once you've narrowed your choices, research the reputations for quality and turnaround time. Avoid companies that you discover use bait-and-switch tactics. As with any other trade service, you can get references, both provided by the company and through your own channels, and they're worth talking to. Several thousand CDs and cassettes cost a nice chunk of change; before you lay your money down, do what you can to ensure you'll be satisfied.

Another important consideration in CD replication is the artwork and layout, both on the CD itself and on the paper insert. Do you recall the adage, "the sizzle sells the steak"? Think of the music on the CD as the steak and the packaging as the sizzle. Musicians commonly get carried away with music. It's easy to shortchange the other important part of the overall presentation, both in terms of the care that goes into it and the money that's spent on it. In planning a DIY record, the art and printing budget should be included right from the start. Within the capabilities of your budget, your record should have eye-catching artwork; easy-to-read layout, lyrics, and liner notes; and a visual message that announces and reinforces the spirit of your music.

Yes, your core fans will buy your record even if the cover art is plain vanilla. For other potential purchasers, though, the decision to pick up a CD and read the liner notes before asking to hear it (or better yet, buying it) is based in part on visual cues. For instance, if your disc is New Age, a cover with an attractive full-color mountain landscape, graceful calligraphy, and a title like *Points to Ponder* will help you sell more discs than a plain white cover with ersatz graffiti lettering announcing a title like In Your Face. This deliberately exaggerated contrast helps illustrate the importance of the artwork and packaging.

RECORDING DIY: SAMPLES AND LOOPS

Increasingly, recordings are made without musicians or a band. This feat is accomplished by using samples and loops: digital prerecorded music tracks that can be manipulated (via cut-and-paste, etc.) into songs, and are available to replicate most instruments. A skilled producer or engineer, or musician who has taught himself the requisite skills, can assemble a seamless-sounding recording without any live tracking except for vocals. Essentially this method of music making is analogous to the collage of visual arts. Little, if any, traditional musicianship is required.

The sonic quality of the tracks is accepted in the marketplace. Many recent CDs by big-selling pop divas, and most hip-hop, have been assembled by producer-engineers with limited or non-existent live tracking. The collage method offers certain advantages: less formal musical technique is required; no studio is needed except to record vocals; easy digital control of sonic parameters prevails; the lead musician doesn't have to endure dissent from contributing sidemen; and so on. Old-schoolers may dismiss music fashioned this way as sterile, soulless, mechanical, or worse, but it has gained commercial acceptance at all levels, including the major-label level.

For DIYers whose resources include more time than cash, the collage method of recording may be the way to go.[37] On the other hand, in music that, by its nature, requires "in the moment" give-and-take between musicians (like jazz), samples and loops are insufficient to create the necessary artistic ambience.

DIY DISTRIBUTION

Distribution—getting your record into stores that sell records—is a weak link in the chain for the DIYer. It's expensive, time consuming, and difficult; those who can find suitable distribution companies for their product let the distributor take care of this part of the business. However, most DIYers start out by distributing their own records.

Distribution begins at the local level. Most independent record stores, and in-town branches of many chains, carry releases by local artists. If you have a regional presence, you may be able to convince independent stores in outlying areas to stock your CD, but it's unlikely that the out-of-town branches of chain stores will carry it. These stores have only so much shelf space, and with the glut of product out there, yours isn't going to get space unless you can demonstrate robust sales.

Whether locally, regionally, or nationally, you have to do everything yourself, which means

- Calling or visiting with the owners or managers of stores to make your pitch
- Giving away promotional CDs for them to listen to (and, if you're lucky, play in the store)
- Making a deal to consign your CDs or cassettes
- Delivering inventory yourself or through shipping
- Following up to monitor sales
- Collecting money due to you (this isn't always so easy)
- Delivering more inventory as needed

These are the same tasks that a record company and a distributor do; but since you are your own company, you get to do them.

Most DIY artists, certainly those whose careers have just begun, are not in a position to attract a major distributor or even a big independent distributor. The larger the distributor, the more probable it is that it deals only with labels. Remember, distribution companies are in business to make profits by selling product. Unless yours is already selling well or there's reason to believe it will be soon, such distributors have no incentive to carry your records. However, as you become better known and begin selling more records, you should be able to locate a distributor that handles music like yours. In all likelihood, it will be a company with a regional presence and strong relationships with the independent stores.

Just working with a distribution company doesn't mean that everything will run perfectly. Many times distributors have less than ideal follow-up. Not only do they sometimes drop the ball in keeping your records supplied to the retail outlets, they've been known to encounter cash flow problems. Translation: You, the artist, will have to wait for your money and sometimes you won't receive all of it. The better your records sell, the less of a problem this will be; companies are much less likely to stiff you if they need you to supply them with product. As in all other business relationships, it's important to have a sense of trust in the people you work with. Still, don't think that merely by finding a distributor, you'll be able to wash your hands of all aspects of distribution. You still have to keep tabs.

Direct distribution is an alternative and less-developed method of distribution. The Internet is its primary vehicle. In its pure form, direct distribution cuts out both the middleman (i.e., the traditional distribution company) and the retailer: The customer orders the CD or cassette directly from the artist's Web site. The typical DIY artist can't expect much traffic other than what he personally promotes. A prospective customer has to have a reason to cruise to this Web site, otherwise he'll never know it exists.

In another form of direct distribution, the artist sells the product through an on-line "record store." At this writing, the most visible such distribution center is CD Baby (*www.cdbaby.com*). This virtual retailer carries the product of any artist willing to pay a nominal start-up fee and a consignment percentage. The distributor doesn't function as a label; there's no screening or evaluation of product for marketability or artistic quality.

The last chapter of this book covers Internet-related issues in greater scope and detail.

KNOWING YOUR MARKET

Even musicians who expect to be as successful as Ani DiFranco and Righteous Babe Records, and who are willing to work as hard, should be prepared for a long road. Without major resources, success doesn't come overnight (and isn't guaranteed). Moreover, it's important for musicians to be realistic about *who* constitutes their market, *how big* it is, and *where* it is. For example,

- *Stylistically*: Is your music of a style that has widespread appeal or is it too esoteric to expect to sell much product? For instance, if no venues are willing to book live gigs for your group, you can't expect the market to be as extensive as if there's a big demand for live performances.
- *Geographically*: Is your music of a regional nature and likely to stay that way? Can you expect to have sales even where there is no established market? The answer is sometimes yes—witness the national popularity of country music in the 1990s.
- *Demographically*: To which age and ethnic groups is your music likely to appeal? For instance, some "teen" music has limited age-group appeal and yet can sell big numbers. Similarly, while some Latin music "crosses over," some sells mostly to listeners with a Latin background. Another common phenomenon is that the market for rock, country, and rap recordings can segment according to sex, with males (or females) accounting for most sales, depending on the style and the artist.

Some of the marketing assumptions you made in the beginning may change, or the music may evolve. Identifying a certain market early on doesn't mean that you shouldn't react to observations you make along the way.

The point is this: You have to be aware of how your strategy is working. Set goals, make plans, and carry them out—but be adaptable. For instance, beginning in the late 1990s, there has been a revival of horn-driven swing music. It gets airplay on radio stations that previously featured only grunge and punk. Some veteran swing bands have found themselves popular beyond what anyone would have expected just a few years earlier. For a swing group, limiting marketing efforts to older people who liked swing the first time around would be a serious mistake.

This chapter isn't meant to provide an in-depth analysis of markets, but these examples should help illustrate the point that, if you're going to sell your own CDs, you'll do a better job "thinking like a record company" than by wondering why things don't seem to be working out as well as you'd hoped. Of course, merely identifying markets in the abstract won't sell CDs; you've got to promote them, you have to distribute them to places where they can be bought, you have to convince someone to buy them, and you have to collect the money once they're bought.

PERFORMANCE AS PROMOTION

For acts on their own labels, the major way to promote themselves is to perform live shows. This gives people the chance to see them and enjoy their music; if they like it enough, they'll be interested in purchasing the acts' recordings. Playing live also provides a venue for direct sale of CDs; plenty of shows today feature a sales table in the lobby. Deborah Liv Johnson, a solo artist who supports herself by performing and selling CDs, says: "More people buy product after a live show than any other time. It's important to catch them in the moment of inspiration. That's why it's important to take 'plastic'—it increases sales in that inspired moment." The recordings themselves end up being a form of promotion; the more people have them and play them for their friends, the more people will attend future shows, buy CDs, and so on.

How often you perform matters a lot. The amount of CDs you sell will be directly proportional to the number of people who see your show. If you play in front of 500 *different* people per month, you're going to sell more product than if you play for just 25. Clearly, you want to develop a following, but you need to do more than perform for just the same small cadre of loyal fans again and again. Even if they all buy your CD, they buy it just once and it's over.

Within the limits of your resources, endurance, and capacity to strain personal relationships, you need to perform as often and in as wide a geographic sphere as you can. Only by doing this will you maximize the number of people who become fans. This process most often builds slowly. Even acts that seem to be "overnight successes" usually aren't. When you find out the long-term story, most of them played for years at the local and regional level, in front of modest crowds, until their audiences and careers grew.

Do your promotional homework. Target clubs that feature music similar to yours. By working with venues where your music fits in, you're more likely to be offered an engagement than if you use the "shotgun" approach. And, if you work smart, there's a positive snowball effect to playing live. The more often the name of your act appears in the advertising in local papers, the more likely promoters and club owners will hire you. They'll key off the other businesses and assume *they're* hiring you for good reason. Once you get a gig, obviously, it's up to you to fulfill your part of the bargain, attract and entertain patrons so the venue operators will make a profit and invite you back.

LABEL DEALS VERSUS DIY—CRUNCHING THE NUMBERS

With a label deal, the artist's real royalty is somewhere between 8 and 15 percent. And, the artist receives no royalties until sizable recording, packaging, and promotional costs are recouped. By contrast, the DIY artist keeps a much higher percentage of the sales price. A big chunk is not given away to the label as profits, because the artist *is* the label. A DIY artist who can get the sales numbers up can earn more money selling 50,000 units himself than by selling five to ten times that on a major. By the way, 50,000 units for a DIY artist, or even an indie label, is considerable.

The following statement contains a very big *if*: If you can sell enough product, then you can make more money with self-released recordings than with a label deal. Our research on several DIY artists bears this out. By all accounts, Ani DiFranco, who's never been signed to a label of any kind, is earning far more than most major label acts—but of course, she's the most successful DIY artist ever. Currently, her CD sales are in the hundreds of thousands per year. Folksinger and DIYer Deborah Liv Johnson, who formerly was signed to an independent label, tells us, "I found I could make a lot more money and put out the stuff I love."

At the other end of the spectrum from Ani DiFranco is the harsh reality of national sales numbers. Andy Allen, the head of independent distributor ADA, told *Music Connection* magazine:[38] "Out of the approximately 27,000 records released in a year, over 20,000 sell fewer than 1,000 pieces—and if you look at the 10,000 sales plateau, the figure is even more daunting."[39] Needless to say, it's hard to have much of a career selling 1,000 units per year, and yet approximately three-fourths of all records don't sell even that many copies.

The DIY route offers financial and artistic control, and therefore independence, from labels. Independence, though, is a two-edged sword. You get to call all the shots and keep a larger slice of the earnings pie. However, the tradeoffs are these:

- You have to spend a large portion of your time and energy on business instead of music
- Resources for production of your records plus artwork and packaging are far more limited than at majors and larger independent labels
- Promotion and tour support are virtually nonexistent, in sharp contrast to major labels and larger independents
- Distribution channels are vastly inferior to those of major labels and all but the tiniest indies[40]
- Although some commercial radio stations have local or indie shows, you receive virtually no airplay at any hour when people are listening. This time is reserved—"majors only"—bought and paid for.

In considering the DIY route, don't lose sight of the fact that record companies have an upside in addition to their financial resources. They offer experience, insight, and expertise. Sure, their decisions can be way off base in this uncertain business, but consider this: Would you rather take marketing advice from people who've worked hands-on in the business for years or from someone with no track record or qualifications?

Still, going DIY may be right for a particular artist. It's strictly a personal decision,[41] but the person or band who chooses this road should be prepared to work very hard and be very patient. For whatever reason, more than 20,000 artists sell fewer than 1,000 CDs in a year, while Ani DiFranco sells several hundred thousand.

LABEL DEALS VERSUS DIY—DISTRIBUTION AND PROMOTION

As previously mentioned, major retailers rarely deal with anyone but an established distributor. Therefore, the DIYer is particularly dependent on sales of records at live performances and through regional mom-and-pop stores. Compared to the availability of CDs at every major chain store in every mall and shopping district (which is what the major labels offer), this is very limited. Relatively speaking, the reach of the independents is not as deep as the majors, but several independent distributors do pretty well for their labels.

Promotion—the building of an artist's recognition factor—consists of airplay, media coverage, advertising, in-store performances, tour support, videos, and so on. These require money, clout, and access, which can be abundantly supplied by major labels, and to a lesser extent, by indies. In contrast, the DIYer has to do all his own promotion. There's no staff, there's no special department with expertise, no outside radio promoter. The artist has no clout. There's nothing to threaten to withhold if the artist doesn't get his way, other than his personal artistry and product—and these are the last things an enterprising artist wants to withhold.

Promotion is important at any level; for the do-it-yourselfer, it's time-consuming and very much "in the trenches." For instance, an artist can arrange to do "in-stores" at local retailers, if he schmoozes it up enough and the owner likes him. Flyers and Internet sites are relatively inexpensive ways to get the word out, although the artist can't be sure how many people are paying attention. Even an ad in a fanzine, a common tool of indie labels, isn't always affordable for the DIYer. By contrast, the majors advertise on heavily watched music television, in big-city newspapers, and in glossy national magazines. Dazzling videos, a tremendous promotional tool, are unaffordable (for all intents and purposes) to all but the majors.

Even though commercial radio is pretty much closed to anyone but the major labels, some airplay is available to DIY artists on noncommercial stations. "I've received substantial airplay on public and college stations," reports folksinger Deborah Liv Johnson, "It definitely helps my sales."

DIY AS A STEPPING STONE

There's no shortage of artists who want to make records, not as a hobby but as a career. Many have no aptitude for business or desire to be in business. All things considered, they're better off on a label, either a major or an indie, which can support the business side. Of course, being on a label is not always an option. An act may be too undeveloped artistically or too unproven in the marketplace to attract attention from labels. As a result, the artist takes the DIY route by default.

Just as indies can serve as a proving ground for acts that move on to major labels, the do-it-yourself route can be a stepping stone to a label deal. Success in selling product is bound to draw label attention. Reportedly, both majors and indies continue to pursue Ani DiFranco and Righteous Babe Records, offering to buy her label or sign her to their own. For both financial reasons (she's doing very well, thank you) and political ones, she continues to fly solo.

By contrast, Hootie and the Blowfish and the Dave Matthews Band, two of the more successful groups of the 1990s, began on their own labels, then moved on to record for the majors, where they sold tens of millions of records. Whatever the commercial goals of an artist, starting by doing it yourself can lead there. Even if running your own business sounds like a drag, it beats the heck out of sitting in your bedroom, waiting for the phone to ring. If nothing else, the experience of going the DIY route will help teach you the facts of life in the music business. This can help you make better decisions for yourself later on, whether you're with an indie or a major label.

CHAPTER 6

Touring—Road Rigor

I f you've watched music television (such as VH-1's *Behind the Music*) or read music biographies, you know that touring can help break an act—in more ways than one. Touring is challenging in many respects. The better artists anticipate the challenges, the more likely they will reap maximum rewards and avoid the obvious pitfalls of road life.

The pop music touring business is now close to fifty years old, and many lessons have been passed down. Today's artists are aware of this history and, by and large, are much better informed than musicians in the early days of touring (particularly rock touring). All of the artists with whom we spoke assert that touring is an important part of their careers. They accept the road's adversity as well as its compensation as a reality, an unavoidable part of the business they've chosen.

Types of Tours

The scale of touring determines the type of tour on which an act embarks:

- The club or coffeehouse tour is a tour of smaller venues, often relatively short in duration. It's most often undertaken by unsigned artists or indie acts.
- The theater or mid-level tour is a step up from the club tour, for acts that have a more widespread reputation. Major-label artists are more visible, and most tours are longer than those on the club circuit.

• The major venue tour hits arenas, concert halls, stadium shows, major festivals, and so on. Usually the domain of major-label artists, these tours tend to be the most lengthy.

Of course, there's a lot of gray area in this set of classifications. For instance, some theater tours also include club dates, and so on.

Club (or Coffeehouse) Tours

The club tour is typically is the first tour an act undertakes. At its most basic level, the club tour earns little income, because ticket prices are low for shows by essentially unknown out-of-town acts, the venues involved are small anyway, and the artist's drawing power is weak. He shouldn't be frustrated or surprised to find the financial returns are poor—on early tours, the artist's main objective should be to spread the word about himself away from his home base.

In the bare-bones club tour, the solo artist drives himself from town to town in his car; if the act is a band, the vehicle is usually a van (sometimes pulling an equipment trailer). The pay on a given night is so low that acts try to book a show for every night of a tour to maximize receipts. This means that a lot of driving is involved. Things most people take for granted, like bathing, eating decently, and sleeping, are hard to accomplish on a basic club tour. Staying in even a cheap hotel or motel is a rare luxury. An artist who networks with out-of-town DIY and indie acts may be able to "crash" for the night on a reciprocal basis. Often, not enough cash is generated to do more than buy enough gas and food to make it to the next show. In these circumstances, vehicle breakdown isn't just an inconvenience, it's a disaster.

Although it's not uncommon for friends of a band to travel as a road crew, bands often haul, unload, set up, break down, load, maintain, and repair their own equipment. This does nothing to moderate the exhaustion of constant long-distance driving, poor sleep, and inadequate nutrition. In addition, artists on club tours typically are their own agents, managers, and so on. So, they have to deal with all the business aspects of the tour—booking shows en route, collecting money from club owners, arranging for in-stores, distributing product, and more.

The words of indie artist Mary Dolan, a solo singer-songwriter, eloquently sum up typical club tour experiences:

> The first time I toured for about one month. I drove up and down the West Coast, playing in coffee shops and bars. I probably played four or five times a week. I broke even, which seems to have been the case each time I go out. I camped quite a bit to save money then, too. This last time I toured I stayed out for three months and traveled from one end of the country to the other and back, with lots of zigzagging in between. I played from two to five nights a week. I broke even this last time, too, though I could afford a few more lux-

uries. I didn't have to camp and was able to get more money per show. I tried to book the tour so that I wouldn't have to drive more than six hours a day (as I travel alone). When my first choices don't pan out, I take gigs where I can get them. I'd rather sing for five people in a bar in a dinky town than spend the night in a motel in a big town, with no gig. I'm out there to be heard. I bring an electric teapot and instant coffee and "cups o noodles" for those times when there is only money for gas. I make stops at historical monuments, roadside attractions, and greasy diners, too, when there's time. I bring a sleeping bag and pillow.

Hardly glamorous, the club tour is not for the unmotivated. But things improve if you work hard and keep progressing. You can do better than break even. Solo DIY artist Deborah Liv Johnson relates that on her longest tour, she covered over 8,000 miles solo in her van and cleared about $5,000 from door and products sales. "It was a hodgepodge tour for the most part—house concerts, bookstores, barn concerts, church concerts, and a few small venues." Of course, as a DIY artist, Deborah Liv stands to make more money off product sales than an indie artist like Mary Dolan, who has to share the revenues with her label.

Considering how exhausting club tours can be under the best of circumstances, the artist should always keep in mind that they're primarily promotional. Each show you do is a promotion for your product and for future shows. The next time you come back to a city, you anticipate that there will be more people in the audience or that you'll even need to play at a larger club. The opportunities to do in-stores, distribute your product to local record stores, and network with local musicians are further benefits of the club tour.

The Theater or Mid-Level Tour

If you're doing the right things, club touring should evolve into mid-level touring. This often includes clubs, too, but usually big ones which may seat from 350 to 1,000 people, rather than the smaller 40–200 capacity venues. On this kind of touring, you have more help:

- Usually an agent is involved
- Tour buses replace cars and vans
- You'll get some overnight stays in motels or hotels
- You'll have a paid road crew
- Your manager (who might be touring, too) and your label will pre-promote your appearance, arrange for interviews, in-stores, and the like
- Your label might be kicking in tour support

This life is still fairly grueling. There are still a lot of hours spent rolling down interstates, thruways, and local roads.

Having professionals such as your agent and manager involved relieves the band of handling the business side of touring. This is important because it helps conserve energy, which can be more productively used on stage. (Also, your agent and manager presumably are better at business than you.) The presence of a road crew means that the musicians don't have to drive, load or unload their gear, set up or break down their gear, repair instruments, or find musical instrument stores for more strings, drumsticks, reeds, or amplifier repair.

Tour support from a record label relieves financial pressure when you're on the road. You know the money is there for bus rental, fuel, bus repair, lodging, food, stage support, and so on; so you don't have to sweat day-to-day receipts. An unexpected expense, such as stolen gear or a hospital visit for one of the entourage, doesn't bring on a money crisis. The other side is that, at the mid-level, tour support is recoupable. This means that the record company isn't so much paying the expenses as financing them; ultimately, the money comes out of the pocket of the artist. In effect, tour support is a loan, which you pay back out of your royalties.

Unlike the small club tour, acts on the theater circuit can make decent money. Ticket prices are higher and venues are bigger; it's no longer just a break-even proposition. Usually, the local promoter offers a guarantee, so if the turnout is disappointing, you still come away with enough money to make the show worthwhile.

This kind of touring is very hard work, which requires lengthy road trips; ten months out of a year is not uncommon. However, for acts whose record sales aren't sufficient to generate revenues to support themselves, the tour is a major profit center. During the peak touring season (roughly May through September), hundreds of acts hit the road to earn most of the year's income. In addition to up-and-coming acts, tours include many performers whose days of significant record sales are far behind them, but who continue to have a strong concert draw.

Major Venue Tours

Although major venue tours are the stuff of legend for sex, drugs, and rock and roll, in truth they are just as much hard work as club or theater tours. Moreover, they are enormous undertakings both financially and logistically. The lodgings, travel, and meals may be far more comfortable, but the high stakes involved take their toll. Every mistake is magnified, every failed commitment is expensive. It costs a lot of money just to have a touring team out on the road. The industry estimate is that it costs *at least* $600 per day for each person (band member, road crew, professional, driver, security, etc.) involved—and some larger tours include forty or more people. The good news is that major tours, if done right, can produce healthy earnings.

Tours are planned by the manager and agent. Once a tour is underway, the boss is the production manager, who is in charge of everything directly connected with putting on the show—lights, PA, stage, crew, buses, catering, wardrobe, local stagehands, you name it. The next-in-line are the stage manager and the backline crew. The tour manager is the act's personal road manager, who can be either their actual personal manager or a representative from the management company. It's his job to make sure the band gets to the shows, to set up interviews, and to coordinate personal matters. His presence is required mainly to protect the tour's investment by ensuring that the artist is ready, willing, and able to go on stage and earn revenues.

The tour accountant handles, and keeps track of, money. The biggest job is to settle with the show's promoter at showtime. Typically, the promoter has paid a 50 percent up front deposit to the agent and pays the balance either just before or just after the show. If the act's take is receipt dependent rather than a flat fee, settling up involves not just collection, but calculation. Remember, this is a major tour, so we're talking about amounts that may be in the hundreds of thousands of dollars.

The tour accountant pays (and makes records of) expenses on the road, including per diem to the crew and performers. Sometimes, expenses must be budgeted against receipts, making decisions about spending priorities from the major to the mundane. For instance, one roadie told us that, when the caravan of buses and trucks is rushing from last night's venue to tonight's concert site, time is so short there's no time to do laundry. Therefore, a run is made for personal items including new socks and underwear for everyone—authorized by the tour accountant.

The added budget of a major tour means that life for the musician is somewhat easier than at lower levels. Food, lodging, travel, and overall comfort are better, with more money to pay for them. However, it's still hard work. Because touring is a major component in selling albums, artists often tour as long as an album still is selling—which may be close to two years. Sometimes, acts record two complete records before beginning a tour, so that as the first one's sales begin to lose steam, the "in the can" album can be released while the act is still on the road.

TOURING—BEHIND THE MUSIC

According to Rod Gibson, a manager for legendary Southern rock group Lynyrd Skynyrd, the two main reasons artists tour are

1. Money: "if it isn't a main reason, it should be"
2. Exposure and promotion: "for record sales, and for your next tour"

He states that, in his experience, the other two ("less important") reasons for touring are

1. Fame and glory: "everybody wants to be loved"
2. Adventure: "there's always someone in a band who's in it for the groupies"

With over twenty years of tour experience, Rod knows that tours don't always meet expectations. For one thing, some tours are either too big or too small to make a profit. In the case of "too big," their costs are too high (often, elaborate staging is a culprit). In the case of "too small," either the tour is too short to generate adequate revenues or the act's draw was over-estimated.

Not all artists on major venue tours are established artists. Some new acts appear as openers for the headliners. Often, the headliner and the opening act belong to the same label and management team, which pro-vides a double benefit. The opener either receives a small percentage of the door or a flat fee of $1,000–1,500, certainly not enough money to cover the actual expenses of the tour without support from the label. For the opening act, then, the primary purpose of touring is exposure and promotion.

Merchandise sales are another way for artists to earn money on tour. T-shirts, baseball caps, and other souvenirs can be sold to an impulse-buyer fan who's willing to pay $30 for a T-shirt that cost the artist $3. If you're not the headliner, you won't do as well in merchandise sales. You begin with the handicap of relatively obscure status. Then, your contract with the headliner will require that your merchandise sell for at least as much as his, so you can't undercut him. Further, the contract will entitle the headliner to an over-ride on each piece of merchandise you do sell. All in all, it's another reminder that you're there mostly for the promotional value.

SPONSORSHIP

The sponsorship tie-in, which began on a large scale in the early 1980s, continues to be a strong factor in the tour industry. In its idealized version, the manufacturers of such products as soft drinks, tobacco, cosmetics, home electronics, automobiles, clothing, or beer sponsor a tour by an artist (or multiple artists) by putting up money to cover tour expenses. In return, the sponsor receives advertising at concert venues (including the main stage) and has its name appear in all promotion in connection with the tour—usu-ally including the name of the tour.

The benefit to the artist(s) is money; the benefit to the sponsor is strong target-group advertising and the psychological association that is created between his product and the artist's image. An example from recent years is the Vans Warped Tour, a traveling summer festival associated with the surfing and skateboarding punk music subculture. Vans makes sneakers worn by surfers and skateboarders, and in theory, everybody's happy—Vans, fans, and bands.

Two main problem issues arise with tour sponsorship. First, what does the artist get for what he gives up? If you've seen the stages for some of the sponsored tours, it certainly appears that the product, not the artist(s), receives top billing. Both for ego and business reasons, artists want to feel that the show is about *them*, not some product. Whenever the sponsor's name is very prominent on the tour stage, it's a lot easier for the artist to feel good about the business reasons if the sponsor is paying top dollar for the privilege. However, when the artists give away too much, no amount of money is worth the submerging of their own identity.

The second difficult issue of tour sponsorship is image. Even though artists are in business to make money, they're still artists. They often take exception to what they perceive as overcommercialization. Moreover, some of the companies that are most eager to sponsor tours make products whose use is, in some people's minds, questionable, even objectionable. Alcohol and tobacco products are most often singled out as controversial. Some artists have ethical problems being associated with unhealthy products or object simply because the long-term harm done to their image seems to outweigh the short-term dollars offered by the sponsor.

Sponsorship offers certain financial benefits for the artist, but they must be weighed against other factors. This is an area where the advice of a wise manager is especially valuable.

DAY-TO-DAY REALITIES

The artists to whom we spoke all stated that being away from home for extended periods is the worst aspect of touring. Travel is very strenuous and tedious; the amount of time spent in cars, RVs, buses, planes, trains, airports, hotels, motels, and depots is far greater than the time spent making music. "If you can't picture yourself sitting in the Houston Airport at 3:00 A.M., waiting for your 7:00 A.M. connecting flight to North Dakota, you might be in the wrong business," says tour veteran Rod Gibson.

Most tours consist of a series of one-nighters. To maximize revenue, you play as many shows as you can in as short a period of time as you can squeeze them in. Typically, an act travels all night after finishing the show. Occasionally, you can relax; if shows aren't scheduled for consecutive nights, there might be a one- or two-day layover in a given town. If you're able to afford to check into a hotel in the next town, that's the first thing you do; but often, just a few hours are left until your sound check. If you have agreed to do interviews with local press or to visit record stores, you have to find the time and energy to do these, too.

The less tour support you receive, the more administrative and logistical work you have to do yourself. Making travel arrangements, checking in, and transporting gear are tasks that wear you down, when you have to do them day after day—and perform as well. The days can get hectic when the same people who have to play that night's show are the ones who are trying to fix the RV so they can get there. Conversely, the better funded the tour, the less time and energy the musician needs to devote to extramusical work. This means you can throw everything you have into your performance, without feeling you left something back on the road or in your motel room.

Staying healthy on tour is more challenging than at home. Constant travel is very wearing, and the demands on one's energy are great. Often there is little opportunity or time to sleep properly. Getting enough exercise and fresh air is a challenge, because the schedule is very unpredictable, and you feel fatigued continually. Eating a healthy diet isn't easy on the road, either. Roadside restaurants have unreliable fare; storing and preparing food yourself is a major (often impossible) chore. Convenience and low cost often prevail over better nourishment.

DAY-TO-DAY REWARDS

To focus solely on how much hard work touring entails and the importance of the business side is to downplay the very real reward of touring: playing music for others. To counterbalance the emphasis on work, money, logistics, travel, budgets, and itineraries, the following is a series of quotes from artists about their rewards from touring:

"Touring is my reward after recording . . . when I'm on the road, I'm able to have contact with the people who listen and relate to my music . . . I live for this interaction. I get to sing through my feelings night after night and experience the emotional evolution I go through . . . hopefully I bring the audience with me where we actually experience some of these worlds together through the music"

—*A young solo pop/rock singer who writes her own confessional material*

"Live performances have an immediate payoff and the interaction is incredible. Especially when you have 11,000 people jumping up and down to your music. Playing a sold out show in any city is a great experience."

—*Drummer for a Celtic rock band*

"Performing live is the lifeblood of our business. We just kind of go with the flow, and people go crazy for our performances. It's hard to live on the road. You're constantly away from your family and your friends, but whenever we hit the stage, it's all worth it. The reality of this business is that if your heart's not in the music itself, you can't put forth that kind of effort; and if your heart's in it, it doesn't seem like an effort!"

—*Drummer for a Funk/acid-jazz band*

"Touring lets an artist make a personal connection with his fans and this creates a bond that is essential in keeping a career healthy and long-lasting. The audience deserves to have something given back to them in a live show. I feel it's really necessary to let the fans know how appreciative I am of them . . . I really enjoy this."

—*Rock/R&B singer who fronts her own band*

THE CONGLOMERATED TOUR INDUSTRY

Just as the record industry and the radio industry increasingly have come under control of fewer and fewer companies,[42] the same forces are at work in the concert industry. In the tour business, there's one word for this trend: SFX. SFX Entertainment is a company that, in just a few years, has acquired concert promotion and concert production companies in the United States to such a great extent that it now controls approximately 80 percent of the major venues across the country. In some cities, SFX controls all the venues, and it's acquiring new ones all the time. In 2001, SFX was acquired by radio behemoth Clear Channel, a purchase which many observers felt was in violation of the letter and spirit of federal antitrust law. Nevertheless, the dominant radio conglomerate now owns the dominant concert company.

The combination of SFX with Clear Channel raises the stakes for artists who prefer not to deal with SFX in certain markets, because they face the real possibility that their airplay will be cut back in a power play or retaliation—not just in a particular city, but in all Clear Channel cities (that is, the entire United States). Artists who prefer to set their own concert ticket prices now find their bargaining power is compromised by the Clear Channel merger. Many observers predicted that higher ticket prices would result from this monopoly, and their fears were justified—ticket prices for major acts rose an average of 35 percent or more in two years.

In the concert industry, change on this scale doesn't just mean "same game, fewer players"; it means the game has changed significantly. Next to the acquisition by Clear Channel, the most talked-about aspect of SFX is its announced policy of tie-ins to advertisers. In the traditional concert setting, virtually all the promoter's income derives from the event itself—ticket sales, parking, concessions, and so on. However, in the SFX universe, advertising sales are projected to be an additional major revenue source. In some sense, the SFX way of promoting shows is like radio; that is, delivering a target audience to the advertiser. The advertiser, not the music fan, becomes the real client. Putting on a concert is the means to an end, not the end in itself.

Does this mean that the quality of concerts will decline? In theory, probably not. If the concert experience fails to please music fans, they won't come back; and if they don't come back, SFX can't generate as much advertising revenue. In practice, though, music fans may not take well to ever-higher levels of commercialization of the concert experience. They could rebel if it feels too much like they're watching TV, being bombarded with ads—that the whole thing is really about separating them from their money. This backlash is occurring already in the professional sports industry, where higher ticket prices, higher concession and merchandise prices, and constant advertising are cited by some fans as symptoms of the degradation of the sports experience. Pro sports revenues are flat and ticket sales are down; the TV audience has declined in some sports as much as 15 percent compared to earlier peaks. No one is certain why this is so, but the disgruntled fans must be at least partially right.

Another issue with SFX's advertising strategy is the lack of choice that an artist will have in a given venue or series of venues. On a traditional tour, an artist has a choice of dealing with a sponsor. However, in the SFX scenario, the artist either plays ball with SFX and its sponsors or just won't get to perform in certain venues. In fact, because SFX controls so many venues, there's always the possibility that the company will find a different artist who does agree to play its game. The upside of higher revenues from corporate sponsors is that there's a larger pie to split. Presumably, this would be an added incentive to artists. In the first edition we stated that "hypothetically, it's even possible that ad revenues can act to moderate the upward trend of ticket prices." The history of the major concert business after the Clear Channel merger has (unfortunately for the consumer), gone the other direction. Since SFX is a corporation, though, you can be sure they'll charge whatever the market will bear. Their first job is looking out for the shareholders, not the pocketbooks of music fans.

Another piece of SFX's strategy is that, by controlling so many venues and production companies associated with those venues, the company will be able to put together entire tours, not just separate shows. This helps the company maximize its profits by keeping down costs through centralized management, increasing the number of seats filled through coordination of the various venues, and selling advertising rights to corporate clients on a national, not just local, basis. Moreover, it creates an opportunity for SFX to usurp the role of the agent by booking an act's tour directly with management. In fact, SFX is purchasing a sizable booking agency. The potential savings of 10 percent can be a huge dollar figure and stands to make the pie bigger for artists, too.

A bigger pie sounds like an artist-friendly trend, but only for big artists who will be able to deal directly with SFX. For the developing artist, it's bad news. Agents make most of their profits from bigger acts. Those profits, in effect, subsidize the agents' nurturing of the small acts, many of whose shows don't earn much for the agent. If the agencies quit working with beginning or less established acts because there's no money in it, while SFX deals only with big acts, who's going to book the developing artist?

Any company with the size and influence of SFX is in a position to change the market. To the average fan, there may appear to be more benefits than bothers: For one thing, a company that controls so many venues and total seats wants to maximize the use of these assets. This should mean more tours by more artists in more places (including some that usually have not been tour stops).

Beyond the prevalence of advertising, the downside of SFX isn't obvious to the casual observer. However, it's still real, and in the limit, the long-term consequences are ominous. A company of SFX's size and scope wants to book tours with only the biggest acts and the highest ticket prices. This makes perfect sense from the point of view of the company and those acts, but it tends to cut out the "middle class" of developing acts. They're too small to be on SFX tours but have outgrown club tours. Demand for tickets is reduced because SFX books so many competing big names. In the long run, the emphasis on bigness tends to help those who already are big while holding down the developing act. Long-time observers of the tour scene already note a fall-off in shows being booked into medium to larger venues of 5,000 to 12,000 capacity; but, in a business with as many variables as music, no one knows for sure how large a factor SFX is in this trend.

Taken to its extreme, SFX's monopoly power can cause big problems for the long-term health of the touring business, including fan backlash and impaired development of new acts. However, the company's announced intentions—that it's in the concert business for keeps—indicate its management recognizes that squeezing the most dollars it can out of the next few years isn't the right course in the long haul. As an example, SFX is planning to place secondary stages adjacent to main show venues, to showcase up-and-coming acts. The tour business ultimately depends on the fans' allegiance to the artists, and SFX claims to grasp the importance of this relationship. It will be interesting to see how this plays out against the backdrop of corporate America's emphasis on short-term profits.

TOURING—THE FOUNDATION OF LONGEVITY

Unquestionably, some acts that rise to prominence (and earn a lot of money) do so primarily via electronic media—recordings, videos, and commercial radio airplay. Many artists today, especially "baby bands," believe that an entire career can be built around such media. Listening to them talk about their career plans, one increasingly hears mention of the Internet. Is the music industry moving away from live performance to virtual performance?

Veteran artists and music business people we interviewed don't think so. They believe that the music concert is irreplaceable in terms of its ability to deeply touch fans. For the concert-goer, this live, in-the-moment experience includes a sharing of feelings with the artist and with others in the audience. This is not a feeling you can achieve sitting in front of a computer or even a big-screen TV. Another factor which makes the concert experience special is that the fan is physically and psychologically insulated from his routine environment, much as he is when he attends a movie theater. The usual distractions—ringing phones, barking dogs, kids clanking dirty dishes in the sink, and the like—are banished, replaced by immersion in the artists and their creation of music. For a few hours, at least, this "bigger-and-better-than-real-life" concert occupies most of the fan's world.

Bonding with fans via live performance is important in the short run (to make money and sell records etc.) and in the long run. Acts that don't tour early in their careers might not have a later part to their careers. A lot of 1970s and 1980s bands that built a fan base through extensive touring are able to maintain careers today, not by record sales but through more touring. One part of their career—selling records—is pretty much over, but the fan loyalty built up in earlier years results in high attendance at today's shows.

On the other hand, consider a different act past its prime, no longer receiving airplay or selling records. If it never toured in its heyday, today it probably has too little of a live-show fan base to support a comeback tour. In such a case, its career is over, because all sources of income have dried up. Touring, then, plays a major role in career longevity—Internet or no Internet.

In just four years since the first edition, prospects for the long-term health of the record industry have begun to cloud. Artists who "win" the pop music lottery and enjoy their fifteen minutes of fame often won't have much of a career (or accumulated wealth) to show for their recording success. As the market for music fragments into more and more sub-genres, and as consumers tire of trend-driven major-label "product," it is more important than ever for career-oriented artists to have a live act that people are willing to pay to hear, year in and year out.

iii

The Varied Careers in the Music Industry and What They Entail

CHAPTER 7

SONGWRITER

Typically, songs consist of words and music, in which syllables of the sung words correspond to the notes of the melody. When it's done right, magic results from both the songwriter's craftsmanship and that intangible ingredient called talent. In the best songs, a great synergy exists. Both the music and the words are highly original, yet accessible to the listener. The lyrics reinforce the mood of the music, and the music reflects the theme of the lyrics.

Songs without words are performed as "instrumentals." Comparatively speaking, you don't hear many of these on music radio and television. Probably, they aren't as widely heard as vocal songs because the typical popular music listener relates better to music that contains vocals. Recently, acceptance of instrumental songs has been increasing, as the "jazz lite," "easy listening," and "new adult contemporary" (NAC) formats have discovered and expanded the audience for this type of music. Commonly, the melody is played by saxophone or guitar, but keyboards or other instruments are used as well.

Some songwriters work alone, producing words and music without relying on partners. Cole Porter, writer of dozens of songs that have become standards (for example, "What Is This Thing Called Love," "Night and Day"), and Irving Berlin ("White Christmas," "Puttin' on the Ritz") wrote by themselves. Some solo artists who are singer-songwriters, like Bob Dylan, Paul Simon, Joni Mitchell, and Sting, write in this manner as well.

Other writers write as part of a team. Some specialize in music only and rely on a lyricist for all their words, while their lyricist partners write no music. An example of such a team is Elton John (music) and Bernie Taupin (lyrics). In an earlier era, Harold Arlen (music) and E.Y. Harburg (lyrics) wrote "Over the Rainbow" and all the other songs from *The Wizard of Oz*. Don Felder wrote all the music (and the arrangement) to the Eagles favorite "Hotel California" before bringing it in to the group, where Don Henley wrote the lyrics.

In other cases, songwriting is a team effort from the ground up. Writers contribute in different ways, but generate both words and music. An example would be any number of Beatles songs in which John Lennon and Paul McCartney wrote the verses, choruses, and bridges by sitting down together and writing "as one." (In the later years of their partnership, Lennon and McCartney tended to write separately but continued to credit the songs as Lennon-McCartney.) Many rock groups write collectively, often by jamming for long periods, seeing what develops, and culling their favorite parts to make songs.

More recently, the advent of sampling technology has made it possible to "write" songs by sampling all or part of an older recording. In the usual case, it is recycled back with special effects, some new words, a superimposed electronic beat, and a new vocal.

TRAINING AND SKILLS OF SONGWRITERS

There are as many stories about the path to becoming a songwriter as there are songwriters. Unlike, say, symphony conductors or principal cellists in classical music, there is no established way to be trained. Relatively speaking, most popular music is simple, basic, and repetitive. That's what sells, because people relate to it. Consequently, writers whose musical experience is entirely with garage bands are just as capable of writing hit song after hit song as writers whose background contains more formal study and "hard knowledge."

Whenever a song is a hit, it's easy to analyze it after the fact. "It has that constant eighth-note pulse" or "the hook does a build by alternating the Sus chord with the major" are the kinds of statements that, while they may contain truth, are insufficient to explain why some songs just catch the public's ear. Otherwise, it would be possible to write hit songs by formula, and anyone with some knowledge of the basics could be taught the ingredients and have repeated success. We all know it doesn't work this way.

The vast majority of commercial songs, although they may not sound just like each other, share some basic characteristics:

- The melody is simple, catchy, and hummable (or seems hummable). Sometimes, the melodies (isolated from the harmony) have the disarming simplicity of nursery rhymes.

- The lyrics and overall theme have an emotional content with a broad base; that is, most people can relate to it because they've felt that way themselves. (Or in the case of story songs, the story is engaging.)
- The song has an inherent structure that provides resolution to the ear. For instance, when the verse has gone on long enough, the hooky chorus enters, and the listener can "feel" it coming. The lyrics have a beginning, a middle, and an end ("I feel bad now, this is how my problem started, this is how I'm going to end up").
- The music and lyrics are mutually reinforcing. If you hear music to what sounds like a sappy ballad, the words are usually a sappy ballad, and so forth. If you read the words to an angry heavy metal song, you can safely expect that the accompanying music will not be easy listening.
- The music or lyrics, or both, have "hooks"—catch phrases, usually repeated, that stick in the mind. These usually are simple and short. Often the rhythmic phrasing of words in the hook contributes (for better or worse) to the unforgettability factor. In many cases, the tail end of a recorded hit song fades while the hook is repeated, which tends to reinforce it more in the mind.
- The music or lyrics have freshness or originality. (This is not absolutely essential, because many songs sound like recycled older songs, but it helps.) Even basic music can have a fresh melody or rhythm over routine chord changes. In the case of lyrics, a nice, original turn of phrase can be applied to a theme that otherwise would seem worn out (lost love, for instance).

Some songwriters have a deep background in classical music and harmony; others can barely play chords on a guitar and don't know what the notes are. Some songwriters have studied music theory and analyzed many standards and other songs, while others just sing melodies to their writing partners and allow them to flesh out the harmonies of the music.

Some lyricists have university degrees in English or creative literature and rely on their study of poetry and prose to create words for songs. Others have very limited language training and just write down whatever sounds good to them at the moment. Some write lyrics and let their musical partners come up with music to fit the mood and rhyme scheme, while others work hand-in-hand with the composer. Still others put lyrics to finished music.

Perhaps the most unusual manner of writing we heard about is that of David Batteau, who has written songs for Bonnie Raitt and Jonathan Butler, among others. David uses his own four-step process:

1. In every case, identify something central to the artist's essence
2. In the case of artists with an ethnic background, try to bring these cultures to a broad audience

3. Research historical, cultural, and topical themes to bring to the music
4. Create songs in blocks of ten or twelve, to tell a story within a set of songs

David Batteau's method is time consuming, almost academic in its approach—"I read at least one book for every lyric"—but this is what works for him and for the artists for whom he writes. The point is, no single formula works for everyone.

In the realm of sequenced and dance music, some of the writers can't sing or play an instrument at all. They assemble their tunes by finding "grooves"—manipulating beats in the computer or drum machine until a basic structure emerges.

STAFF SONGWRITER

In the "old days," the staff writer was a salaried employee who gave up all claims to the songs he wrote. For that, he received a salary from the publisher. The writer no longer had to face the uncertainty of not paying his bills, but he gave up the possibility of making "big bucks" on songs that went high on the charts. Nowadays, a staff songwriter is simply one who writes exclusively for one publisher in a formal contractual relationship. The writer writes in exchange for money, the publisher has free rein to use the songs as it chooses, and the writer is prohibited from writing songs for the benefit of any other publisher for the term of the contract. While this is similar in appearance to the old arrangement, it's much more favorable to the writer.

The usual terms of the contract provide that the songwriter signs over one-half of his publishing rights to the publisher in exchange for advances against royalties—that's certainly more favorable to the writer than surrendering 100 percent of his rights. The writer is obligated to deliver ten or twelve marketable songs per year, and the publisher is obligated to attempt to place the songs. During the term of the agreement, the company pays the writer annually, as if he's getting a salary, but such payments really are advances. So, to the extent the publisher generates royalties by placing the songs, the writer begins to receive payment only when his advances have been recouped.

At the larger publishers (the only ones that can afford staff songwriters), the atmosphere is similar to that of any other office, except that the product is music. "Writer's rooms" containing a piano are provided, and songwriters sign up for access to these rooms. In recent years, this arrangement has evolved to on-site recording studios, which have a staff engineer at the ready. Demos of this sort tend to be much more elaborate than piano and the writer's voice. In some cases, the amounts expended to make them are treated as a further advance against the writer's royalties.

Of course, the songwriter has no obligation to use the publisher's facilities to record demos or otherwise work on his songs. If he doesn't need or want to go by the offices, he may work in his home studio to record demos or provide sheet music to the songs he writes. His obligation is only to deliver songs; how he does it, within reason, is his business.

If the royalties generated by the songs don't cover the advances, does the writer have to repay the excess to the publisher when the contract is expired? As a practical matter, no. The publisher assumes the risk that this will occur. Usually, the songwriter has used the money for living expenses and isn't in a position to pay it back.

What about songs that are placed before the expiration of the contract but don't generate royalties until afterwards? Such royalties are shared between the writer and the publisher as the contract provides. Songs may generate royalties over many years, and the publisher's right to receive its share of the royalties for songs it placed under the contract last as long as the writer's, unless limited by the contract to a fixed term of years.

If the songs delivered by the writer during the contract term aren't placed by the publisher within a specified period of time (often three years after the contract expires), most contracts provide that the songs revert to the sole ownership of the writer. The rationale for this is that a publisher that hasn't succeeded in placing them by this time isn't going to keep trying. Therefore, the songwriter gets back the rights, to do what he might with the songs.

There is no absolute "standard contract." Terms of the contract will vary with the company you're dealing with, your bargaining power, how effectively you negotiate, and conditions within the industry. For instance, in an era where self-contained groups are the hot item, there is less demand for staff songwriters—the industry is more "group driven." In other times, it's "song driven"—less emphasis is placed on performers and more emphasis on songs, with a correspondingly greater demand for staff writers. Of course, this can vary among genres; for instance, as it has evolved, country music has never been group driven.

Most staff writer contracts contain option periods for the publisher, that is, to extend the contract. This often is a series of one-year options. Should the company decide not to exercise them, the contract ends, whether the writer wants it to or not. Obviously, the publisher will exercise the options where it has been successful in placing the writer's songs (or, when it hasn't been, it still thinks it will).

Conflicts between the publisher and songwriter can arise when, shortly after the contract ends, the writer publishes what turns out to be a hit song. The publisher is inclined to believe that the song is one of the "good ones" the writer kept for himself as the contract neared expiration. On the other hand, the writer will maintain that it was merely coincidental that this song was written soon after his staff deal ended. To cover this situation, contracts often contain a provision that gives the publisher rights to the writer's unsubmitted songs that generate income within a specified (brief) time after the contract expires. Still, this can be a bone of contention—in most cases, there's no sure way for the publisher to know if the song was written while the writer was still under contract.

GETTING STARTED AS A STAFF WRITER

So how does a songwriter become a staff songwriter? For that matter, how does a person secure any position in the music industry?

One question at a time. The way to find a position as a staff songwriter is the same as for many other jobs in the industry. You have to be in the right place at the right time—by design. You should know which companies hire staff songwriters, who the head honchos and other decision makers are in those companies, what kinds of material they handle, whose songs they've placed with major artists—and, you have to be able to show them you've got something to offer.

Obviously, the best credential you can bring to the table is that at least one of your songs has been a hit. Publishers want you to write for them once you've shown you can write and place songs without them (it's a bit like the bank being willing to loan you money when you prove you don't need the loan). They're looking for a "sure bet"—even though really there's no guarantee that any of your subsequent songs will be placeable or become moneymakers.

If you don't have a hit, you have to show the publisher some marketable songs you've written—an audition, if you will. Most of the time, this will be a demo recording. If the song is strong, the demo need not be elaborate—piano and voice or guitar and voice can do the job. Of course, a convincing vocal delivery will be important to sell the song. If the song is more production and performance dependent (like a sequenced dance track), the demo should present the song in a more finished version, to simulate the way you expect the final product to sound.

Still, having a marketable demo is just a start. Despite the occasional exception, an unsolicited demo you mail to the company probably won't even get you more than a polite form rejection letter—sometimes you get no response at all. This is true even if it is addressed directly to a contact person you've found out about. You need to approach people in the publishing business to get your demo heard. They're already busy; they get approached each day by many people as it is. When soliciting by mail, lesser-known writers often have more success with a polite letter of introduction unaccompanied by a demo tape, particularly where they include a response card. By not bombarding a stranger with a demo right off the bat, they give the publisher a chance to request the tape and to know what to look for when they do receive it.

Don't expect a publisher to know about you unless you sell yourself. You have to hang around with the right people—other songwriters, session players, producers, demo singers, managers, or anyone else in the business. All business is a game of contacts (who you know), and in the music business, this is even more true. Having a credible person recommend you to the publisher is the best way to get your foot in the door.

Suppose one of your musical friends, who's close with someone who works for the publisher, has hand delivered your package. After allowing a reasonable time for the person at the publisher to play your demo, you make a follow-up call. Your name will be recognized by this person, who'll take your call. Instead of plunging right into business, you start off on a lighter note, talking about your mutual friend.

If the person hasn't already listened to your demo, speaking to you will remind him to do so, and he will make sure he finds time for it. If you get along personally, if he feels you're a clever and entertaining person, he'll make a personal connection. You'll be a person he wants to help, if he can. Plus, he'll be inclined to think that your personable nature translates well into your songwriting.

Of course, none of this guarantees he'll think there's any future for you in the songwriting business. Ultimately, he will make a totally subjective judgment based on his experience. Either he'll try to sign you to a deal, reject you, or advise you to come back later when you've already had a hit song. But at least you will have had access to someone who's in a position to advance your career—and access is necessary, even though it's not always sufficient.

As more and more pop songwriting takes place at the "groove" level by making use of samples, loops, and other collage methods, fewer and fewer staff songwriter positions are available. Producer/engineers are often credited songwriters, supplanting the need for staffers.[43] If popular music goes around "full circle" to the artistic style and business structure of the 1950s, staff songwriting may make a comeback, but we see no indications on the horizon that this will ever occur.

A COMMENT ABOUT BUSINESS

This isn't a "how to make it" kind of music business book, so we won't go into detail on the subject of the musician as businessperson. However, we do wish to stress that in any discussion of a career, a business component always goes along with the purely creative component of writing, playing, producing, and so forth. Reasonably talented people with great business skills and work ethics generally get further in all occupations than major talents who are poor businesspeople. The music business is no different. The industry is interested in the bottom line; it doesn't care how talented you are.

Selling yourself, doing research on the market for your abilities, being responsive to the needs of others in the industry, making contacts with the right people—these and other business skills are plentiful in the repertoire of most successful songwriters (and others). Yes, there always will be some exceptions to the rule: The brilliance of a very small number of people is so undeniable that it overcomes their weaknesses in business; others are just lucky and get discovered through no efforts of their own; and so on. These exceptions are overpowered by the rule. In the main, you have to go looking for success—it won't come looking for you.

Probably, you've read interviews with famous songwriters (or film actors), in which their considerations seem to be purely artistic. "I want to bring more classical elements into my songs" or "I'm tired of tough-guy parts; I'm rejecting scripts that don't let me play a sensitive role" are the kind of comments you see. How can these artists seemingly ignore business?

- They can afford to. They're already well known and in demand. Even if their new venture fails, they still get royalties from their older work. They turn away more offers than they accept. By contrast, someone trying to break into the business has to work a lot harder on business and has the creative part under better control.
- Because they're established (and financially comfortable), they have the luxury of concentrating on more purely artistic issues. You can bet that, when they were coming up in the business, they jumped at the chance to do things to make money, make contacts, and get noticed, usually with scant attention to the artistic merits of the endeavor. If you do research to find out about their early careers, you usually discover they were trying very hard to sell out.

Songwriting as an Independent

The independent songwriter is more of a free agent than the staff songwriter. He's not tied into one publisher for a period of time or a fixed number of songs. He's in a position to get his songs published on a one-by-one basis, by working with various producers, artists, and managers. Each one of these will try to bargain with the writer for portions of his publishing rights (for more on these, see Part I, "The Publishing Business"). Remember, performers and writers are the people in the industry to whom sales and airplay royalties accrue; therefore, everyone else is trying to get a piece of their action.

Independents often write songs with a particular recording artist or style in mind. Then, they record demos and pitch these tunes directly to the artist, the producer, or the artist's manager. If there is a desire to use the song, an interesting game starts: How much of the publishing is the song-writer going to have to bargain away to get the tune recorded by the artist?

This is determined by the relative bargaining power of the parties. For instance, a writer just starting to move forward in the business might be able to get a better percentage deal working with a small label, an unknown producer, and a fledgling artist. However, even if the song is terrific and performed well, it might go nowhere because the clout behind the recording is much less than that of a big-name artist, top producer, and major label. To "break" the song and get a career off the ground, the writer, in most cases, will be better off settling for a smaller piece of a much bigger pie—and this means giving up more of the publishing rights.

Of course, many factors enter into this equation: For instance, compared to the first example, a somewhat proven songwriter coming off a hit will be able to strike a more favorable deal with the team of a big-name artist. At the highest level, the work of the major songwriter can be in such demand that the writer keeps all of his publishing (owns his own company). The manager of this company gets paid to place the songs with artists in the position to sell the most copies and get the biggest airplay, that is, generate the greatest income for the songwriter. In this case, the give-and-take is reversed; compared to the early example, the songwriter calls most of the shots, not the producer, manager, and artist.

The less-established songwriter may be in a position to try to keep more of his publishing if he feels that the song is strong. He can risk failing to make a deal with a given team because he perceives that the song is highly marketable—he can find another buyer. If he senses that an artist, producer, manager, or label strongly believes in the song and wants to record it, it works to the writer's benefit. Of course, if he's wrong in these situations, it helps if he has alternate sources of income, from a day job, royalties, or wherever.

The independent songwriter lacks the resources of a publisher available to support the daily writing—no piano room or recording studio with an engineer at the ready. Fortunately, though, songwriting can take place anywhere; for example, many writers carry portable cassette recorders and sing their ideas to save for later. Independent songwriters often work out of their homes, where they have a music room, office, or home recording studio. Some songwriters find it unproductive to work out of their homes and have a separate office they go to every day, just like a stockbroker or insurance agent. Since separate offices are an added expense, the writer who has one normally is well into his career.

THE SINGER-SONGWRITER

The songwriter who is also a solo artist writes a little differently than the independent writer. He doesn't have to worry about placing songs—he's writing them for himself, and he knows what the singer is looking for. Still, he has to sit down and write regularly, in whatever place and manner work for him.

When dealing with a producer, record company, or publisher, the singer-songwriter also is in a different position in that he is playing a more complex game. He's trying to get established in two careers, not one. He has two colors of bargaining chips, if you will—his songs and his potential as a performing artist. Publishing rights are commonly used as a bargaining tool in negotiating record deals.

In hard terms, the major label and producer will say, "If you want us to put out your album, you're gonna have to fork over part of your publishing." It's a package deal, and because the newer artist doesn't have much bargaining power, he has to give in to this demand. In most cases, there isn't much choice, because the company is taking a risk—after all, the singer-songwriter hasn't established a track record.

On the other hand, once he's been successful and his contract has expired, he'll be in a position of greater bargaining power. If he's good at business (or has a manager who is), the next deal he makes will be much more in his favor. Occasionally, a new artist generates a "buzz" and is able to negotiate a better deal, not only for publishing but for all aspects of his career. The major labels can get into bidding wars and become desperate to sign an unproven act. Partly, this is because they're convinced the act will be a big moneymaker for them; and partly, it's because they want to prevent their rivals from landing the artist. In a bidding war, bidders react because other bidders are reacting, which is why the process can get out of control.

Ordinarily, a publishing demo needs to be only strong enough to present the song. However, the singer-songwriter is showcasing more than the song—he's also selling himself as a performing talent. The double purpose of this demo means that it should be produced to a higher level of finish. While this is more expensive, it's a necessary investment. Moreover, it allows him to work both sides of the street. He can use the demo for its primary purpose and, at the same time, to pursue a pure songwriting track. He can work the demo with publishers, managers, producers, and artists just like the independent songwriter.

Songwriter–Band Member

In the 1950s, a few recording artists (Sam Cooke, Little Richard, Carl Perkins, and Paul Anka come to mind) performed their own material, but they were exceptions. The great majority of the time, artists performed songs written by others. Performers weren't songwriters, and songwriters weren't performers. Singers were backed by bands selected by a producer, record company, or manager.

The mid-1960s brought in the era of the self-contained musical group that writes, sings, and plays the instruments on its recordings. The most prominent, successful, and trendsetting of these groups was The Beatles.

The Beatles did start out as a rock and roll cover band, but the albums of original songs are considered to be their major achievements. Ever since they rose to prominence, self-contained musical groups pretty much have been expected to generate their own material. It is now the rule rather than the exception that the group (or some of its members) write the songs they perform.

As with the singer-songwriter, groups trying to get ahead in commercial music wear two hats, writer and performer, and face similar issues with respect to trading off some of their publishing rights to get a foothold as recording artists. What's different, of course, is the group dynamic. The more people involved in decision making, the more likely it is that there will be disagreements.

For instance, some members of a group might be in favor of allowing an outside artist to be the first to record a song written within and for the group, while others would be opposed. The in-favor faction would argue that placing a song would raise the profile of the group and help earn money. The opposed faction might argue that they can do it better, that the song is too personal to allow someone else to do it first, or that they were saving it to be the first single on the debut album.

Another area of potential major disagreements has to do with who writes the songs, and who within the group gets the royalties. It's implausible that all members of a group are equally talented and prolific writers. More likely, one or two members generate most of the material, while the others lend their playing and singing talents or occasionally contribute songs. If the publishing spoils are distributed strictly along the lines of who the writer is, then comparatively speaking, the nonwriting members of the group stand to lose out financially.

Some groups solve the problem by simply splitting the publishing royalties in equal shares among the members, no matter who in the group really wrote most of the material. This team concept can work very well, especially in bands that started when their members were very young and that have been together a long time. The rationale is that they've all supported each other to get as far as they have and are like a family. Clearly, if the main writers would feel shortchanged, this doesn't work!

Other groups go the alternate route and let the individual writers keep the royalties to the songs for which they're responsible. In this case, the more unevenly the writing is distributed within the group, the more likely it is that disagreement will follow. The group members who don't write might feel cheated. On the other hand, perhaps they feel fortunate to be part of a group whose success is dependent on its writers. If other sources of group income (CD and tape sales, concert receipts, etc.) are large enough and everyone agrees that this solution is fair, it can work, too.

THE PRODUCER/SONGWRITER AND ENGINEER/SONGWRITER

Music created from samples, loops, and beats forms the basis for many or most songs in dance music, hip-hop, and rap. Increasingly, these songs result from the efforts of a producer (who may also be the engineer). The producer collaborates with the vocalist or rapper (the person who most often provides the lyrical component of the material) to co-write the song.

Since no actual session players or traditional "outside" songwriters may be involved in creating a song, the rise of these styles to prominence has increased the prominence of producers and engineers. To a great extent, a hot production team such as the Neptunes is the twenty-first century version of a hit pop act. Their input to records they produce is more significant than the contribution of the singer/artist whose name is associated with a song or album—and they receive songwriting credits.

OTHER SONGWRITING OPPORTUNITIES

Writers have other avenues to pursue in addition to writing for themselves or other artists. Songwriters and composers are responsible for commercial jingles for radio and TV, film and television scores, and background music; the skills required are not much different. The markets for these are relatively smaller and more specialized than the popular music industry, but they are very real. Sometimes, people move between industries; for instance, pop songwriter-performer Barry Manilow began his career as a jingle writer. Similarly, pop writer and group member Danny Elfman moved into film scoring and is known for his work in the movie *Batman*.

As the commercial popular music industry is the basic thrust of this book, a full discussion of these other careers is outside of its scope.[44] Interested readers should approach them with the same attitude and business savvy as other careers we cover here in greater depth.

CHAPTER 8

SOLO ARTIST—ON YOUR OWN

T he solo artist—the talented and charismatic person in front of the microphone—is the most recognizable and enduring symbol of popular music. While it's true that many recording groups have achieved significant recognition, the majority of music fans give the name of a solo performer when they're asked to identify their favorite artist.

Although a few instrumentalists enjoy successful popular music careers, most solo artists are singers. These days, it's not uncommon for them to write (or cowrite) their own material, which both personalizes the songs and provides an additional source of income for the singer. However, it isn't necessary to write to be successful, and many of the most distinguished solo artists don't write much, if at all.

Far more than music is involved in being a solo artist. The solo artist is an entertainer, so writing, singing, and playing are just the beginning. Factors in his popularity (or lack of it) include personality, look, energy, stage presence, sexuality, and even politics. Added together, these are the "image"—that all-important intangible people think of when the artist's name is mentioned.

SOLO, BUT NOT ALONE

A very tiny number of artists write, produce, play, and sing on their albums without the involvement of any others. These rare exceptions prove the rule, though. Listen to a record by a typical solo artist or attend a live show: The artist has plenty of help. In a larger sense, what makes an artist a solo artist is the appearance of only that individual's name on the front of the album cover. The casual fan of an artist may not bother to read the credits on CD liner notes, but if he does, he'll discover that the music he's hearing is a collaborative effort, a partnership between the artist and other team members.

Even if the artist is credited as the sole writer, the producer often is responsible for working out the arrangement, instrumentation, and form of the songs; putting together introductions; and generally making the tunes radio-friendly. Especially for computer-generated pop, dance, and hip-hop records, the producer-writer is the true artist. This person has the greatest responsibility for creating the sound the audience really listens to. The artist is no more than a voice—an important part of the mix, to be sure, but a lesser contributor *to the music* than the producer.[45]

For a singer who doesn't write at all (or writes lyrics only), finding a good match in a writer and producer is critical. A producer who genuinely understands the artist's image and musicality can be of great service in finding and choosing songs which will "work" for the artist, as well as the right session musicians. Not uncommonly, a singer may have particular empathy for the songs of certain writers and seek to continue performing songs by those writers. In successful situations, these talented songwriters pen songs with their favorite performers in mind. This is a symbiotic relationship, to be sure.

Solo artists who write music often accompany themselves on piano or guitar, but they rarely perform or record "naked." In most cases, such artists are backed by other musicians (usually at least bass, drums, another chordal instrument, and a solo instrument like electric guitar) on stage and in the recording studio.[46] In the studio, the accompanists may be session musicians or members of the artist's touring band. In the case of the rare solo artist who is strictly an instrumentalist, the touring band and the studio band usually are the same; the accompanists are a big part of the artist's overall sound.

Sometimes, sidemen work faithfully (and nearly exclusively) with one performer for years, both recording and touring. The artist's audience recognizes and appreciates the continuing contributions of this family of regulars, who in their own right are part of the show the fans come to see. Usually, a musician from the regular band serves as musical director for the solo artist and may share writing and production credit.

In the case of a solo artist who isn't just a well-packaged marketing ploy, the essence of the music springs from the artist. Even if he doesn't do it all himself, the final product represents the artist's unique personality and musical vision.

CHOOSING SOLO STATUS

None of the solo artists we interviewed said that they had an early driving ambition to be a solo act. Nearly all of them were in bands before going on their own. One of the reasons cited for going solo it that it's simpler than being in a group: "You don't have to worry about getting everybody on the same page," says one artist. "I enjoyed being in bands, but in my experience, everyone wanted to be the leader and we never got anything done. That's when I became frustrated and started performing on my own," says another. Singer Leah Andreone, who has released two major-label albums, relates:

> I did not consciously set out to become a solo performer. I had absolutely no idea how the process of getting a record deal played itself out. I went along with the advice of people I trusted and learned later why I made many of those decisions. When the opportunity presents itself to make a record with a major label, you move quickly. Everybody moves quickly . . .

Leah Andreone's decision, then, was based on the opportunities presented as much as a carved-in-stone intention to work solo.

Singer Mary Dolan, who accompanies herself on guitar, sums up the practical side:

> When I decided I wanted a fuller sound to accompany my music, I began to work with other musicians in a band situation. Though the benefits of a full ensemble are great, I found that they usually did not outweigh the benefits of performing solo. For example, as a solo artist I can rehearse whenever the heck I feel like it, choose all of my material without conflict, and take home all of the meager pay at any given gig. With a band, rehearsals are scheduled and rescheduled, people don't always agree on set lists, *and* one-fourth of $50 is not enough to live on.

The majority of solo artists we spoke to are singer-songwriters. One who is not is smooth jazz saxophonist Pepper Williams, who records and tours under his own name. Pepper puts together session musicians to play on his albums, who may or may not be the same players as in his live band. He pays his studio and road musicians as an employer:

> I didn't so much choose to be a solo act as gravitate that way by virtue of being the one who gets the band together and steers the ship. It's partly ambition, partly leadership skills, and partly that some musicians don't want to be bothered doing anything besides playing. You have to be willing to risk some money to do what I do . . . a lot of people are used to showing up, playing, and getting paid, but they don't want to be businessmen. That's the way it's always been in jazz . . . you have the leader who is the 'name,' and he calls the shots.

What these various solo artists have in common is that once they went on their own, there was no looking back. This type of career was the best fit, and they knew it.

IMAGE

Consider these names: Salvador Dali (painter), Ernest Hemingway (writer), Bette Davis (film actor), Rudolf Nureyev (dancer), Wolfgang Amadeus Mozart (composer). They're generally considered to have been leading artists in their fields. Yet, in each case, the famous name conjures up much more than the achievements of a great painter, writer, actor, dancer, or composer. As remarkable as they were, each seems seem to stand for something in addition to his or her artistic legacy—something bigger than life. What these magic names possess is *image*.

Having an image that is evoked by your music, your look, or the mention of your name is a significant selling point and may even grow beyond the music itself. In commercial popular music, images abound. Some solo artists are unabashedly romantic, others are cynical about romance. Some sing about politics, others are strictly personal. Some are drop-dead gorgeous, others are "regular folks" and proud of it. Some are raunchy, others are overtly religious. Some are depressed, others are upbeat. Some are urban, others are rural. Some are suave, others are down to earth. Of course, there are endless variations and combinations.

Usually, an artist develops an image naturally. Particularly if you're writing your own songs, the "real you" emerges in your performance and your recordings. It's important to be conscious of what this evolving image is, so that you can avoid sending conflicting or confusing signals. This isn't to say you should be coldly calculating or insincere, because these are unnatural and not believable. Rather, the awareness aids in the professionalism of your overall presentation. For instance, if you're a male country singer, you're better off wearing jeans and boots than dressing like a gangsta rapper.

Image is important whether you are a solo act or part of a group, but the solo artist's image is utterly dependent on a single personality. In a sense, a group has more leeway with its image, because fans accept that individual group members have different personalities. In the majority of groups, a large part of the image is based on the teamwork, contrast, or interaction of the distinct members—in short, their chemistry. The nature of being a solo artist means that you can't rely on group chemistry for your image. Because you're the whole team, you have to be that much more conscious of your image. Of course, an observant, conscientious, and astute manager should be of tremendous help in identifying, nurturing, and projecting your image. It's part of what you pay him to do.

Music is a way of communicating feelings and emotions, many of which are very complex. These emotions come in bundles, and the music evokes them beyond mere words and music. The overall emotional package you convey is your image.

THE LOOK

In an ideal world, spiritual beauty matters more than outward beauty. Society has coined sayings to reinforce this concept ("it's what's inside that counts"). However, in the world we live in, looks matter, and often they matter a great deal. Study after study shows that attractive individuals have an easier time achieving or gaining status, money, power, sex partners, career advancement—most of the things in life that everyone's always fighting for.

Nowhere in society do looks matter more than for solo artists in the music industry (and entertainers generally). Especially for an act trying to break through, an attractive appearance is a major asset. In the age of the music video, looks may be the determining factor in whether an act is offered a record deal. This may sound cynical, but turn on music television and watch videos by solo artists. The odds are you'll see far more physically attractive people with limited musical ability than you'll see talented musicians with major flaws in their appearance.

While it's true that some fairly ordinary-looking (and in some cases, homely) artists have broken through, they're in the minority. Often, despite the lack of classic beauty, they have (or at least project) an interesting, intriguing, or exotic appearance. Appearance is part of the overall image; having the look to match that image is the name of the game. If the image is threatening, or rowdy, or "just folks," stunning looks aren't necessary. But, if you're shooting for a glamorous, desirable, sexy image, the opposite is true. It's all about marketing—who the target audience is and how you want to be perceived by it.

One fact of life in the popular music business is that looks are more important for women. Our society perceives women as objects of desire, and the music business amplifies this as a sales tool. If you have any doubt, open the Sunday newspaper to the entertainment section and peruse the display ads for upcoming concerts by female solo artists. Look closely at the photos: Lighting, makeup, and professional expertise are used to create come-hither facial expressions, seductive poses, and cleverly displayed bodies. Few of them resemble your Aunt Debbie, who never got her figure back after her third child.

One female solo artist tells us that her A&R rep has been known to keep track of her weight. An executive laments the harmful effect that a psychological disorder, leading to binge eating and weight gain, had on his client's career. (She's recovered now.) A producer tells us that he can't envision much of a career for a singer because "she looks like a guard at a women's jail." The sentiment behind statements like this isn't very enlightened, but it represents how the industry thinks, which in turn is a reflection of prevailing attitudes in the culture.

In this environment, the artist must take her appearance into account with the utmost seriousness. Personal fitness trainers, strict diets, beauty consultants, cosmetic surgery, and dental implants are just a few of the means solo artists use to enhance or maintain their looks for the benefit of their careers. These things apply also to male artists but not in the same degree. A male artist with an angular, craggy face can get away with being "rugged," but a female artist with equivalent looks just has a big nose and funny teeth.[47]

You want to be judged on your music, but the visual component of your image is inescapable. Unless this ingredient is at least commercially acceptable, you may not get the chance to be judged on your music beyond the local level. You ignore it at your own peril.

HOW OLD ARE YOU NOW?

Much of the concern over appearance also reflects another obsession of society and the music industry: youth. It's often said that popular music is a young person's game. Of course, if enough people in the industry feel that way, it's a self-fulfilling statement; and largely, it is. Attractiveness is defined almost exclusively in terms of attractive *young* people. For women, this means generally, the ages of eighteen to thirty; major labels very rarely sign new female solo artists who appear more than thirty. Again, the same rules apply to men, but they get a better break on the age—maturity (up to a point) is considered sexy in men but not in women.

Here is a reproduction of a display ad from *Music Connection* magazine:[48]

LATIN
FEMALE
(17–22) Singer Needed
for well connected manager.
Songs and studio provided.
Send photo and bio to:
Fictitious Productions
Los Angeles, CA 90016

Note that a demo is not requested and that singing ability is not mentioned. Not only does appearance matter, it overwhelms the music itself. Based on this advertisement, it's clear that there is a demand for performers who possess the right look but scant musical abilities. Our purpose here isn't to criticize, much less reform, society's prejudices. Moreover, it would be pointless to argue that the industry should change its marketing assumptions. We're just showing the business the way it is.

What are the consequences of age-based bias for the aspiring solo artist? In the case of a forty-five-year-old singer-songwriter who's never had a major label deal, it probably means you're not going to get one, at least as a solo artist. This doesn't mean you shouldn't try. If you can establish yourself on a smaller or niche label, you may be able to "move up," but be aware of what you're up against. Remember, age bias is all about marketing, not talent.

Although authoritative figures are not available, the music industry believes that most pop records are purchased by listeners from ages twelve to twenty-five and that they want their artists to belong to their own generation. This is a complex, and again self-fulfilling, situation. Considering that the big promotional push on commercial pop radio and music video stations is oriented to teens and people a few years older, it makes sense most sales would be made in that market. (Either that, or all those major label promotional dollars are being wasted.) If the industry concentrates on marketing its product to a particular audience, no one in the business should be surprised that other, essentially neglected, market segments account for a smaller proportion of sales. In large part, this is the result of increased concentration of power in fewer and fewer major labels, a trend that will be discussed in chapter 14.

THE LOOK YOU WANT

Within limits, the way you choose to present yourself is within your control. Obviously, if you're short, you can't become tall, and if you're seventy-five years old, you can't look like you did when you were twenty. However, in between extremes, there's room to maneuver. Muscle-toning, hair dye, flattering clothes—there's almost no end to the things you can do to maximize the marketability of your look. The choice of how far to go is yours, but most people do something—even if that just means putting on a cowboy hat when you don't feel like it.[49]

Some solo artists feel that relating to their audiences live and on their recordings does not require any particular concessions in their look. Singer-songwriter Mary Dolan tells us:

> Comfort is more important to me than appearance. I've found that if an artist has the goods to deliver, people 'get it' regardless of the artist's appearance. I've encountered lots of people who have advice and ideas in regard to my looks, and despite their intrusions I do what I feel is right and I continue to move forward.

It may be that the sincerity of appearing in whatever feels comfortable is part of a performer's image and enhances appreciation of the music. At the same time, if he hasn't tried any other manner of visually presenting himself, then it's quite possible that by some measures, his career progress could be improved. Correctly or incorrectly, he may think he's not making much of a trade-off. If dressing very casually on stage is important to an artist, and he's satisfied with his career progress—well, you can't argue with satisfaction.

TRAINING

Despite the industry emphasis on image and looks, most solo artists are real musicians. They become involved in music because it means something to them and they exhibit a talent for performing or writing. In contrast to a group, the solo artists' skills can't rely on group chemistry; they must sink or swim on their own.

The extent of formal training of solo artists varies widely. Some are formally schooled, others just pick things up along the way. By contrast, session musicians generally are much more highly trained. This is understandable, as the skill requirements of a session player are more technically demanding, with less emphasis on personality and no emphasis on songs or lyrical message. Although we found in the folksinger-songwriter genre that the musicians tend to go more for feel than for virtuosity.

Smooth jazz saxophonist Pepper Williams majored in music at California State University, Hayward, to study his instrument, music theory, composition, and arranging. In his genre of music, all of this knowledge is called upon. Pepper composes and arranges music for the band he fronts, transcribing and writing in traditional music notation. Although he could have learned how to do all this on his own, he considers his formal training invaluable. On the other hand, singer-songwriter Deborah Liv Johnson relates:

> Most of my training as a singer was from listening to other vocalists on radio and records. I picked up the acoustic guitar in college, and started writing songs and singing as a solo act. I don't consider myself a very schooled player, but I do take lessons sporadically. I'd love to do it more, but there just never seems to be enough time.

In the area of voice, the distinctive sound of many artists derives in part from the fact that their early vocal style was not formally acquired. Singers tell us that this is an advantage, because many voice teachers are unfamiliar with popular singing and tend to push students toward a generic classical style. Fortunately, in recent years the community of voice teachers has grown to include an increasing number who are able to coach singers in popular styles without this bias.

The solo artists we interviewed believe that, while formal training can help, dedication, passion, and development of an individual vision are more significant. Major label vocal artist Leah Andreone, whose two albums have been in the pop-rock-alternative genre, seems to speak for all when she states:

> I am classically trained in piano and have studied music all my life, in col-
> lege and through private lessons. But more importantly, I studied other peo-
> ple's music and paid attention to other people's styles of writing a song,
> singing a song, and feeling a song. I have learned much more by watching
> my peers than by reading a book about chord structures . . . Music allows me
> to face pain in a way that I am not able to express through spoken words.

The performer (especially a singer) is giving his talent to his audience, but more than that he's giving his personality. In light of this, it's understandable that the solo artist would emphasize personal expression over other aspects of music.

Singers generally agree that some vocal technique training is important once you begin singing often, not so much for musical direction as for the preservation of the vocal instrument. Singing in any style is very physically demanding. While proper technique does not guarantee that a singer won't encounter voice problems, it does help to minimize the probability of their occurrence. Further, it cuts down on the severity of vocal difficulties that may be encountered by a singer who, for instance, sings all the time or needs to perform despite upper respiratory infections.

If you're a singer, your voice is your career; when it's gone, you're done. Vocalists who push their voices, either through chronic overuse or improper technique, can develop nodes (small growths) on the vocal cords. Nodes interfere with proper vibration of the cords. In severe cases, you can temporarily lose your voice entirely. If they become chronic, nodes can limit the singing voice to a squeak or hoarse whisper. We spoke to several singers who have required surgery for nodes. All of them are recovered, and heartily endorse training and vocal health programs to maintain the singing voice.

PRODUCTION AND ENGINEERING TRAINING

As more and more commercial music is created using studio technology as the primary instrument,[50] it is increasingly helpful for solo artists to develop familiarity—if not intimacy—with engineering and production. Knowing how to manipulate computers, digital music workstations, and other devices is rapidly becoming as important to dance music, rap, and hip-hop artists as learning to play acoustic guitar is for a traditional folk singer. Increasingly, the production *is* the song, so performers and writers in loop- and sample-based genres must be up to speed in technology in order to create their sound.

We expect there will always be popular music that is created the old-fashioned way; that is, by musicians playing instruments rather than by producers pressing buttons and working hard drives. Nevertheless, it is wise for artists in certain genres to acquire skills as their own engineers and producers, since this will not only give them greater capacity to control the artistic product, but also maximize their ownership rights in the songs and recordings.

THE PRODUCER RELATIONSHIP

In live performance, there's room for experimentation. Which songs go over best, whether there should be a solo or harmony vocals, and finding the ideal tempo and groove are just a few of the components you might scrutinize and continue to refine. If you try something, and it doesn't work, there's always tomorrow night. In recording, however, there is no tomorrow night. Once the recording is "in the can," your judgments are forever frozen. This is why a capable producer is so important to an act, whether the act is a group or a solo artist.

In the case of a solo artist, the role of the producer looms even larger than for a group. Consider that, when you're a member of a group, musical judgment is applied collectively, even if group leaders tend to have more say. Each person in the group (drummer, rhythm guitarist) plays a specific part in making the music on the finished product; and most of the time, no one who isn't a group member plays or sings. By contrast, most solo artists are singers. They may or may not play an instrument on their own recordings. Even if they do, most of the instruments are played by studio musicians— musicians who might be playing on a dozen other, dissimilar sessions that week. Under these circumstances, for the solo artist's record to have a cohesive sound, someone has to take the initiative. That someone is the producer.

Some artists begin with a concrete vision of how their record should sound, but most of the time, it isn't well developed. The artist's chances of properly assembling the music by himself are pretty weak.[51] To pull together all the loose ends which form his vision, he needs to bounce ideas around with another musician who's committed to the success of his recording—the producer. In a group situation, band members can gang up on the producer if they disagree with some of his ideas, but a solo artist has no one else to back him up if he disagrees. Because the producer is virtually a partner, his effect on the finished product of a solo artist is even greater than for a group. Singer Mary Dolan sums it up nicely:

> While the success of my career is dependent upon me, the success of my CD is heavily dependent upon my producer. I am responsible for 'promoting,' but the producer has the job of directing my music in a tasteful, hopefully marketable way. Sometimes tasteful and marketable don't coincide. Nevertheless, a good producer is *very important* to me and my success.

The significance of a producer is a two-sided coin. The right producer for an artist can help make recording magic happen. He can mold and polish basic songs into little gems, he can find the perfect rhythm section to play behind the artist, and so on. However, the producer who is mismatched with his artist, despite his best intentions, will help create a record that is directionless or that sounds all wrong for the artist. For example, consider a producer who's known for his mammoth string arrangements; often, he feels compelled to provide them. However, for a record that should be much more raw, the effects of such production will be harmful. So, the solo artist needs to be especially sure that he feels comfortable with his producer.

PROFESSIONALS

Groups as well as solo artists rely on professionals, particularly attorneys and personal managers. But, as in the case of the producer-artist relationship, the importance of professionals is magnified in the solo setting. In a group, some members have more music business smarts or experience than others, and their collective wisdom can help to monitor their professionals. By contrast, the solo artist has no bandmates to buffer these relationships. This aloneness makes the initial choice of the manager (for example) even more critical than it is for a group.

Solo artist Leah Andreone relates that she was very careful in assembling a team of professionals and feels comfortable taking their advice:

> When it comes to decisions pertaining to my career, I listen very intently to my lawyers, record company, publishing company, and managers. I know that they have probably been doing this for more than double the amount of time that I have and definitely have some wisdom that I have yet to attain. I wanted the feeling of a devoted family . . . I feel I am very lucky.

Solo artists who are out of the DIY school understand how important, in particular, personal managers are. Do-it-yourself success story Ani DiFranco began by doing everything herself but now employs a personal manager. DIY folksinger-songwriter Deborah Liv Johnson has a different take on managers and the music business in general:

> I've mostly been a lone wolf in the music biz. I do everything myself. But, I do like to ask questions, especially when it looks like someone is doing things well and I can learn from them. I make excellent contacts at Folk Alliance when I attend their conferences . . . If someone offers you a record contract, run the other way!

Deborah Liv Johnson's view and Leah Andreone's views and actions are far apart. Nevertheless, they aren't so different in their origins. Each recognizes that, as a solo artist, her career is especially susceptible to the input of industry professionals.

A DAY IN THE LIFE

Because a solo artist is the whole show, so to speak, solo artists are some of the busiest people we've met. Being an artist is a "twenty-four/seven" job, far removed from the taxing but predictable nine-to-five grind. Artists are constantly working the widely varying aspects of their careers, and there's no telling what part of the day they'll be busiest. By contrast, songwriters, session musicians, producers, and engineers usually can choose to work something closer to regular hours, more like most working people.

Because most artists tour, much travelling is involved. But, even when the solo artist isn't out on the road, career-related demands on time are great. Working out of a home base, the artist usually keeps so busy that he doesn't remember what day of the week it is. Early in the day, he may meet with his producer to preview and work on new songs. Later, he'll work out to keep up his health, appearance, and stamina. Although many people exercise regularly, few face the draining work days, weeks, and months of the touring artist. Fewer still are in careers in which such a premium is placed on appearance.

In addition to keeping his body fit, the solo artist also tries to keep his music in good shape. All the solo artists we interviewed state that they try to practice their instrument every day and to keep progressing in terms of understanding music. Singers especially say that it's important to work on the voice, to keep that crucial instrument in peak condition. Citing lack of time, none of the solo artists we talked to pursues regular formal study with teachers. Most say that they take lessons here and there and try to learn from their performing peers.

Solo artists who aren't touring usually are recording or preparing to record. For most, part of this preparation is writing material. So, in addition to working on music generally, the solo artist has specific goals and work to do to achieve them. Sure, solo artists have personal lives and hobbies, but they truly don't have as much time as regular folks. Being a solo artist is comparable to being an Olympic athlete, like a swimmer or pole vaulter:

- The competition is very tough. The others are working twenty-four/seven on their careers, and if you don't also, you're at a disadvantage.
- Your chosen occupation is very grueling, taking both a physical and emotional toll. To hang in, you need to stay fit, healthy, and sane.
- Your career is likely to be compressed into fewer years than ordinary careers. You have to make the most of it while you're young, competitive, and "hot."
- You have expert assistance, but when you go out to do your thing, everything rides on you alone. Success requires an obsessive mindset and determination.

Long-time artist manager Ron DeBlasio, who has worked more with solo artists than with groups, says:

Though the first things I seek in an artist are talent and uniqueness, they're just qualifiers. The very next attribute I look for is a burning passion and dedication to be in this business. It's a very brutal business. If you're not willing to accept the sacrifices, you'll either give up before you succeed or destroy yourself succeeding. Being an artist can take a huge toll on your personal life; often your career requires you to put a higher priority on its obligations than on your family, for instance. It might mean that you're on the road when your kid graduates from school or has a birthday party, and you just can't be there. . . .

Like the Olympic athlete, the solo artist isn't just a regular person who happens to pursue an extraordinarily demanding career. You're so busy making the career happen that it becomes who you are, not just what you do.

INCOME

The manner of earning income is just one more way that being a solo artist is unlike a normal job. In such a job, you perform services for your employer, and you receive wages, salary, or commissions (and if you're really lucky, some other benefits). In terms of income, it's a one-on-one relationship. For the solo artist, there are many sources of income, and the only one that is technically an employer is the record label.[52]

At early stages in their careers, not all solo artists can support themselves adequately through music. In which case, they take the proverbial day job. Once they get rolling, though, solo artists have varied sources of income, particularly if they're also writers. These include performance royalties, mechanical royalties from records and videos, live performance fees, sales of licensed merchandise, synchronization rights, and so on. You can see why, if your career is successful, you need a CPA to keep track of all these sources and to help make sure that you receive all that's coming to you.

Please refer to other chapters in this book for a more detailed discussion of the specific mechanics of the various sources of income.

CHAPTER 9

GROUP MEMBER—IT'S A TEAM EFFORT

I n the 1950s, solo artists still ruled the charts. The era did see its share of singing groups, even a few rock and roll groups such as Bill Haley and the Comets. Still, in rock and roll the dominant names were solo acts such as Little Richard, Chuck Berry, Jerry Lee Lewis, Buddy Holly, and others. In the mid-1960s, though, the business changed dramatically. The popularity of what came to be called "rock" music displaced the tamer, "adult" pop that had preceded it. Led by The Beatles, many artists began writing their own material. And, the prevalence of self-contained groups skyrocketed as such groups became at least as common as solo acts.

Being in a group has both advantages and disadvantages, rather reminiscent of a good news–bad news joke. For example, the more people involved in a task, the less reliance there should be on any particular individual. However, problems can arise if some members don't pull their weight. Contrast the saying "Two heads are better than one" with "Too many cooks spoil the broth." There can be strength in numbers, but also there can be disagreement and strife.

We asked record company executive Paul Fishkin whether he prefers to work with groups or solo artists. He hesitated, then replied, "I was going to say I don't care for groups, because they break up. On the other hand, solo artists break down."

THE RIGHT STUFF

"So you want to be a rock and roll star, well listen now to what I say
Just get an electric guitar, then take some time and learn how to play . . ."

—*Roger McGuinn of The Byrds*

Most newspaper accounts of the rise of a newly successful band read like an itinerary: "First we played here, then we recorded our first demo, then we caught the eye of our manager," and so on. Because the articles are about the people who are in the group now, they understandably gloss over the history of what happened before that lineup crystallized. The untold story, though, is that finding the right people to be members is the single most critical element in the career success of a group.

There are several reasons for this. First, the musicians must be able to sing and play together in a way that is musically valid. Very often, young bands are so desperate to complete the lineup that they choose the wrong person(s), someone whose ability level isn't up to par or whose style is too far from the basic musical direction. Under these circumstances, something always sounds "wrong" and keeps the band from developing a unified, listenable sound.

Does this mean that, ideally, all group members should have identical tastes and musical preferences? Not at all. The musical chemistry of the best groups is based as much on the differences among the individual musicians as on their similarity. The creative tension between the members plays itself out as a blending of personalities and influences. Thus, the music they make together takes on a special flavor that is recognizable and enjoyable to listeners. But, the differences need to be reconciled into vibrant, cohesive music, not rambling, unfocused music. The Beatles are a famous example—the pop sensibilities of Paul McCartney seemed to clash with the raw rocker in John Lennon, but the group made it all work.

The significance of chemistry and synergy between members cannot be overemphasized. Some groups make magic creating music together, even though no individual in the group is surpassingly accomplished as a writer, singer, or instrumentalist. Time and again, when a member leaves the group that made him famous or does a solo project, the albums he releases fare poorly on both the commercial level and the artistic level.[53] What's missing is that special "something" that he enjoyed in partnership with the other group members.

The *musical* chemistry inside a group is partly a result of *personal* chemistry. Where the individuals within that group share not only musical but also other interests, where there is a genuine tie of camaraderie, where they genuinely believe in each other's talent, and where they feel so strongly about each other that they're able to overcome petty differences and ego trips, the power of this bond will be reflected in the music. All of this may sound corny, but it's true. Bands in which people really don't like each other almost never get anywhere, mostly because they break up before they have a chance to get anywhere. The odds are that music made not in a spirit of cooperation, but with animosity, will not be very appealing.[54]

Often, groups that manage to make commercial music despite severe personal differences break up or lose key members just as they're on the brink of a record deal (or, sometimes, right after signing a contract or putting out their first record). While it may seem ironic that they manage to progress so far, only to pretty much wreck their own chances, it isn't coincidental. Increased career pressure brings out deep, inherent personality conflicts within the band; instead of cementing the unit, the pressure causes irreparable fissures. Our advice is that personality and chemistry matter a lot. In the long run, they are *equally as important* as musical talent. If you just can't work together, there's no point in going into business together, because it won't last.

One other very important aspect of choosing the right people has to do with compatibility of business and life goals within a group. As groups form, some members may be more ambitious than others about a long-term musical career and, so, may be more accepting of the personal sacrifices required. For example, if your group is absolutely determined to "make it" but your prospective new bass player is unwilling to be separated from his wife and kids to go on tour, it doesn't matter what a great person he is or how well he plays—forget about him. Find someone else, whose goals match yours. Or, suppose you consider yourself a pure artist, unwilling to "sell out" by signing a major label contract. If the objective of others in your group is to make pop records that reach the widest possible audience, there's potential for some serious disagreement down the road.

In real life, most musicians begin in groups strictly for fun and the love of music. Often, they're young, inexperienced people more concerned with enjoying themselves than with making plans. Under these circumstances, we don't expect that they will approach the issues just discussed with reflection and maturity. In all likelihood, they will barely consider them. But, as they develop as a unit and as individual musicians, career questions begin to appear where there were none.

As much as possible, issues like these should be worked out early on in the life of a group. If they can't be resolved to the satisfaction of all, changes should be made for the good of everyone involved. These changes may seem painful at the time, but we guarantee that things even as unpleasant as firing someone from a group or getting fired from a group seem much worse if they happen when more is at stake. Of course, not all changes are necessarily this radical. Sometimes people compromise successfully.

GROUP LEADERS

As much as chemistry and personal compatibility are essential, in no group of any kind—from law partnership, to tennis club, to homeowners' association, to rock band—do all members see eye to eye on every issue. Yet, groups succeed in accomplishing their major objectives. In addition to having the right people on board, such groups have leaders—people who, by virtue of inclination, talent, vision, character, and interpersonal skills, are most suited to guide decision making.

In music, leadership exists on two levels: artistic and business. On the artistic level, songwriters often are the leaders of a group. Because they generate the material that is performed, in some sense, they speak for everyone. Rarely does a successful group write songs collectively or enjoy a situation in which songwriting ability is distributed equally in band members. Since artists generally have large, sensitive egos, this disparity has the potential to cause friction among members. Just as significantly, it has powerful business consequences. Songwriters earn publishing royalties, but nonwriters don't—a situation in which some people in the group stand to earn far more than others.

The imbalance doesn't have to result in resentment. First of all, non-writing band members usually are savvy enough to recognize that without high-quality material, the group will not enjoy much opportunity for success. They're glad to be part of a group that actually has a career. In addition, it isn't uncommon for the songwriters in a group to share writing credit with bandmates who helped work out the songs or share publishing royalties with them in some other contractual manner.

We asked John Mattox, drummer for the Young Dubliners, a group that has enjoyed success touring and on independent labels, whether it bothers him that he's not the star or the main writer. His reply:

> Not at all. There have to be certain parameters or frames that the band works inside of. Any ideas beyond those of the group can be explored by solo projects and freelance work . . . 'Chemistry' is an interesting word. If the music sounds great and people respond positively to it, you know something is working. However, this does not mean that everyone in the band is like-minded and gets along with each other . . .

In a similar vein, Jimmy Crespo, who joined already famed rock band Aerosmith as lead guitarist, says:

> When I joined, I wasn't made a member at first; I was a hired gun on a salary. The other guys made it very clear to me it was *their* band. I knew my role in the scheme of things. It was understood that the front man was always going to be [vocalist] Steven Tyler. Sure, I like the spotlight when I'm taking a solo, but basically I'm a band kind of guy. I'm happiest when my ideas and playing contribute to the whole . . . Having a role to play doesn't mean you're a second-class citizen.

Good team play includes the willingness of individuals to subordinate personal glory, power, and control for the betterment of the team. With each member understanding his role and executing it to his fullest capability, the group can get much further than if each individual tries to be the leader.

Things don't work as well when everyone's a queen bee and no one's a worker bee.

In the business realm, some group members always will assert leadership. Others don't want to be as pro-active; they're more likely to evaluate, critique, and vote on plans made by the leaders than to take the initiative themselves. Group decisions should reflect a consensus; and the leaders forge that consensus.

The recognition of leaders should not mean that some members are "more equal than others." Most of the time, the nonleaders are not blind followers. They simply recognize that the leaders are the most capable of watching out for the interests of the band. Just as democracy doesn't mean that everyone's the boss, having leaders doesn't mean having dictators. No member should cede a voice in band affairs out of laziness or ignorance; doing so is a disservice to everyone in the group. Leaders don't have a monopoly on good ideas. The input of all members is important not only to preserve the group relationship but also to make the best possible collective decisions.

GROUP AGREEMENTS

What prevents many groups from dealing with the business side of being in a band is that it doesn't come naturally. Particularly in their early stages, groups are something like marriages—the partners are driven by a common passion, overflow with good will toward their mates, live for the moment, and can't imagine that anything can come between them. In fact, making partnership agreements appears to be the antithesis of how they feel about each other, because they contain provisions with potentially nasty contingencies no one wants to think about. Under these circumstances, entering into such an agreement seems unappealing at best.

Still, one of the first things that motivates musicians to seek legal advice is the desire to firmly establish group agreements. A group agreement is, in most cases, a partnership agreement,[55] which in its generalities is not very different from a partnership agreement between, say, the operators of a restaurant or other business. In its major points, a well-thought-out agreement:

- Clearly identifies the partners, the name of the business in which they have an interest, the business purpose of the partnership, and the time parameters.
- Defines the obligations of the partners in operating the business, individually and collectively. Sometimes, a managing partner is designated.
- Lays down the ground rules for operating, including voting rights and dispute resolution, day-to-day operations, sharing of income and expenses, and amending the agreement.

- Outlines circumstances and procedures under which new members may be admitted or old ones may leave, including what an ousted partner receives on termination from the group.
- Provides a formula and a procedure in the event of dissolution of the partnership, including divvying up the assets and liabilities of the partners.

These aren't all there is, but they're the biggies. These provisions can get pretty long and complex where the group has been around for awhile selling a lot of records.

A band member often asks a lawyer if the existence of a fair agreement prevents getting ripped off. The answer is that no agreement can stop partners from cheating you or pushing you around, if that's what they want to do. But, a good agreement defines your recourse if, for example, you feel you haven't received your fair share of group income. In this way, the agreement may act as preventative medicine—partners are more likely to stick to something they've signed. Where there's no written record, it's easier to play fast and loose.

If you've only been in fun bands or local groups in which little money is spent or made, the chances are you haven't signed a partnership agreement. But, when the economic stakes get higher, you should seriously consider it. For example, producing and releasing your own CD is becoming increasingly common and may easily involve an investment of $10,000–$15,000. This is enough money to give rise to certain questions:

- What happens where certain members contribute more hard cash, because others just don't have the resources?
- What if the group breaks up before all the CDs are sold or before all the expenses connected with it are recouped?
- Suppose the main writer leaves and joins another band? Should he have to buy the CDs from the group, which now has little interest in promoting them?
- What if, as a result of the CD, the lead singer is offered a major label contract without the group? Does the group have a right to part of his income?

These are just a few issues that may arise. They demonstrate that any group embarking on a business venture with significant financial consequences should consider the contingencies, agree on how to handle them, and create a memorandum of their understanding—preferably with the help of a lawyer.

Even though some major partnerships operate as handshake deals, the vast majority of high-earning groups have formal partnership (or, as noted earlier) corporate deals. Again, the analogy to marriage is apt. Few people who get married young and broke enter into prenuptial agreements, but prenuptials are very common among wealthy people who remarry after a divorce. It may seem unromantic, but there are times when people feel too much is at stake not to protect their economic interests.

What's in a Name?

One of the biggest sticking points in band relationships is this: Who owns the name by which the group is known? In a number of high-profile cases, some members of groups that had broken up tried to resume operating under the old name, only to be prevented from doing so by legal action of the nonparticipating members—Jefferson Airplane (Starship), Creedence Clearwater Revival, and the Talking Heads, to mention a few. In the case of 1950s singing groups with few surviving members, there have even been multiple groups touring under the old name (the Coasters, the Drifters, and the Platters), each claiming—without authorization—to be "the original."[56]

In a well-publicized case, famed New Wave group Blondie reformed in 1998 after a fifteen-year hiatus. Former members Frank Infante and Nigel Harrison, who were not included in the reformed group, claimed an ownership interest in the group name. They instituted legal action to try to prevent the others from getting together again under the name Blondie or, failing that, to receive damages and be compensated as if they were participating. The reformed Blondie released a new album and played many shows before the matter was later resolved against Infante and Harrison.

Based on the example of groups like Blondie, the best time for group members to deal with band name issues is while the original lineup is intact. Rights in a name should be part of the group agreement. Recall that groups can agree on any allocation of rights; members are not obligated to share rights equally. Musicians are often reluctant to discuss property rights and down-the-road, worst-case contingencies when they'd rather be making music. However, being in a music business career involves business as well as music and, sometimes, more business than music.

Band names are not just names. Fans are often faithful to their favorite groups over a period of decades. Serious goodwill is tied up in the name of a recording group that has had a number of hit records. Whoever holds the rights to that name owns an asset that is capable of producing significant income in personal appearances and (depending on circumstances) new as well as old recordings.

We've all seen people sporting T-shirts, bumper stickers, baseball caps, and other paraphernalia proclaiming the name of their favorite group. Since a group's name is part of their image, it's intimately tied into their success. The name is analogous to the brand name of tangible products. For instance, people are loyal to brands like Harley Davidson motorcycles,

Fender guitars, and Nike shoes. The plain fact that a product bears the name makes it more likely that certain people will buy it instead of a competing brand. When a name of a product is fully protected by law (Coca-Cola, Pepsi), it's called a "trademark." In the case of playing music, which is a service rather than a product, legal protection is called a "service mark."[57]

A group should pro-actively try to make sure that the name they've chosen isn't already taken and protected by law. Names have a value, which translates into dollars of revenue from record sales and appearances. To use a name someone else has been using creates a possibility of confusion in the marketplace, which may result in:

- The intruders' receipt of income that by rights belongs to the originals
- An inaccurate or inferior representation of the original group; this is not only unfair to the fans, but it also damages the value of the band name—perhaps irreparably

A famous case in point is Fleetwood Mac of the early 1970s. Due to internal problems, the band quit in the middle of a tour, apparently having split up. Trying to keep income rolling, the band's manager put together a band with different personnel using the name Fleetwood Mac. The new band didn't include either Mick Fleetwood or John McVie, the members from whom the group name was derived. Members of the "real" band brought suit to prevent this action by the ostensible manager. They prevailed on the basis of protecting their property interest in the group name. Of course, in the Fleetwood Mac case, the misappropriation of the band name was intentional and rather larcenous; more commonly, name duplication occurs inadvertently, because there are so many groups in so many places.

As a legal and practical matter, name duplication means much more if at least one of the groups is earning, or imminently stands to earn, significant income or, based on geography, musical genre, and group sound, the bands are likely to be mistaken for each other in the eyes of the fans and industry. Unless one or both of these factors is present, the issue of competing group names should be susceptible to amicable resolution. Without these factors, the groups really aren't stepping on each other's toes anyway. In most cases, one group agrees to stop using the name. The group that has developed it more extensively may pay the other for this privilege, at least to cover the administrative expenses involved in changing names. It's a much cheaper, simpler, and less aggravating resolution than litigation.

Various databases, including federal and state trademark registers, are available as sources for an attorney to research whether the use of a group name is first in line. Be aware that even a diligent search does not always turn up the existence of a group that has been performing, perhaps recording, under the name your group would like to use.

IT'S THE MONEY

We noted earlier that to be a member of a group, the ability to get along on a personal level with other people in your group is as important as the musical side. As drummer John Mattox points out, it's unrealistic to expect that everyone's going to be buddy-buddy. However, if a group is going to move forward together, it should be able to keep its eyes focused on major goals rather than bogging down in the things the members don't like about each other. While maintaining a stable lineup is not a prerequisite to success, common sense tells us that it helps.

The simplest and (for obvious reasons) the best method to preserve peace is for group members to be equal partners in business matters.[58] However, sometimes a new musician may join a group that is already well into a career. Here, there are three basic ways to go:

1. Make him a full member (partner) from the get-go.
2. Make him prove himself within the group for a probationary period. If he passes this test, he is admitted as a full partner.
3. Keep him in the group, not as a partner, but as an employee (hired gun). Sometimes this mutates into choice 2.

Bassist and co-lead singer Jason Scheff is with the venerable and highly successful group Chicago. He was admitted as a full member immediately upon joining:

> I was told I did really well at the auditions and that [keyboardist-singer] Robert Lamm wanted me. In effect, Robert is the managing partner, and the others generally agree with what he says because they respect his judgment. A few days later, Robert called me and told me they were going to make me a full member. I couldn't believe it, I was this twenty-three-year-old kid and I would've taken the gig for rent money just to play with Chicago. Robert explained that the group wanted me as a full member from the start, to show how much they believed in me . . .

Jason joined Chicago in 1985, has written hit songs for the group, and in 2004, is still in the band. In large part, he attributes the long, cordial, and profitable relationship to the trust shown when he was admitted as a full member.

Not all "new kid on the block" scenarios are as gratifying as Jason Scheff's. A musician (let's call him Ray) who replaced another player in a famous band[59] initially joined as a hired gun. As Ray assumed a more prominent role, he was told he would be admitted as a member, but the group dragged their feet even as he wrote songs to be included in upcoming albums. Once in the recording studio, the other members informed Ray they'd record his songs only if he'd give up some of his publishing—a favor that ran in one direction only.

Finally, Ray was admitted as a full member, but only after the band was in artistic and business disarray due to various personal problems, including substance abuse. In short order, he found out that, in addition to becoming a partner in a group which wasn't earning much, he'd taken on substantial back tax liabilities. Unable to make anything of the situation, Ray quit playing with the group but didn't surrender his partnership interest. In a few years, the original lineup successfully re-established itself in the commercial music world. Ray asserted a claim that he should be compensated for the tax problems he'd been caused, for fraud, and for his share of the profits. Ultimately, a settlement was reached under which Ray surrendered his partnership interest and all other claims in exchange for a lump sum cash payment.

The contrast between Ray's experience and that of Jason Scheff is night and day. Both musicians became part of established bands, but the similarity ends there. Respectively, their experiences illustrate the worst and the best of business relationships in a group setting, but they're more than war stories. In a group, business relationships are *internal*—within the group—as well as *external* (for example, with third parties like promoters and record companies). The career-minded recognize that getting along in business is part of the big picture.

IMAGE AND APPEARANCE

All the information contained in chapter 8, "Solo Artist," about the importance of an artist's image and appearance (the bias toward youth and beauty and so on) applies to groups as well, but with a twist. For starters, groups, more so than solo artists, are categorized—some might say pigeonholed—that is, identified by the industry (including the music press) with a movement such as Seattle grunge rock or California ska-punk of the 1990s.

When your band's image and career are coming together, you should carefully consider the industry's tendency to pigeonhole. It can cut both ways for your group: It's helpful to be considered part of something that's hot, but it's deadly to be connected in people's minds with something formerly hot, and now passé. Not entirely, but to some extent, you can control how people think of your group. Let's say you'd prefer not to be thought of as part of the grunge scene. In that case, try to obtain gigs in "nongrunge" venues, and play on bills that aren't dominated by grunge acts. Further, avoid dressing like a grunge band and minimize obvious grunge influences in your music. If people in the business still want to slap a grunge label on you, at least you've tried to avoid easy categorization.

A group's typical fan can always tell you the lead singer's name and often that of the lead guitarist. However, it's much less likely that he can identify the group's drummer or bassist. For better or for worse, the star of a group is the focal point of the group's image. Usually, it's the lead singer, although it may be a flashy instrumentalist; in rare cases, each person in the band carries an equal weight of image.

Even as early as when you're putting your group together, you need to consider the charisma factor and appearance of the band members. For instance, if your lead singer is a sexy twenty-one-year-old with great charm, dynamite stage presence, and a fantastic, unique voice, *and* happens to look like a swimsuit model, you shouldn't have to worry so much if your bass player is an immobile, stone-faced geek (assuming, of course, that he gets the job done musically). This is not to say that image and visuals are everything, but they are more important than they used to be. It still helps to have catchy songs and make great-sounding records.

TRAINING

The musical preparation of group members is not so different than that of a solo artist. Their backgrounds vary from the completely self-taught musician to the highly schooled player. In contrast to session musicians, the majority of musicians in popular music groups do not read music. Since the only songs they're going to play are their own (or ones of their own choosing), they don't have to sit down cold and play tunes they've never heard before, with a rotating cast of musicians. The self-contained group learns the songs working as an ensemble.

One of the most valuable things to develop is a readily identifiable group sound. A big part is often the lead singer's voice (Guns and Roses, Heart), but it can also be based on the grooves of the rhythm section, as in the case of The Rolling Stones or the Dave Matthews Band. It can be based on particular instrumentation, such as The Byrds' twelve-string electric guitar or the honking saxophone of Bruce Springsteen's E Street Band. It can be based on the harmonic content of the music (Steely Dan) or the use of vocal arrangements (The Beach Boys).

These are just a few of the many factors that make listeners say, "Oh, I know who that is!" For groups, recognizability is a component of marketability. There's no formula for creating this asset. Usually it materializes as a group grows musically. Forcing it ("we're the first heavy metal group with a lead bassoonist") won't sound right. Certainly, groups should listen to feedback from their audiences to discern what fans pick up on and try to play to their strengths.

In classical music,[60] a premium is placed on virtuosity. Popular music, by contrast, is oriented to a group's distinctive sound, the personal statement, or message of the music, and the psychological image it conveys. If a group is a little rough around the edges but has a strong personality and catchy tunes, it's got more than enough to be marketable. In fact, the rough edges are often part of the charm and work in the group's favor by strengthening its image. The art of a pop group lies not in its musical accomplishment or sophistication, but in how it touches people's emotions. Often very simple, basic music sells even when it clearly is a rehash of older stuff, because a new generation is hearing it for the first time. We're talking about show business here. What sells, sells, regardless of whether it represents advancement in the state of the art.

Solo artists are usually singers or, if they're instrumentalists, play a melody instrument like saxophone or lead guitar. In pop music, few (if any) solo artists, for instance, are drummers. That's just not the nature of the instrument; drummers join or form groups rather than pursue solo instrumental careers. In a group, there's a greater opportunity for musicians who play support roles rather than lead roles—drummers, percussionists, bassists, rhythm guitarists, and so on. They're no less important than the other musicians; for that matter, a rhythm section player may write, sing lead, and be the best musician in the group.

GROUPS DAY TO DAY

Like solo artists, group members are busy people. There isn't much distinction in their activities because they're part of an ensemble. Dealing with management, lawyers, and a record label, recording, touring, staying in shape, rehearsing—all of these are common activities. The major difference is that, in a group, certain time demands can be spread out among the members. For instance, an interview with a journalist doesn't require all four members of a group; the reporter will probably be happy to talk to anyone. In the case of a solo artist, burdens like these fall on one person, since there's no one else to take care of them.

INCOME SOURCES

Again, the ultimate income sources of group members are no different than for solo artists. Because there is an internal agreement among group members as to how to share income, the final money path for each member may be somewhat more complicated, but that's the major distinction. Also, since group members play different instruments, more of a variation in instrument endorsement deals is available. In the scheme of things, such relationships with manufacturers usually are not the most significant source of income, but they're a nice perk.

DECLINE OF THE GROUP AND THE ALBUM?

In the "classic rock" era that prevailed for approximately thirty years from the early 1960s, groups became the dominant form of act, and albums replaced singles as the major medium fans listened to. Acts like Fleetwood Mac, the Rolling Stones, the Eagles, Pink Floyd, Led Zeppelin and many others recorded albums and toured. Some solo acts (Elton John, Joni Mitchell, James Brown), were huge, but by and large the music industry was propelled by groups making music known in the radio trade as "album oriented rock" (AOR).

In the early 2000s, the genres of heavy metal and alternative rock remain dominated by groups, and other popular acts like the Dave Matthews Band and Phish are still groups. However, more and more often, acts which rise to prominence are solo artists like Shania Twain, Beyoncé, and 50 Cent. And, increasingly, the medium listeners use to enjoy these artists is the single, rather than the album.[61] This trend towards solo artists and singles is more reminiscent of the late 1950s era in music industry than of the AOR era.

Unlike some other changes we have discussed, which are by nature "one way," it is not clear that the recent trend towards singles and solo acts is other than a cyclical one. To the extent it stays around, songwriters interested in breaking their groups commercially might be well-advised to focus on crafting catchy singles rather than entire concept albums.

CHAPTER 10

SESSION MUSICIAN—IN THE STUDIO AND ELSEWHERE

The most-recorded musicians in history aren't famous solo artists or members of venerable recording groups. They're session musicians—players whose names do not appear prominently in liner notes or on album covers.[62] Session musicians play on pop recordings in all genres, as well as on advertising jingles, TV shows, movie soundtracks, and everywhere else there's music. Session musicians often accompany performers in concert settings, either as a member of a "touring band" for a solo artist or as an extra hand to augment a set group.

Session work is a different scene than being a group member or solo artist and requires a different approach. For example, the focus of a recording by a solo artist (usually a singer) is on the artist—so if you are that artist, it's all about *you*. By contrast, for the session drummer playing on the recording, it's most emphatically *not* about you. Instead, your role is to subordinate your personal artistic goals, ego gratification, and spotlight-grabbing tendencies to the wishes of the producer and the artist. In short, the purpose is to present someone else's music rather than your own. "Its all about serving the song," says one session veteran.

MUSICAL BACKGROUND OF SESSION MUSICIANS

One common thread we found among studio musicians is that they usually began in music, and demonstrated an aptitude for it, early in life. Studio guitarist Mitch Holder relates:

It started when I was about seven, with a school mate bringing an acoustic guitar to school singing folk songs. I became interested in the guitar, not the singing. I studied from the age of eight, and my first teacher, William Pellegrini, taught me how to read music. Subsequently I took more lessons from another teacher, John Frisco, who taught me harmony . . .

Carol Kaye, one of the foremost studio bassists ever, began as a guitarist. Both of her parents were professional musicians, and she started playing at age nine. She explains:

Through a girlfriend, I met Horace Hatchett [teacher of renowned jazz player Howard Roberts], who loaned me a guitar . . . within three or four months of lessons, I was working for him as a teacher, and I was playing jazz gigs professionally by age fourteen . . .

The experiences of other session musicians were similar in tone if not in detail. Most session musicians are people who took playing an instrument seriously as they were developing. It was a consuming passion, not a casual pursuit of youth. In response to our question, "Did you set out to have a music career at an early age?" they answered "yes." Significantly, the "I wanna be a star" mindset does not appear to have played much, if any, part in this process.

Does this mean that if you're a late bloomer, you won't have the goods it takes to be a session musician? Not at all, but it does mean that you'll be facing competition from talented people who've earnestly pursued music from an early age. The point is not that you must start young to have a chance but that, to develop the skills, you must love playing so much that you're willing to put in the time, the effort, and the dedication to craft.

READING MUSIC

Although numerous talented singers and players in all genres do not read music, many sessions require reading skills. For certain sessions, those players who cannot read are usually excluded out of hand, even if they have a great ear and many other definite attributes. All of the session players we spoke to are adept sight readers and stressed the importance of reading in their ability to secure work. Even if the bulk of their work is on pop and rock sessions, they consider training in classical music or jazz essential insofar as reading is concerned.

Sight-reading of parts written out in musical notation is the rule in movies, television work, and jingles, particularly for orchestral players (strings, horns, etc.). In other sessions, especially pop and rock, the music is "charted" with written chord symbols corresponding to measures. The recording scene in Nashville, home to most country sessions, is known for its "number" system in which charts are written out with numbers that correspond to the chords and intervals of the key center. No matter which method is used—standard musical notation, chord charts, or the number system—the session musician must be able to work with it. The most versatile session players read in each of these formats.

Occasionally, one encounters a successful session player who doesn't know how to read music. However, such a player is rare; we're talking about someone who has both an uncanny ear and a faultless ability to memorize music the first time it's heard. These are abilities very few people are born with. You can't learn them, but you can learn to read music. A person who's serious about being a well-rounded session musician should learn to read.

VERSATILITY AND OTHER MUSICAL SKILLS

In addition to being able to play his instrument well in the craft sense, a studio musician must be sensitive to the music he's called on to play. In response to our question "What qualities do you have that makes people want to hire you?" guitarist Mitch Holder, a thirty-five year studio pro, replies:

> The ability to sight read and play many different styles on demand, with little or no rehearsal time. I also found that I had a knack for coming up with hooky rhythm parts on R&B stuff and got a lot of calls to do that, along with the other 'reading' dates.

Thus, he established a reputation for being effective on almost any session and being particularly empathetic in one context. This combination of versatility and specialization has led to the busy career he enjoys.

Being known for playing one style or with one sound can keep a session player busy, because a producer or artist who is looking for that particular style or sound will know exactly where to get it. On the other hand, if the musical winds shift, it's possible that there will be less call for this player's specialty. Another studio guitarist, Jimmy Crespo, tells us what had transpired once he acquired a reputation based on his years of playing in blues and rock bands and sessions:

> I began to specialize, without really trying. I was getting calls to play in that particular style more and more. I had learned to read so I could get more work, but the fills and licks I was asked to do usually didn't require reading, it was more ear-playing, feel-playing. It was great to get a lot of calls to just show up and play, but you can also get to be trapped by what you're known for. You know, people think you can only do one thing . . .

In his case, there's plenty of demand for the blues and rock style—he's not suffering from any shortage of work, and he isn't complaining about the sessions he does. Having worked on his instrument and his reading skills, Jimmy Crespo tells us he'd like to stretch out more than he sometimes does, so the full range of his music can be utilized.

Bassist Carol Kaye feels that experience and training in jazz is what makes for the best session players:

> Jazz is improvising, and most of us [studio players] were fine jazz musicians. The arrangers were pretty good, but they still needed us to 'pad' the parts by adding our own ideas . . . we used to say, 'Shh, don't tell anyone we play jazz' on the [recording] dates . . . we all had the groove, the technique, the musicianship, the experience . . . if you take the singer off the recordings and really listen to the musicians in the background, then you get an idea of where the power of the recording of the 1960s hits comes from . . .

Kaye began doing sessions in the days before session musicians were credited and continues to this day. She states, "very few 'rock' players recorded the 1960s rock records. Most of the studio musicians were jazz players." Whatever the "sound" of the group (and there were many different ones), the studio players had to come up with parts that were appropriate to the music and voices. Due in part to the insistence of players like Carol Kaye, today's studio musicians receive more credit. And, thanks to the standards they set, the skills needed today to play in different settings must be at a high level.

Clearly, the more specialized the style or instrument a musician plays, the more specialized his calls will be. For instance, if he plays Latin percussion, he probably isn't going to hear from a lot of country producers, because his instrument just isn't used in country music. He'd be well advised to work out of Los Angeles or New York rather than Nashville. If, on the other hand, he plays pedal steel guitar, which is considered mostly to be a country instrument, then Nashville is the place to be. If a music career is important, the musician will go where the work is. Similarly, musicians branch out to keep their options open. For instance, many Latin percussionists are excellent trap drummers, too, which widens the range of playing opportunities.

More versatile players have more stylistic and geographic options, but both the specialized and the versatility-based approaches can lead to a busy career as a session player. Either way, you have to be good. As the studio players say, "the tape don't lie."

TOOLS OF THE TRADE

The studio musician must bring to the session not only talent and experience but also the right instrument(s) to get the job done. The old saying "It's a poor carpenter who blames his tools" applies just as well to musicians. Again, the requirements will vary depending on the type of music and the instrument played. For instance, if you're a tenor sax player, you'll probably show up at a session needing only your main instrument. But, if you're a guitar player on a country session, you may show up with five electrics, three acoustics, and a banjo, as well as an assortment of amplifiers. For guitarists and bassists, amplifiers are part of the instrument, too—even though they sometimes record "direct to tape."

When in doubt, show up with more of an arsenal than you need. It's better than needing an instrument you didn't bring with you. Check ahead with the producer. Even after talking to him, you can't be absolutely sure; as the day's session progresses, the tracks might be turning in a different sonic direction. Obviously, a keyboard player with a massive Hammond B-3 organ rig should find out up front if there is any need anticipated for it. If the producer says no, then changes his mind, he'll bring you back next time with the B-3. He'll have no one but himself to fault for not saying yes on your initial inquiry.

If you play sessions, your instruments should be in perfect working order, and you should bring spare parts (strings, reeds, drum heads, etc.). Producer Josquin des Pres tells the story of a recording session he produced where the drummer brought drums with old heads that were so battered, they appeared ready to tear. The drummer came well recommended, but his kit was in such disrepair that three hours of tuning were needed to get it to sound anywhere near reasonable. Because the other musicians who had been assembled would not be available again soon, the session was recorded anyway. In the end, the drum sound was so poor that the tracks were not usable. It didn't matter that the drummer played well, because he sounded terrible anyway. In addition to this being a frustrating situation, it was also expensive—the drummer and his poor kit wasted not only the money that was spent on him but what was spent on everything and everybody else at the session. No producer with any choice at all is likely to call this musician back.

THE MORAL OF THE PRODUCER SWITCH

Studio lore has it that an electric bass player invented a musically useless "producer switch" in response to being asked to perform repeated takes at recording sessions.[63] The bassist would play what seemed to be a great performance, with feel, tone, accuracy, and originality, then a producer would say, "that was pretty good, but do you think you could make the sound more . . . I don't know . . . could you try a different tone?"

After hearing this (or something like it) enough times, the musician realized that the producers were unsure what they themselves meant. To fight back, the bassist installed an important-looking toggle switch on his bass. Utterly ineffectual (because it wasn't wired to the electronics), it was mounted prominently on the instrument's body. Even peering into a darkened studio area through the control room window, a producer could clearly see it being thrown.

When asked to redo a performance that he knew was already as good as it could be, the bass player simply hesitated, smiled, and said, "I've got it!" Then, with an exaggerated gesture, he threw the producer switch and proceeded to play the exact same lines with the exact same tone as the previous take. "How was it?" the bassist would say, removing his head phones. More often than not, the producer's response would be, "Perfect take. You nailed it, just the sound I was after!" The legend goes on that most studio bass players of this era modified their instruments with producer switches.[64]

In fairness, the producer's job is complex, and he must take into account what everyone does—the big picture. By contrast, studio musicians and artists worry mostly about just their own parts. It's only natural that a producer would begin to split hairs about the tone of a bass or another instrument. The moral of this story is not that producers are dolts or don't have good ears. Rather, it illustrates the point that the studio musician's job is to adapt to the situation at hand. Always remember that you are there to support the big picture, not to argue with the producer or artist. One session musician says, "It's OK to question a part [you're being asked to play] once— but *just* once."

A producer may change the part of a studio musician during a session or ask the musician to play with a different technique or an altered tuning. Any number of "curve balls" may be thrown at the player. These things can catch you off guard, because they go beyond the scope you thought was expected. It's natural to be apprehensive. The musician who can think on his feet, who can refrain from acting flustered, and who can deliver the performance that the producer or artist wants—even if it's not what he thought he was being hired to play—will get the calls for more session work. Although he may have confidence in his abilities, not every musician enjoys working in this environment.

Adaptability is a matter of temperament as well as musical skill and experience. It's a job requirement for session players, one that should not be overlooked by those contemplating the career.

SMILE WHEN YOU PLAY THAT

Session musicians find some of the music they're called on to play tedious, dull, worthless, or otherwise unfulfilling. This is understandable, since the session musician doesn't choose the music. Even though you may choose to turn down a session if you don't think you'll enjoy it, there are several reasons you probably won't:

- If you're like most people, you can always use the money
- You don't want to acquire a reputation as someone who says no too often
- You want to maintain your relationship with the producer, rather than strain it by turning down work
- You want to play with as many different musicians as you can, the better to "keep your name out there" for prospective calls

• The player who could be hired instead might make such an impression that he will be the one the producers start calling

Session work is very competitive; there are more qualified players than lucrative studio jobs. You've got to continually prove yourself to hang on to your turf.

The more established a session player you are, the more likely you'll have competing calls and be able to choose the one you prefer from among them. Nevertheless, even for the most experienced veteran, there's a "day job" aspect to session work, which implies playing things you wouldn't play if it was your call.

The attitude that the player brings into any session is important. Off the top, it's assumed you wouldn't be there if you couldn't play; therefore, your professionalism is what the producer, engineer, and other musicians will notice first. Professionalism means smiling, playing the music as well as you can, and keeping the expression of negative feelings to a minimum—preferably zero. There are several reasons for this. First of all, you're in a cooperative work environment, and whether you're making music or doing something else, people don't like working with someone who has a bad attitude. "You can't go in there wearing a long face," says guitarist Jimmy Crespo, "work is demanding enough without someone complaining or bringing personal problems into the studio."

Even more important, since music is a medium of emotional expression, a person who exudes a negative vibe drags down the music. At the very least, it's a harmful distraction, as if trying to play music with integrity while the clock is running isn't demanding enough. Worse yet, a poor attitude adversely affects the musician's playing and that of others, impairing the feel of the music. This can mean, for instance, having to do more takes than should be necessary when recording tracks. More takes means more time, and time is money. The studio, the engineer, and the other session musicians all cost by the hour, so wasted time gets expensive.

Session drummer Ron Wikso sums up "attitude" this way:

Of course, you have to be able to play! But after that, I think the most important thing [in getting hired] is that I can get along with most people. People want to work with other people that they're comfortable with and enjoy being around. I think that, if given a choice between someone who is an unbelievable musician but is a real jerk, or someone who is just a good musician but is a really nice person, the really good musician who's a nice person will usually get the gig. Especially, when it's a road gig and you have to, essentially, live with the people you're working with.

As with most other aspects of life, excellence, by itself, isn't enough.

Some of the most accomplished jazz and classical players (even some big names) have had long careers as faceless studio musicians, playing TV show themes, commercials, movie soundtracks—whatever the gig calls for. It can be steady work with a nice paycheck, not always the case in the music world. The level of musical professionalism is high, and the working hours and conditions beat being on the road. The trade-off is that there's a certain amount of monotony, of commerce taking precedence over art. If you can accept this and play with integrity and positivity, then you may be cut out for session work. There's no room for "star" attitudes and self-important egos here.

COMPENSATION OF SESSION MUSICIANS

Recording session work for television and movies is American Federation of Musicians (AFM) union work.[65] The person who does the hiring of musicians for these sessions is called a "music contractor." The music contractor's business is to put together musicians for sessions, and he's required to be in the union to handle the job. In many cases, players double as contractors. For pop music recording sessions, sometimes music contractors handle the hiring of musicians, and other times the record producers call the musicians themselves. Jingle houses use contractors, too, but sometimes directly call the musicians for their sessions.

Under agreement with the AFM, payment must be made to the musician within fifteen business days of a session played on. Technically, a fine applies if this requirement is not met. According to session player Mitch Holder, this is not policed as rigidly as it used to be: "If the check is a couple of days late, nothing much happens." The name printed on the top of the check is that of either the film company, the production company, the record label, or one of several payroll companies commonly used by them.

Every union job requires a written contract. The paperwork is done by the contractor, the producer, or the company paying for the session. Under the collective bargaining agreement, the companies themselves are required to be AFM signatories in order to hire musicians and fill out contracts. The written contract is far more than a mere formality. If there's a problem getting paid, it's proof that the musician played the session in question. Further, the contract is a way of enforcing the employer's pension contribution to the musician's account (like many unions, the AFM has a pension fund for its members).

The rate of pay, called "scale," is set by the AFM for each type of contract. Different scales apply for different kinds of work, most notably, TV-film, motion picture, phonorecording, and jingle. Another job that has a separate scale is called a "sideline." In a sideline, a musician who "accompanies" a singer in an apparently live performance on a TV show just pretends to play—the music has already been recorded in a "prerecord." The actual recording session pays much more than the sideline—it seems fair that a musician would be paid more to actually play rather than to pretend to play.

Some session musicians who are "hot" or whose particular skills and sound are deemed particularly appropriate to a project, earn above scale—double or even more. There aren't many of these musicians who can "write their own ticket," but the ones who fit this description are in a position to make quite a bit of money. This type of "studio star" is most common in the popular music industry, more so than in film, television, and jingles.

Can a musician earn a good living doing sessions? The answer is, absolutely yes, but the trick is to keep working as much as possible. According to guitarist Mitch Holder,

> Doing records can be very lucrative while you're 'hot,' in the producers' eyes and the contractors' eyes. Most record players are hot for a few years and then someone else comes along. A longer career can be obtained by doing 'everything' and being versatile and flexible. In addition, movies have a Special Payments Fund which all the movie companies contribute to.

The companies pay into the Special Payments Fund annually. The amount paid in on behalf of a musician is based on all the motion picture sessions he's worked on within a five-year span. It includes payment for movies run on network television as far back as the 1960s. In essence, this is a royalty payment for session musicians, albeit a modest one.

Over the years, some prominent longtime studio musicians, in conjunction with the AFM, have pushed for a change in the compensation system whereby session musicians would receive mechanical royalties (see chapter 2) in addition to their wages. So far, there have been few signs that the major record companies will agree, which isn't surprising, since the payment would come out of their pockets.[66]

BREAKING INTO SESSION WORK

Breaking into session work isn't easy. First of all, the music scene is populated by many talented players who are competing for too few jobs. Second, there's no tried-and-true route to getting your name and talent known to the contractors and producers who do the hiring. By way of illustration, consider the story of legendary bassist Carol Kaye, whose first session work was as a guitarist. She first got noticed in jazz clubs, wielding her guitar at night alongside musicians who were working days in the studios. Her playing made such a positive impression that these players recommended Kaye for her initial studio gigs. Interestingly, she began playing electric bass by accident—when the scheduled session bassist didn't show up, she put down her guitar and picked up the bass, even though she had never played before. The rest is history—who would've played bass on all those 1960s and 1970s hits if Carol Kaye had stayed with guitar?

The session players we talked to agreed that there is no formula. "I've never heard the same story twice," affirms guitarist Mitch Holder. We were able to discern some broad patterns, however, leading to these generalizations:

- You have to be in the right place at the right time. Part of this is luck, but part of it is preparedness.
- You have to meet and play with the best musicians you can, both to hone your skills and to make a reputation.
- You have to play as much as possible. The more people you meet and play with, the more positive impressions you can make.
- Do all these things, and eventually you'll get a shot—then you have to do a great job.

Drummer Ron Wikso paid attention to his early experiences and persevered:

> After my first paying gigs, I learned that the best way to get hired as a musician is by word of mouth, so when I got out of school and wanted to play for a living, I just tried to meet as many people as I could. I would go to clubs where there were bands playing and other musicians were known to hang out in and try to get to know some of them. I would meet people on gigs and try to get to know them. I would take any gig I could get and do any rehearsal I could. Just anything that would keep me playing and get other people to hear me play. Some of the things you wind up doing aren't a lot of fun or maybe aren't very musical but, you can always find some positive aspect to it . . . like, I'd rather be playing for a living than having to dig ditches for a living!

"Keep playing, keep growing, keep loving it, and hang around with the right people," says guitarist Jimmy Crespo, adding, "I never 'planned' a career like a doctor or lawyer would. I took jobs because I liked the music—I didn't care if they paid well. I just loved to play as much as possible, and eventually I was able to do it for a living."

CHANGES IN THE SESSION SCENE

Like other businesses, the music business changes over time. The principles stay the same, but demographics, market conditions, and technology greatly influence the way music is made, marketed, and sold. In general, the session player is one of the costs of making music, and if there's a way to reduce that cost, companies will try to find it. To some degree, they've succeeded. The musicians we interviewed (even ones who remain busy) agree that overall, there's less studio work than there used to be.

To begin with, technology has made it feasible for producers to have studios in their homes. With so many people recording at home, they actually don't get out much to mingle and meet new session musicians. Naturally, they call the ones they already know. While it's human nature to go with the tried and true, it's also human nature for a creative person like a producer to try an exciting new player. The result of the home studio is fewer new opportunities—more work goes to the same small circle of players.

Another aspect of technology that has affected the session scene is MIDI (musical instrument digital interface). MIDI enables a person who plays one instrument (usually keyboard or guitar) to sound like other instruments as well and to program rhythms, sequences, and sounds. The heart of a MIDI setup is a synthesizer (or "synth"), a digital keyboard that contains downloaded sound samples. All parts are patched through the synthesizer, which is a computer-controlled instrument. MIDI recordings are often immediately recognizable for their "drum machine" sounds, which often are far bigger, somewhat artificial sounding versions of real drums.

Although full exploitation of MIDI requires computer proficiency, such skills are more readily learned than the ability to play ten or twelve different instruments. Particularly for forms that are repetitious, like rap, hip-hop, and dance music, MIDI tracks not only fit the bill but form the sonic basis—the recordings wouldn't sound "right" if everything was played instead of programmed. Needless to say, this way of recording reduces the demand for studio players. "If MIDI had been around during the disco era, when I averaged 600 sessions a year, no one would have been working at all," comments guitarist Mitch Holder.

In the mid-1980s, the use of MIDI caused work to slow down for movie, TV, and jingle musicians, especially for orchestral players. One synth programmer took the place of what might have been a dozen or more musicians. As it turned out, skilled synth players charged a lot for their services. By the 1990s, movie producers realized that they could afford to hire a whole orchestra for what they were paying for a synth score. In movie work, this brought the orchestral players back into the studio. Synth scores fell from favor for aesthetic reasons as well, and now most movies feature played music rather than programmed music.

Another technology that took root in the 1980s is sampling, which consists of digitally slicing off chunks of older recordings and incorporating them elsewhere. In practice, sampling is used by producers or programmers to create "loops," or backing tracks, to form the basis of an ostensibly new song.[67] This is common in rap and hip-hop, which most frequently use samples from 1960s and 1970s funk and soul recordings. In essence, the new recording relies heavily on music from original sessions done many years ago. As with MIDI, many recordings feature no live players. Thus, sampling means less work for today's session musician.

After the mid-1980s slowdown in studio work for orchestral players, demand has come back strong. However, for rhythm section musicians such as guitarists, drummers, and bass players, at least some of what they do has been replaced by sampling, loops, synths, and computers. Moreover, the winds of fashion in pop music have blown toward sequenced tracks and self-contained "alternative" and punk groups in the 1990s, compounding this effect.[68] Guitarist Mitch Holder relates:

> When I started in the early 1970s, there used to be three or four guitar players on every date. This means that if there were ten dates (and there were actually a lot more), then thirty or forty guitarists would be working. Now, there's less work and most dates don't have any guitars (usually orchestras). You don't have to be a mathematician to figure it out.

The changes wrought by trends aren't necessarily permanent, and pop rhythm players may stage a major comeback sooner or later, just as orchestral players have done. In the meantime, plenty of session musicians are branching out as producers or in other parts of the industry, and some have left the music business altogether.

MUSICAL TRENDS DRIVE SESSION PLAYER DEMAND

Commercial music recently has moved more in the direction of producer-driven forms such as rap, hip-hop, and dance pop. As digital equipment and techniques enable making this music with fewer and fewer (or no) musicians, the demand for live session players has continued to decline. With evolving tastes, more "organic" forms of music such as country and folk may well re-emerge as the more popular forms, and with them, a greater demand for session musicians. However, for now the market for such players is not expanding.

CHAPTER 11

PRODUCER OR ENGINEER

Most people listening to a recording listen only to the "name" artist. Perhaps, if they like a solo by a guest artist or a session player, they'll search the credits to find out who that might be. It's unlikely they'll notice (much less remember) the name of the producer and engineer—even though anyone who's ever listened to a cassette, CD, vinyl record, mini-disc, or any other format of commercial popular music has heard the work of producers and engineers. These relatively anonymous people play an enormous role in making recorded music listenable and marketable—sometimes, their roles can be as important as the artists themselves.

Producers and engineers often play broad roles, and the manner in which they work varies widely among individuals. Sometimes, producers also have a hand in engineering recordings they produce; sometimes engineers are the de facto producers of recordings they engineer. In other cases, a producer or engineer may stick very closely to his narrowly defined job. In the creative chain (musician → producer → engineer → tape[69]), producers are a step closer to the source.

WHAT PRODUCERS DO
One of the least-understood careers in the music industry is that of record producer. The tasks involved (and skills needed to address them) are so variable and comprehensive that describing the job is difficult, even for those who practice this most demanding of arts. When we asked producers

to tell us just what it is they do, there was always a hesitation. "Wow, that's a tough one," "I'm not even sure myself," and "I'll try, but I'm not certain I can describe it" were typical responses. The way different producers work varies so widely that it's difficult to be specific. By examining the history of record production and working forward, we can help reveal the role of today's producer.

The producer of a record is like the foreman of a construction project or the director of a motion picture. The foreman doesn't draw the plans, operate the bulldozers, or drive rivets; the director doesn't write the script, act, or operate the cameras.[70]

The producer of a record, being responsible *to both the artist and the label* for the finished product, oversees and guides the work of others making that product. Principally, he's working with the artist, the engineer, and session musicians who may participate. Typically, the producer brings the session musicians (and the engineer) on board.

In the old days—that is, until the mid-1960s or so—pop records were pretty much a captured live performance. In the recording session, the artist performed his stage act in front of microphones, with a tape machine running. In the studio, the producer's job was to make sure the artist did enough takes to get a good one, coach the artist to achieve this goal, and deliver that take to the record company. The producer's job also included other duties, at least with certain acts. For example, prior to the actual session, the producer would find songs for the artist to perform, arrangers to write charts, and musicians to play on the recording. Because producers were label employees, there was no question that, if conflict arose, their loyalty belonged to the label's vision of commercial product rather than to the artist's vision of his work.

Beginning in the mid-1960s, the producer's job was radically transformed, because of changes in both music and recording technology. For the first time, many artists wrote their own material. Obviously, this usurped the producer's role of finding songs. Equally important, the writer-artists were more musically autonomous and protective of their sound, which tended to shift artistic power away from the producer and to themselves.

Yet, even as musical changes seemed to be diminishing the importance of producers, new technology (most notably, multitrack synchronized recorders and effects processors) was working in the opposite direction. Before these recording advances, the live performance was the work of art, and the recording merely chronicled it. The new technology ushered in the modern era, in which *the recording itself is the work of art*, an aural experience far more adventurous and far-reaching than a live performance could go. The studio itself became an instrument—one of dominant importance and very difficult to master. To fully exploit its possibilities, an experienced producer is needed.[71] Such is the situation in today's music business.

Some producers—notably those with a strong musical background—become very involved musically with the artist. If the artist is a group, the producer is like an extra member. Such producers are inclined to make very specific suggestions, for example:

- Starting a song on the chorus, with no separate introduction
- Recommending a different beat and tempo
- Suggesting the lead singer phrase differently (the producer might sing it the way he thinks it should sound)
- Asking the bass player to come up with a less busy bass line (and maybe even writing one)
- Calling for a bridge to be written to heighten the dynamics of a song (perhaps suggesting the chord it should start on)

Of course, these are just a few examples of getting involved musically. There's literally no end to the changes that can be, and sometimes are, made during the recording process.

In contrast to the hands-on, extra-member producer is the "get out of the way" producer. Often, this type of producer is not a musician himself, and is not capable of providing clear musical examples of his opinions. Operating more like a well-informed fan than an extra musician, his way of working is much less specific. During the recording process, he's more likely to let the artist "do his thing." Then he'll ask the artist to make changes he feels are warranted. He may be at a loss to demonstrate or express in musical terms exactly what he's looking for, but he's skilled in getting the point across in words and phrases.

The "get out of the way" producer can be very effective, for example, working with certain jazz groups and artistically mature rock groups—musicians whose ideas are already so well-developed that they just need to be fine-tuned. In each case, the musicians have an artistic vision, and the producer is able to connect with it. By feel more than anything, the producer can tell whether the artist is realizing his vision and help him along in the process, as well as making sure the record is acceptable to the label. His suggestions may tend toward the specific (for instance, "this song needs more drive"), despite being unable to hum, play, or write a different rhythm. What's important is the quality of the producer's ears—the artist trusts them, picks up on the ideas he expresses, and gets it right.

The "signature sound" producer is another breed altogether. In vivid contrast to the "get out of the way" style, the "signature sound" producer leaves a strong, individual, and recognizable sonic stamp on all the records he produces. The stamp may have to do with the instruments used, the session musicians brought in, use of effects processors, vocal layering, and other factors. Sometimes, he's criticized for taking over the production too much and crowding the artist; that is, making a record that sounds like him more than it sounds like the artist.

Even though such criticism is understandable, remember that the "signature sound" producer gets hired because he's hot—his records are hits. Often, he's identified with a genre in which he's produced some of the big albums; artists and labels come to him because they're trying to duplicate (better yet, exceed) the success of prior artists.[72]

Since these clients are seeking (and paying for) his sound, he wants to deliver it. Unless there's a gross miscalculation, matching the artist with this type of producer isn't inappropriate, where the artist is looking for a guiding hand or new direction. Sometimes well-established artists look to work with a "signature sound" producer for this very reason—they think they're getting stale or they see him as a collaborator whose sound will mesh well with theirs.

Just as many of the hands-on "extra member" producers started out as accomplished musicians, many of the "signature sound" producers began as engineers and gradually evolved into producers. There's another species, too: the engineer-producer. This wearing of two hats can result from a producer turning into an engineer as well or vice versa. This is the ultimate responsibility in the studio, but some people can do both jobs simultaneously—and do them well.

PRODUCER-DRIVEN COMMERCIAL MUSIC

During the heyday of the self-contained band, the producer's role began to diminish, at least for a time. However, in certain styles of today's music, not only is the producer just as important as in the past but even more prominent. Specifically, many of the modern recordings of rap, hip-hop, and what is known in the industry as "dance music" are *producer-driven* rather than artist-driven. In the basic form, these recordings are pretty much the work of one person: the producer. He needs the "artist" only as a voice to sing the song and as an image to appear in photos, videos, and (sometimes) live, often lip-synched, performances.

If we define the "artist's sound" as the aural composition people *really* hear when they listen to a record, then the producer himself is the artist—in producer-driven pop, the name of the singer on the album is just part of the marketing. In this common scenario, the producer writes the material and records it himself by programming various tracks using drum machines, sequencers, synthesizers, samples, and other digital marvels.[73] If he feels the need, he brings in "real" session musicians to flesh out the track—the decision is his alone.

Even for do-everything producers in great demand, hooking up with a name recording artist is desirable. The producer usually has no marketable image and therefore needs the front person as much as he needs the producer. Such partnerships can be particularly lucrative for the producer, who gets writer's royalties in addition to his producer's compensation.

SONG DOCTORS AND PRODUCER-ARRANGERS

A step removed from the do-everything producer is the "song doctor." This producer isn't a denizen of the rap, hip-hop, and dance music world but, rather, of the pop-rock world. And although the records he makes are not producer driven, he in essence is a partner with the artist, because he is responsible for a major portion of the songwriting.

The artists the song doctor works with usually fall into one of these categories:

- An artist who sings but writes only lyrics, and so requires a cowriter for music
- An established artist whose songs are weaker than they used to be and whose new material needs shoring up by a pro
- A new artist who needs the same sort of help as the established artist—polishing songs and writing new ones if need be

The song doctor–producer tends to have a background as a musician in his own right. This style crosses over significantly with the hands-on, "extra member" style—really, it's just the next step.

Another variation on this theme is the producer-arranger. He's not really a song doctor, and he does even more than the hands-on guy. The producer-arranger starts with the artist's undeveloped raw material of basic, simple songs and builds a lavish production from the ground up, often writing fully orchestrated parts. Typically, he works with solo pop singers, not groups. This genre is more artist driven than the rap, hip-hop, and dance sphere of producer-driven pop, but not by much. Compared to music of the self-contained rock group, this is a producer-driven realm.

THE PRODUCER AS PSYCHOLOGIST

All the experienced producers we interviewed told us that the most challenging and important part of what they do involves the psychology of the artist. To do the best possible job (in addition to the purely musical contribution), the producer must

- Get inside the artist's head to share his vision (while setting aside personal preconceptions and biases)

- Motivate the artist and hold his hand
- Communicate with the artist on whatever level is required
- Understand what the label is looking for from the artist

The late producer-engineer John Mathias summed it up this way:

> I try to understand the essence of an artist through communication . . . the more the better . . . I want to get inside the artist's head. Then I focus on what he/she is trying to say. Then I blow it up to larger-than-life. Simple, huh? . . . the job [of producer] is *heavy* psychology, because every artist needs different stimulation. Some need to be mollycoddled, some need to be "abused." Some need an audience, some need seclusion, etc., etc., etc. It's my job to deduce (quickly) what it is an artist needs to give his best, or, hopefully, better than his best . . . and then make all the elements work to that end.

This answer was the response to our question, "How do you describe what you actually do as a producer?" Interestingly, the producer emphasized the psychological aspects rather than the purely musical ones. Like the Olympic athlete who tells us that a sport is "90 percent mental," the accomplished producer has reached the stage where he can take the sum of his natural talent and training to its highest level by focusing on human psychology.

The psychological aspects of producing artists cuts across production styles. Whether we're talking about the hands-on, extra-member style; the get-out-of-the-way style; the "signature sound" style; the "song doctor"; or the producer-arranger, the name of the game is to get the best and most essential (and most marketable) performance from the artist.[74]

COMPENSATION OF PRODUCERS

A producer's input is usually considered to be of critical importance in whether a record will succeed, and top producers are considered to be artists in their own right. It's not surprising that they are among the best-paid people on the creative side of the music business. Producers are paid by the artists whose recordings they produce.[75]

For producers working with major label acts, 3–3½ percent of sales is the percentage we most often heard (naturally, superstar producers command more). This percentage is called "points," although it just as easily could be called a "producer's royalty." As is the case with the artist, "sales" means actual sales less return allowance, breakage allowance, promotional goods allowance, and all the other deductions that reduce the sales base on which royalties are paid.

Producers also receive advances when beginning major label recording projects. We heard numbers like a flat rate of $25,000–$30,000; sometimes, the advance is on a per song basis ($2,500–$4,000 seems to be the common range). As with artist's royalties, these advances are recoupable; the producer receives no payment on his points until earnings exceed the advance. Again, the compensation figures and contract terms are generalizations; at the higher and lower ends of the pay scale the numbers can be much different. Most significant, points give the producer "a piece of the action," an opportunity to share directly in the success of his work. This was not the case in the old days of staff producers, who were salaried employees of the labels.

PRODUCTION DEALS

There are many variations on the "production deal." In contrast to the major label–artist–producer deal, it's even more entrepreneurial and speculative. One common type begins life as the relationship between a producer and a new (or at least unproven) artist and works this way. An artist hooks up with a producer, who for a relatively modest fee, produces some songs for the artist. Usually the recording is high-quality demo but not necessarily master quality. Using his connections, the producer shops it to labels, hoping to get a deal.

If the artist secures a label deal, the agreement between him and the producer provides for the producer to receive points (in the 3–7½ percent range). In a sense, the producer is investing in the artist's future. If no deal is made, the points are worthless; and in the end the producer receives only the fee he was paid for developing the product, which often is minimal. But, should the artist sign a label deal and go on to be successful, the producer stands to do well. Sometimes, these deals obligate the artist to hire the producer for his label release. This works only if the label agrees, which it often does, viewing the artist and producer as a package. In either event, the artist is obligated to pay the points.

In another variation with greater out-of-pocket costs, the artist and the producer sign an agreement, again with no label involved. The agreement calls for the producer to record the artist—that is, to produce finished masters just as he would for a label deal. Since the producer receives no fee and no advance, he's the one taking the financial risk. In return for this, the artist signs over half of his publishing and agrees to a royalty as if the producer were a label.

For the producer and artist, the object of the deal is to sell their contract to a major label. If this occurs, then in effect the contract between the label and the producer (or his production company) is now substituted for the old one between the producer and artist. "The danger here for the artist is that he can be asked to give away a lot to the producer, then more to the record company. Caution is called for," says artist manager Laurent Besençon.

In essence, this type of production deal shifts the initial financial risk of developing the artist and getting a high-quality master to the producer instead of the label. The label takes over for the producer and runs the show, provided the artist consents.[76]

ENGINEERING: TRACKING

In industry generally, engineers are scientists and technical experts who design products and systems, but that's not how we're using the term. In the music industry, the engineer is the person behind the recording console.[77] This person is responsible for microphone placement, channel routing, recording gear (including the recorder, mixing board and outboard gear,[78] and more)—and, most importantly, setting it up and operating it during the musical performance to capture it as a recording.

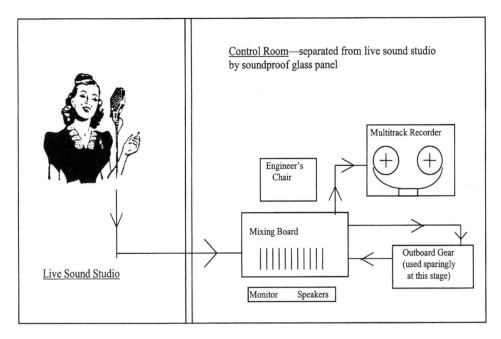

Figure 1. The initial recording process (tracking).

The simplified diagram of Figure 1 shows the working environment of a recording studio, where engineers and producers spend much of their time. The multitrack recorder (which may be analog or digital) captures the performance of musicians. Because the tracks of various instruments and vocals are *synchronized*, most tracks on the tape[79] may be played back while others are being recorded. This greatly enhances the flexibility of the process; a "perfect" performance can be captured without everyone having to be perfect at once. For instance, if a band does a great performance of a song but the bass player makes a bunch of mistakes, it's not necessary to scrap the take. Instead, the bass player can rerecord that part while playing along to everyone else's tracks and listening through headphones. With modern synchronized recorders, it's no longer necessary for all the musicians who perform on a recording to play at the same time or even to meet each other.

The levels at which the various instruments "go to tape" are controlled by fader knobs on the mixing board.[80] During recording, the engineer and producer listen to the performance on studio monitor speakers. The monitors are used again when the artist, producer, and engineer listen to the playbacks to check the performances. Outboard gear and plug-ins (reverbs, compressors, digital delays, and more) are used mostly in mixing. This is because effects can be added as desired to the stereo mix, but if they're on the 24-track masters, they can't be altered afterward without taking a chance of ruining the sound.[81]

The nature of synchronized recorders means an artist can suspend work on a song and come back to it later, add new instruments or backing vocals, or to redo an unsatisfactory part, all after the initial sessions are over. During this working period, *rough mixes* are made to a stereo medium (usually CD, cassette, or DAT). The rough mix gives the artist and the producer the general idea of how the final recording will sound if made from the available tracks. The balance of the various instruments may be off (for instance, the lead guitar isn't loud enough), but the essence of the performance is audible. Trained ears can project what the finished product will sound like.[82]

The tracking process continues until the artist and the producer feel that the tracks are as good as they can reasonably be made.

MIXING

In mixing, the engineer, working with the producer and (in some cases) the artist, sculpts the multitrack tape down to a two-track stereo mix. This mix contains the balance of the instruments and vocals, the effects (such as reverb on the vocals for a "full" sound), and equalization.[83] The mixing engineer may or may not be the engineer who tracked the recording sessions.

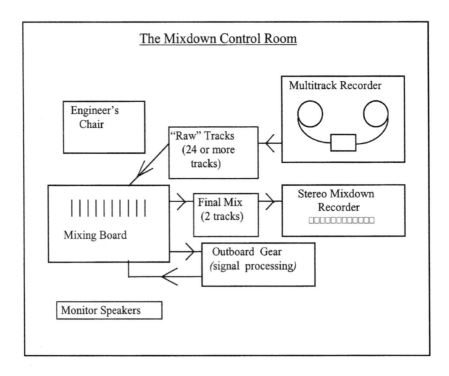

Figure 2. The mixing process.

In mixing, as in the earlier stages of the process, the mixing board is essentially a master control panel. All signals pass through it on the way to tape, and it controls the level of each track that goes to tape. For example, the signal path of a lead guitar track might go from multitrack master, through mixing board, then to outboard equalizer, then to the effects processor, then back to mixing board (which sets its volume level and spacing on the stereo "horizon"), then to stereo tape. Figure 2 illustrates the mixing setup. The logic of this signal path is maintained even when the mixdown is performed on a hard drive setup—often generically called ProTools (after an actual product). In practice, the entire mixing process takes place within the digital domain. Thus, all recording hardware and software is contained within one hard drive, rather than in separate machines.

As mixing down to two tracks takes place, the relative levels, stereo pan, equalization, and effects *for each track* on the master have to be right *at the same time*. The engineer must have an understanding not just how to operate the equipment but of the ultimate product that results from the process. An engineer's ears are just as important as the ears of a musician or producer. The most sophisticated studios (and ProTools setups) have automated mixing boards that allow the engineer to program the sequence of changes that must be made during the mixing of a song. However, at every stage, human judgment is responsible for the decisions programmed into the board.[84]

COMPENSATION OF ENGINEERS

Until the mid-1960s, engineers on major recordings were the employees of the record label (which also owned and operated the recording studio). Today's engineer, however, is more an independent small businessperson than employee. He works for himself, and provides services for multiple labels, studios, and artists. Like most small business people, he has to be part sales rep, because he always has to obtain new work to keep business going. And, as in most trades, word-of-mouth for a job well done will bring more work to his door. There's nothing like a hit record to make artists, producers, and labels want to work with you.

As with other music business careers, the rate of compensation of engineers varies widely. If there is any rule of thumb, it's that the bigger the artist and more important the project, the more the engineer will be paid. As in other jobs, the more competent, experienced, and savvy an engineer is perceived to be, the higher the fee he can demand. On the other end of the scale are assistant (or apprentice) engineers, whose earnings won't pay the rent in a medium rent district.

Generally, engineers base their fees on hourly rates. Often, an engineer charges a flat rate for a project by estimating the number of hours, multiplying it by his rates, and then cutting the resulting total somewhat. This helps cinch the deal with the client, and it also works for the engineer because he knows he's booked in advance. The experienced engineers we interviewed have contracts that provide a per-hour surcharge if a project goes over a certain number of hours. This "safety valve" protects them when clients work so slowly that the flat rate would turn out to be unprofitable.

How much engineers charge also depends on how badly they need the work. Despite what hourly rates may be printed on rate cards, many will work for a lower rate if they have no other paying projects on the horizon. There's more competition than there used to be, and this drives down the pay scale. In recent years, ever-cheaper recording gear (resulting from the digital technology explosion) has made entry into the studio business easier, and as a result, there is an oversupply of studio owner-engineers willing to work cheaply.[85]

Of course, the most in-demand engineers in the industry don't worry about having to cut their rates. Often, they work with a select group of labels, producers, and artists, and they're always booked up. A busy producer or artist who favors working with a particular engineer will keep him busy, too. Since successful producers are aware that their success is intimately connected with the engineering quality of their recordings, such working partnerships are common.

Even though they're not the wealthiest or most famous engineers, home studio engineer-owners have grown in number. For some, it's a full-time gig; for others, a second job. Those studios that keep busy often specialize in:

- Making demo recordings for aspiring artists and songwriters to shop to labels and publishers
- Making recordings for the increasing number of artists who self-release and self-distribute recorded product (DIY)
- Making recordings for independent labels

Such artists and labels are often short on money, and can't afford more expensive studios and engineers. For them, the home studio's lower overhead and rates are a great fit.

Some of the larger commercial studio operators and engineers resent the home studio engineers for driving down prices and taking away business.[86] (Wherever there's competition, there's going to be some resentment.) Of course, you get what you pay for: The gear, the studio working space, the atmosphere, and (most of all) the engineering expertise of a major recording studio are sought after by the major producers, artists, and labels. There, they know they can get a better product, and they're willing to pay more to get it.

TRAINING OF ENGINEERS

No single well-defined path of technical training leads to a career in engineering. On the one hand, some schools and colleges offer specific training for recording and audio engineering. Some of the engineers we interviewed had attended such schools and felt they benefited from learning "the basics" this way. On the other hand, many engineers have no formal engineering training. They learned the old-fashioned way: by hanging around studios, watching what the engineers do, asking questions, helping out, and soaking it all up.

All of the engineers we spoke to, no matter what their background, stressed the importance of on-the-job training. Most started as assistants to experienced engineers, gradually earning, and being entrusted with, increased responsibility. In each case, the time came when the assistant was ready to engineer projects alone. Engineer John Mathias eloquently summed it up this way:

> I have a degree in arranging and composing, as well as a four-year degree in audio engineering. I also consider my years at [famous studio] the Record Plant before I became a staff engineer as 'graduate studies' in practical

recording. Although I had the degree in audio engineering, I didn't really learn how to be an engineer until I did the on-the-job training a big studio gives you.

Working with microphones, recorders, wiring, mixing boards, effects processors, computers, ProTools rigs, and the rest comes more easily to some people than it does to others. Engineer Barry Rudolph graduated college with a bachelor's degree in electrical engineering, fully expecting to follow a career in the aerospace industry. Only after an aerospace job layoff did he drift into the music industry. Barry feels his college training was of some direct benefit: "My electronics background helps me a lot as I want to know how everything I use works!" Even in Barry's case, though, the on-the-job training is what he considers most valuable. Finally, he got his "break":

> I hung out at the studio. I was an assistant and learned miking, tape editing, and recording methods . . . I learned about recording all types of orchestral instruments since we used to do film scores and commercials. I learned the basics about studio acoustics by helping to build a few rooms. My first actual experience as a first engineer was when I was assisting, and the first engineer passed out from drinking a lot during the course of the session. He couldn't continue so I was it! The next day after the session went well, I started doing all the sessions that came through the door.

If a generalization can be drawn from the experiences of engineers we spoke to, it's this: The job of engineer is technical, but more than *just* technical. In the music recording industry, what engineers do is so specialized, it has to be learned in context. In addition, virtually all the engineers we interviewed had some background in music (playing in rock bands, being a choir member, etc.) before heeding the call to engineering.

iv

CAREER DEVELOPMENT

CHAPTER 12

MAKING A NAME FOR YOURSELF—EARNING A REPUTATION

As noted in the Introduction to this book, many people we interviewed didn't enter into "the business" to have a career. Rather, they couldn't find anything else they enjoyed as much as playing, singing, writing, or being around music generally. We kept hearing variations on "I didn't choose music, it chose me." However, at some point all of them—whether solo artists, band members, session musicians, songwriters, engineers, or producers—realized that getting serious about a career means getting down to business. Each story is different, but each person did what it took to make a name in the music business.

Some fields of endeavor, such as sports, lend themselves to objective, even quantitative, evaluation of potential and talent. It's hard to ignore the basketball prospect who runs the fastest, makes all of his shots, scores the most points, and grabs nearly every rebound. Even in civil service, exams are used to test knowledge and aptitude for specific jobs and to rank applicants. The music business (like the entertainment business generally) is much different.

In the popular music business, image, perception, and reputation are everything. Year after year, record companies, music fans and critics are surprised by hit records that no one predicted could enjoy such popularity. Bands and singers with very modest talent become stars and climb to the top of the charts. In popular music, many observers believe that the importance of videos has de-emphasized music in favor of looks, image, and "attitude." In this environment, there is no formula for having the sound and the image that sell.

Of course, to succeed you must work hard, realistically evaluate what you have to offer, believe in yourself, and hang in there. Keep in mind, though, that no matter how much talent and originality you have, no matter how marketable you might ultimately be, the phone isn't going to start ringing just because you're worthy. You need to be conscious of what it takes to make a name for yourself and take the necessary steps to do just that. The truth is, if you and your music aren't known and earning money, you don't have a career, you have a hobby.

Musicians are marketing themselves to two groups: people in the industry and music listeners. For example, a session musician or a producer is interested primarily in what the industry pros think, because they're the ones who do the hiring. But, ultimately, the listening public's positive response to the work product of that session musician or producer is why that person gets hired again and again.

At all levels, and for many different roles in the music industry, making a name for yourself is a critical element in success. Public relations firms, managers, and other consultants can handle much of the work as your career matures, but in earlier stages, you most likely have to do it all yourself. If thinking about and executing this task seem uninviting, ask yourself whether you prefer a career in music or a hobby in music.

PERFORMANCE

Every time you play or sing in front of others, you're not just entertaining. You're also trying to make a sale—of your talent, your personality, your charisma, your essence. If you win people over, you flourish; if you don't, you've got to go back to the drawing board and figure out how to do it right. Even though the night's music vanishes once you leave the stage, its effects should not. Your show is the most direct form of advertising. The impression you make should encourage listeners to attend future performances, tell their friends about you, buy your product, and request airplay.

The most immediate feedback on your music is provided live. Like stand-up comedians, musicians don't have to ask anyone how they're doing. They can feel it. As in live comedy, the audience lets you know if your performance is working. If you don't sense it's working well enough, you can adjust on the fly. For instance, if a band that plays both rockers and ballads plays a club it's never been in before, it should be prepared to alter its set list to go heavier on one or the other as called for, depending on the audience's response.

Whether you're in a mega-selling veteran recording act, an indie musician, or a DIY musician who's just getting started, the same dynamic applies: When the audience hears and watches the act, they're either going to feel some bond with you or they're not.[87]

Of course, you can't expect to please everybody in the crowd. There are some audiences in which most everyone loves you; then, you perform the identical show in front of a different crowd, and hardly anyone "gets it." This phenomenon is just one among the many, often confusing, ups and downs of the music business. Music deals with emotional responses and is far less predictable than other market choices. By contrast, for instance, almost everyone likes chocolate.

In music, the salesperson (the performer) and the product (music) are inextricably tied together, far more so than in other businesses. It's fair to say they are one. Contrast this with, say, car dealers. If they're selling a great car at a great price, customers will buy even if the salesperson is surly or aloof. In music, however, if the audience thinks the performer is boring, condescending, a jerk, or in any manner is unworthy, they won't buy his CD, they're not going to attend any more of his shows, and they'll make a poor report to their friends. Conversely, if they feel good about a performer, they're not just an audience—they're fans! For this reason, no matter what, you've got to give every show all the preparation, effort, and sincerity you can. Sure, you're human, and there will be times you're worn out or just aren't getting enough energy back from the audience to pump up your adrenaline. But you still have to try.

Performance as promotion means *professionalism*. Professionalism means treating the audience with respect, courtesy, and warmth—and putting on a show. This book isn't meant to be an encyclopedia of stagecraft, but here are tips and examples:

- Arrive on time and be ready to play when you hit the stage. Listeners who've had to wait will be quicker to turn off and tune out; it's human nature.
- Know your material, and have a set list prepared. You don't want a lot of dead time between numbers and you don't want to "drift." The performer should appear to be in control of the agenda.
- Relate to the audience. Introduce the songs you play and acknowledge applause with due modesty. The front man should identify the musicians on stage and their contributions to the band ("and on my left is Jack Davis, rhythm guitar").
- Dress appropriately. This might mean tuxedos for jazz at Carnegie Hall, jeans and cowboy hats for country. Some show-biz flair never hurts—the audience wants to feel as if the performer is one of them, but also that he is special.
- Make the listeners feel that you're performing for *them*, not just for yourselves. This job falls more on the front man, but it's important for everyone to appear engaged with both the music and the crowd. Enthusiasm is infectious.
- Give a great show. Play and sing your tail off—"It's the music, stupid."

- Acknowledge the club or other place of performance, and if there are acts going on after you, talk them up. Use this opportunity to announce your upcoming shows and other pertinent news.
- When your show is over, thank people for coming out to listen, and mean it. If you're selling product, it's OK to tell the audience it's available on site or at local stores. As much as possible, make yourselves available to mingle, sign CDs, and so on.

Doing everything right doesn't guarantee your performance will be a success; it just maximizes the probabilities. If you've ever been in a rock band, you've had some performances ruined by things beyond your control, such as sound system difficulties or tone-deaf sound engineers. Life goes on. The next show will be better.

THE PROMO PACKAGE—BIOGRAPHY

If you're looking for a corporate job, you should have a résumé; if you're looking for a job as a professor, you should have a c.v. (curriculum vitae), which is Latin for résumé. If you're a musician, you should have a promotional (promo) package (which, by the way, includes a résumé). Your promo package is a set of materials intended for the eyes and ears of people in a position to do your career some good: club owners, agents, managers, music critics, disc jockeys, record companies, and so on down the line. It should contain information that presents you in your best light and makes them want to do business with you.

If you're a producer, engineer, or session musician, a résumé might be all you need for a promo package. It should contain pertinent information, especially a discography or compendium of recordings or sessions to your credit. As part of our research, we received several résumés from prominent producers, engineers, and session players. The lists of hit recordings and TV or film scores we read told us, "This person must be really good, that's why he keeps getting called to work on sessions with top-quality talent." Clearly, the information presented should be well organized and easy to read. The more professional it looks, the more professional you're presumed to be. The contact information (that is, phone number, address, fax and e-mail address for you or your manager, agent, etc.) should appear prominently.

For a solo artist or group, the résumé is called a "biography" (bio). For most artists who make their own music, it isn't relevant to describe themselves by listing their credits; instead, they have to characterize their music in words on a piece of paper. It isn't easy.[88] These things that are important for a bio:

- Keep it short. We've never met anyone in the business who will read beyond one page.[89]

- If you're a group, give the names of all members and what they do ("Jeff Jones, lead vocals," etc.), plus a brief, descriptive, individual background: "Bob's jazz career began when he started playing along with Miles Davis records when he was thirteen."
- The information should be specific; avoid descriptions such as "eclectic" or "new music." Help the reader understand *something* about your music without having to listen to it. If your music can be categorized, do it in a way that won't pigeonhole you (for example, "though direct comparisons are difficult, we've played many bills alongside bands that are part of the 'alternative country' movement"). If flattering comparisons have been made, by all means allude to them.
- Tell the reader *where* you've played—clubs, festivals, concerts, cities. If you've opened up for bigger-name acts, go ahead and name drop. Use bold fonts to highlight your most noteworthy achievements.
- The bio will be part of the first impression that precedes hearing your music—most people can read it faster than it takes to load a CD in a player or boot up an MP3 online, much less listen. Its layout should look professional. All spelling and grammar should be correct. Keep the tone breezy and amicable. Avoid clichés, especially bragging ones like "unique" and "dynamic."

In writing a bio, put yourself in the shoes of, say, a club owner or concert promoter. Stand back and think about what *you* would want to find out about an artist you didn't know much about. Guided by this principle, you'll write your best bio. This is not the time to be bashful—it's fine to cast yourself in the best possible light. Just don't get carried away making claims you can't back up, and avoid coming off as conceited, immodest, or arrogant.

THE PUBLICITY PHOTOGRAPH

If you're going to perform in front of the public, appear in videos, and so forth, then a photo must be included as part of your promo package.[90] It may gall musicians to think that they're being evaluated on something other than their music, but the music business is part of show business. And in show business, looks count—a lot.

Chances are, when people open your package or click on your Web site, the first thing they do is look at your photograph—before reading your cover letter or your bio and before listening to your tape, CD, or MP3s. It's human nature to want to see who you'll be listening to and reading about. The visual impression is made within a few seconds. If it's positive, you acquire favorable momentum; if it's negative, the rest of your package has to dig you out of a bit of a hole. So, try to start off on the right foot with an effective, well-done photo.

The first thing to know about photos is that they should be black and white, 8 × 10 inches. This is the standard of the industry.[91] The reasons? Black and white lends itself to newsprint reproduction, which is important for advertising (and it's far cheaper than color—so much the better). The 8 × 10 size is convenient; big enough to see detail, small enough to mail without folding. If your photo deviates much (it's in color or way too big or small), you'll probably be perceived as unprofessional.

Your photo should portray your act in the way that fits your overall image and presentation and that is likely to make people take an interest in you and want to know more about you. For instance, a photo that presents a group as petulant, angry, and decadent might be perfect for punk rockers but totally wrong for a gospel band. If your group contains a featured performer with sex appeal, that person should appear prominently and (depending on the genre) tastefully.

Publicity photos should play up positive features and play down negative ones. If the people in your photo aren't "beautiful," don't despair. Model-quality features are nice, but they're not necessary. In the final analysis, the artist's image—what you project to the viewer about your character, personality, and appeal—is what matters. Body language, facial expression, and clothing go a long way in making this statement.

An effective photo is the product of much thought. Even though you're a musician, not a visual artist, you can form valid ideas of what will work—the setting, pose, costume, props, and overall image. Resist the temptation to save money by getting your photo taken by your bass player's brother who had a photography class in high school. This is the time to secure the services of a professional. A true pro will dig deep to find out what you're looking for. He'll ask to listen to your CD or attend one of your shows, to focus in on what you're about. Professional expertise with lighting, cameras, lenses, film, makeup, and so forth is worth every cent. We're talking about your career, not a driver's license picture.

In a photo session, a pro photographer makes many exposures, and later will deliver "proof sheets" containing miniature versions of all of them. Of course, some will be awful, but at the end of the winnowing-out process, you should be able to choose from at least two or three excellent shots. In making up your mind, invite your fans and advisors to tell you what they think. Ask them to give reasons for their preferences; sometimes, they notice things you miss. Make sure you get the opinions of objective or disinterested parties—people who can take a step back and critically evaluate the photos without letting sentimentality get in the way.

Once you've chosen the photo, have it replicated by a photo service that caters to musicians and actors. Make sure the service inserts your name and contact information on the bottom edge of the promo prints. The typeface should be bold and plain, not ornate or highly stylized.

THE DEMO

Some acts gain popularity because of their look, image, or attitude, rather than how they sound. However, they are the exceptions. For most artists, the music is the determining factor in whether they sink or swim. So, the demo CD, tape, or MP3 is the most important component in the promo package.

Demos are music; bios and photos are not. A superb demo will overcome shakiness in the rest of the promo pack. After all, an artist who has great music can get a better photo easily enough. On the other hand, with weak or poorly presented music, there isn't any real substance to work with—the problem's harder to repair. A listener who hates the demo is unlikely to say, "who cares, the bio and photo look great." Therefore, you need to make the best-sounding demo you can. Achieving this technically is really the same process as making your best DIY recording; refer to chapter 5 for guidelines on making your own recording.

In making a pure demo (that is, "demo only"), the most significant issue to consider is the songs to put on it. First, a demo should have no more than three songs.[92] If you're trying to get a gig, three songs is enough for a club owner to know whether your sound is good enough to hire you. Remember that music business people (managers, promoters, A&R reps, etc.) are busy. They make rapid decisions about whether they like something and want to hear more. And if they want to hear more, they'll ask for it.

The songs on a demo should not necessarily be your personal favorites, but the ones you believe will be most readily liked by your target audience. Avoid songs with long introductions; people in a hurry want to get to the vocals and the basic tune right away. We've heard some A&R reps say that if an intro is too long, they just skip to the next track; and if *that* one has a long intro, they stop listening altogether. The songs on your demo should be sequenced in order of "best song first," and so on down the line.

If you are an indie or DIY artist with your own CD or tape, it usually serves as your demo. After all, it gets expensive to manufacture one CD that is only a demo and a different one that is an album. This can create some problems, because an album has something like nine tracks, not three. Its song choice and sequencing might be quite effective as product but less effective for demo purposes. So, we recommend that your album open with your three best songs. If this isn't feasible, make sure your promo package includes a CD, not a cassette. This way, it's easier for the listener to rapidly skip tracks.

Remember, the purpose of your demo (particularly if you play your own material) is to showcase two things: the songs and the performances. The guiding principle is to keep things simple so these elements shine through. Most music industry professionals are no different from the average fan—they listen to the singer first, then the words, the melody, and the overall energy or vibe of the demo. Deliver these straight up.

Stay away from overproduction. It's tempting to make each song its own magnum opus, but that's wrong. Too much gloss can distract from, even bury, the fundamental strength of the songs and performances. Almost no one will notice, much less be favorably impressed, that you creatively use reverse reverb on the hi-hat cymbals. And, to some people in the industry, too much production can be a turnoff; they suspect you're trying to pass off middling product using fancy packaging. Avoid this risk by keeping the production straightforward.

Some artists manufacture their own demos from their full-length CD album. This can help your budget—blank CD-Rs and cassettes are inexpensive, and you can purchase them as you need them. With a home computer, you can print your own labels and inserts. Properly completed, your demos will sound and look professional. They require decent home equipment and some time, but these things are available to many artists. Another advantage to making your own demos is that you can "custom build" them to fit your needs. For instance, if you have a nine-song CD, you can make different three-song demos to try for dissimilar gigs.

Your demo and its packaging, should have contact information printed on it.[93] This means on the CD (or cassette) as well as on the sleeve or box, since these items often become permanently separated from each other. It would be ironic to have your package stir the interest of a record company or agent, but not to get a call because your group name and the information on how to get hold of you aren't on the demo. Remember, the purpose of your promo package is to get people to like you, to know who you are, and to call you. So, your name, and at very least a valid telephone number, should be on everything, as in this: Demo: The ShoeLaces, call Mike Brandon @ (555) 989-7237.[94]

THE PRESS KIT

A press kit is a collection of reviews, interviews, advertising, and anything else where your name appears in print. In effect, it's a scrapbook meant for someone else's eyes. Early on in your career, you won't have much of a press kit, because you won't been around long enough to accumulate one. But as you continue to perform, release product, tour, get airplay, and so on, it will build.

You want the press kit to be inclusive; after all, you're using it in your campaign to convince the industry that you're for real artistically, that you're actively "out there" pursuing your career. The press kit should be neatly arranged and not too big or unwieldy. The more clippings you accumulate, the more you have to decide what's really going to make a difference and what's unnecessary. As with your bio, brevity goes a long way. Even if you have hundreds of pages of material, you should limit the kit to one or two pages, unless there's some stuff that's so glowing and so authoritative that you can't leave it out.[95]

Using a photocopier or scanner and cut-and-paste methods, you can compress multiple clippings onto a single page, especially if you use the "size reduction" feature of the copier. Lay out the page so that headlines containing your name appear prominently and repetitively. Not only does this have the benefit of fitting a lot of information into a convenient package, its dynamic appearance can make you seem exciting and important. Spurring the reader's interest is very much a process of evoking emotional responses; although reason plays a part, feelings play a greater role in whether people buy.

A well-done press kit enhances your credibility: "It seems that plenty of people have taken an interest, so I'd better check out this act carefully!"

SMOKE AND MIRRORS

In "The Emperor's New Clothes," no individual has the courage to comment that the king actually isn't wearing any clothes at all, because everyone else around him acts as if he is. His subjects begin to doubt their eyes and their sanity. This fable points out that people often look to what others think before forming their own opinions. Nowhere is this more true than in the music business.

If a lot of what happens in the music business seems to defy logic, it's because we're dancing on the slippery slope of emotions. Tastes and trends move very fast. What's hot today is largely forgotten, and sometimes ridiculed, tomorrow. People in the business frequently don't trust themselves to make decisions; they look for a "buzz " or at least outside validation before they take an interest in an artist. A buzz is a fast-growing (and often vague) reputation that an act is hot, coupled with emotional excitement on the part of those spreading the word.

To a degree, musicians can manipulate their own buzz. A few years ago, some employees of an independent record company created a rock band called Thorpe, just to find out how much industry buzz they could whip up. Thorpe was completely fictitious; the "band" had no music, no product, no members, no gigs, no pictures. The buzz was generated from phony word-of-mouth, fake press releases, articles, concert reviews, and the like. When the pranksters started a rumor that a riot broke out after a Thorpe concert, calls from major label A&R reps rained down in buckets. Finally, the bluff was called, and Thorpe was revealed for the joke that it was. The A&R heads of the majors were not amused. This incident made them look like a bunch of particularly gullible lemmings, and it made the popular music industry seem vapid and devoid of substance.

By working smart, you can create and maintain an interest with only threads to work with. For example, let's say that you pick up a cheesy gig playing at a benefit music festival where all the proceeds go to a worthy cause (that is, you don't get paid). You play at 2:00 P.M. on Saturday (when no one is there except the vendors, the sound man, and a few drunks), while

Famous Artist plays in front of a great crowd at 8:00 P.M. (when you're long since gone). You can treat this show as a meaningless experience, or you can use "smoke and mirrors" to derive significant career benefit.

Truthfully (if not entirely accurately) tell promoters, club owners, and others that you shared the stage with Famous Artist. Add it to your bio. This can help you get your next gig; perhaps you'll talk yourself into a slot opening for Famous Artist when he next comes to your town. After that, you'll be able to say you played with him at the Prestige Theater. That you performed at such a prominent venue will impress future music business contacts, both locally and elsewhere. When another artist in the vein of Famous Artist comes into your area, you now have a leg up on talking to the promoter to open *that* show. It doesn't take much imagination to understand that this process can snowball into some pretty valuable opportunities, if you're clever enough and bold enough to play your cards right. You can build a pretty large structure starting with some very modest building blocks.

And, unlike Thorpe, you really exist. When your "bluff" gets called, you're in a position to deliver the goods.[96] As you progress in your career, your credibility will rely less on wisps of accomplishment and more on solid grounds of your track record.

Just Get Out There and Do It

In practice, there are three reasons why someone chooses to work with you:

1. He thinks you can do the job (competence)
2. He knows you or knows about you (familiarity)
3. He likes you (personality)

Competence is a prerequisite. The field of music is so competitive, a record label or music contractor, for example, can't afford to hire people who might not be able to do the job. To a degree, competence is the factor over which you have the most direct control. Although you can't increase your genetic endowment of talent, you can work hard to develop it fully and be ready to handle the kind of work and career you're seeking.

Familiarity grows with exposure. Within the music business, simply being busy is a big endorsement. It means that you're willing to get off the couch and work, which not all "artists" are motivated to do. Whether you're an engineer, solo artist, songwriter, or part of a heavy metal band, keeping busy also suggests that what you have to offer impresses others enough to induce them to work with you. The music industry person feels more secure getting involved with someone who's already been given the "seal of approval" by a known and respected peer or industry contact.[97]

Your promo package (photo, bio, demo, and press kit) and Web site can be formidable tools, but they are no substitutes for people knowing and liking you. The more your name is in circulation and the more people you meet and get to know in the business, the further you're going to progress. The saying "It's not what you know, it's who you know" is especially true in the music industry. This isn't to say that artistic ability is merely an afterthought. Rather, so many talented people compete in this arena that access, track record, visibility, and personality take on heightened importance.

In a recent *New York Times* article[98] about Broadway dancers, a successful dancer says, "There's a glut of qualified, trained people in New York. The directors don't have a problem finding good dancers, so they do what you'd expect—they work with the ones they know." Especially in fields like producing, engineering, and session work, this principle carries over into the music business.

Personality—the kind that induces people to want to work with you—is a hard quality to define. Just as with your musical ability, personality is combination of innate traits and things you've learned. Establishing rapport comes easily to individuals who are naturally outgoing and relaxed. Others, whose temperaments are naturally more reserved or high-strung, need to augment their instincts by learning to mix, mingle, and yes, relax. This isn't to suggest putting on a phony, backslappy air; that turns people off right away. Rather, the more restrained individual should understand that, sometimes, other people mistake an introverted manner for arrogance or aloofness. Someone can readily overcome this, but he'll have to be more self-conscious about breaking the ice than would a more naturally gregarious person.

Of course, no matter what your innate personality type, you've got to follow up with professionalism, courtesy, and responsibility.

NETWORKING

Networking means integrating yourself into the musical community. It means forming and nurturing relationships that are professionally rewarding as well as personally rewarding. Although this may sound like a rehash of "just getting out and doing it," it isn't. Networking is more subtle and more personal. Many times, networking takes place within the context of socializing, where your abilities and credentials aren't even on the line.

For example, many rock musicians "hang" with other rock musicians or with people connected to rock music, on their off time. They attend each other's shows, they have lunch together, they chat on the phone, they attend sports matches, they go to parties (lots of parties). This is hardly surprising—it's natural that people who have much in common would choose to spend time with each other and emotionally support each other. In addition to the friendship and mutual interests, these musicians are bound together by their membership in a musical community that, given a chance, will help out and sustain its members in tangible ways.

From time to time, musicians hear snippets of information about, for example, an opening in a band, the quality of a recording studio, or the trustworthiness of a manager or lawyer. Some of this is in the nature of industry gossip, and some is "hard news." As stories circulate, people in the community naturally pick up on them and contribute to the flow. "My old rhythm guitarist would be perfect for that band," or "I heard about someone else who had a great experience with that studio," or "Tell your friend, he should see my lawyer" are examples of some of the helpful responses that can flow through networking.

By stressing the significance of networking, we are not suggesting that you approach it in a self-serving, calculated manner. Instead, we believe you should allow networking to work for you in a natural and mutually nurturing way. That's a far cry from a cynical, selfish approach. Likewise, it's hardly helpful to isolate yourself from the musical community (whatever your particular community is) by being a loner, either. Doing so is no less selfish than the calculated approach, because by choosing not to take part, you're neglecting your responsibility to be a citizen of the community. By not contributing or giving back, you're letting others down—whether you're aware of it or not.

ADAPTABILITY AND SURVIVAL

When you scratch beneath the surface of prominent people in the industry, you often find that they originally made names for themselves doing something else within music. For instance, many performing artists started out writing songs for other people to sing, many producers began as engineers or session musicians, and so on. For some people, the road to the career where they ultimately land passes through other territory.

Part of this progression might be simply a matter of finding yourself by moving, seeking, and experimenting. However, a deliberate process is also at work: *I really want to do music as a career, and at present certain avenues seem to be opening up for me. Since they offer the opportunity to establish a reputation while earning a living, I'd be a fool to ignore them. Once I've made something of a name for myself, I can focus in more on my primary interests.* Plying your talents in one area paves the way to the next.

Suppose you think you've done all you can to have a music career and it just isn't moving fast enough. Before you give up and try an altogether different profession, think about whether you've really given it your best shot. Perhaps you haven't been inventive enough or open-minded enough about seeking out a niche for your talent. For example, let's say you're a musician who starts out with the intention of establishing a career as a member of a major label recording group, but you find yourself stymied by poor luck or poor timing. The group breaks up, and you consider doing other things like producing or session work, but they're hard to break into directly. You're so frustrated you're ready to become an insurance salesman.

It's important to pursue opportunities you hadn't previously taken into account. Have you thought about giving lessons or writing instructional books? Have you thought about writing a column for a guitar magazine? Have you thought about working on product development and design with musical instrument or equipment manufacturers? These examples may sound far-fetched, but they're not; in fact, they're real-life examples. Each one of these avenues really exists, as do many more. They work for you in three ways:

1. You still do music or a music-related career, instead of selling insurance
2. The visibility and credibility you gain will be vehicles for growth of your career on many levels
3. You may find you really enjoy branching out

The willingness to adapt and the inventiveness to adapt constructively are keys to survival in the music business.

CHAPTER 13

PROFESSIONAL HELP— LAWYERS, MANAGERS, AGENTS, AND OTHERS

Furthering your career is very much a hands-on effort. Obvious examples include manufacturing and selling your own recording (DIY, for "do-it-yourself") and making a name for yourself in the business. Yet, even at early stages of your career, you might consider it useful to consult with professionals or substantially delegate certain tasks and responsibilities to them. Usually, the busier and more successful you become, the more you delegate.

Some people with music industry careers handle nearly every aspect personally. Not necessarily "control freaks," they just prefer a high level of involvement. They're right about one thing: Even if you delegate, your career is still your own responsibility. It's up to you to monitor your professionals. As much as you'd like to wash your hands completely of the business aspects of music by hiring specialists, you still have to "check in" with the people you're paying to help you. Think of it this way: If you hire someone to paint your house, do you want the painter to decide what colors it should be? Of course not.

The major categories of professionals most musicians deal with are lawyers,[99] managers,[100] agents, and to a lesser extent, business managers, accountants, and publicists. In our experience, many musicians are confused about the function and role of each. Such confusion is heightened further in situations if one of them wears multiple hats, which is not uncommon.

MUSIC LAWYERS

The stereotype is that lawyers write documents containing impenetrable language and interpret equally incomprehensible ones written by other lawyers. Although this image has some basis in fact—try making sense out of an eighty-page major-label recording contract—lawyers can help you in your career and sometimes keep you out of serious trouble.

The technical part of what lawyers do is ascertain what your legal rights are and make sure that you get what's coming to you. This isn't meant to sound vague; it's just there are legal ramifications to so many things you do. Consider the following examples:

- You are a member of a band. Who owns the band name? Do you have any recourse if you're kicked out? These and like questions can be preempted by having a partnership agreement, which summarizes the members' understanding of their relationship. Who drafts the agreement and advises on the topics it should cover? A music attorney.
- You are a producer working on a production deal with an artist you think shows great promise. Since you'll be investing time and money in the artist, you want to make sure you'll participate in his success if the masters you produce lead to a record deal. You should consult a music attorney to draw up an appropriate contract.
- You are a solo artist with a buzz. A major label contacts your manager to express interest in signing you to a deal. Your manager tells you the good news and acknowledges he wouldn't know a great deal from a lousy one. Who negotiates the deal? An experienced music attorney.

These examples hardly represent the limit of what music attorneys do, but they should start you thinking about when you need one.

Lawyers and Contracts

Whenever you commit yourself in a significant business relationship, you want to understand all the ramifications and negotiate terms as favorable as circumstances permit. As a participant, you may think you know what you're agreeing to, but what happens later if your understanding differs significantly from the other person's? After all, by signing a contract, you both agree that it accurately summarizes the agreement you bargained for. If the final agreement contains provisions unfavorable to you, it's hard to go back and say, "Gee, but that isn't what I meant." The search for objective meaning begins, and ends, with the contract. A skilled attorney helps ensure that what you sign is what you mean.

The word "legalese" is often used disparagingly to describe the language of attorneys, as if it's just so much useless jargon. By and large, this isn't accurate. Because the wording used in contract terms is critical in determining their meaning, language must be used very precisely to unambiguously express the concepts agreed to. Think about how difficult it is to fully and correctly describe on paper any complex deal:

- It must accurately include *all* the deal points you agree on
- It must internally define certain of its terms with specificity—for instance, "net" and "gross" don't mean the same things from contract to contract
- It must anticipate and provide for contingencies that may be expected to arise during its lifetime
- It must be clear and unambiguous. Ideally, independent outsiders looking in should come away with identical interpretations of its meaning

Much skill is involved in drafting and interpreting legal language. The result of this care and expertise may look like legalese, but the reason for it is to protect the client's rights.

Contracts are like surgery—if you sign something you don't really mean, it's hard to go back and make things the way they would be if they were done properly to begin with. Huge dollar swings can hinge on seemingly small variations in language, such as if the word "or" instead of "and" is used to connect two clauses in a sentence. Paragraphs that make reference to other sections may seem straightforward but contain traps for the unwary. For example, a friend may report signing a record deal with a 14 percent royalty. On its face, it sounds like a decent rate, but what does this number really mean? Not a whole lot, unless you understand the sales base against which the royalty is paid. For instance, if the base is reduced by enough returns, breakage, giveaways, and offsets, 14 percent may really be closer to 5 percent.

Invariably, certain business relationships result in disagreements. One or both sides think the other isn't upholding its end of the bargain—or one side may simply decide to cut its losses if it senses the deal just isn't paying off. If they can't resolve differences any other way, the parties end up in court. Naturally, some contract lawsuits are about the facts (who did what to whom when or who failed to do what should've been done). Whatever the circumstances, almost always courts look to the written document to interpret the facts and find a resolution of the disagreement.

Legal problems often occur because business expectations and conditions change during the course of a relationship. Sometimes, parties breach contracts because they've changed their minds. For these and other reasons, a well-drafted contract can't guarantee you won't encounter disagreements arising out of it. But it can protect your interests should they occur.

Other Legal Settings

The bulk of what music attorneys do is negotiate, review, and draft contracts; but, be aware of other legal services they often provide "especially" for musicians:

- Copyright services and consultation (see chapter 1)
- Trademark services and consultation (regarding, for instance, band names and logos)
- Negotiation, arbitration, and litigation services
- Immigration services related to permits and visas to work in foreign countries or for noncitizens to live and work in the United States

It's rare for one attorney to have extensive, in-depth experience in all these fields.

For some services, then, consulting lawyers are brought in. For example:

- Many attorneys don't handle lawsuits—they might help prepare a case that gets this far, but usually defer to litigation specialists for courtroom work
- Immigration law is its own demanding specialty. Most music attorneys "farm out" this work
- Intellectual property attorneys often limit their practice to trademark and copyright law

You may wonder why one lawyer can't handle all a musician's needs. The answer is that too much is going on in each specialty for one person to keep up with all of them and still have time left over to work.

In this way, law is like the field of medicine, where specialization is the norm. In medicine, you visit your personal physician for most of your medical needs. However, if you develop chronic wrist pain from playing your instrument, you'll probably be sent to an orthopedist who specializes in musicians' joint injuries. To develop expertise, there's no substitute for the experience of dealing repeatedly with similar issues. The same philosophy applies in law. Responsible attorneys are quick to bring in help when they're out of their depth.

More Than Lawyers

Many music lawyers do more things for their clients than fit within the narrow definition of legal work. That is, some of the services they provide are more in the realm of business consulting or personal management. So many music lawyers are gregarious types who readily mix, mingle, and schmooze. Whenever they perform work for their clients, they're meeting producers, musicians, executives, record company lawyers, and many others. Rubbing shoulders with movers and shakers of the business, they develop a network of contacts that grants them superior access to the corridors of music industry power. Such attorneys become movers and shakers themselves.

The best known nonlawyering job handled by music attorneys is *demo shopping*. Demo shopping (demo selling, really) is just what you'd guess—the artist's demo is presented to labels or producers with the intention of procuring a record deal. In interviews, major label A&R reps often state that, because of the volume of demos received, they listen to "solicited" demos only; that is, ones received through a contact such as a manager, an attorney, or someone they know already. A music attorney, especially one with a stable of star clients and a great track record, possesses the clout necessary to make people pay attention to his submissions. Of course, this doesn't guarantee that the company will sign his client, but the artist will get an opportunity that otherwise might be denied.[101]

Ideally, the musician wants a lawyer to have the influence to get phone calls returned by industry higher-ups and the technical expertise to tie down all possible loose ends. However, this package isn't always available. In practice, some of the most powerful music attorneys act more as deal makers than lawyers. They bargain, negotiate, cajole, demo shop, take meetings, do lunch—all on behalf of their clients. The actual legal work—drawing up contracts and performing other tasks you need a bar license to do—is left to other lawyers in the firm. This isn't a bad thing; as in all fields, capable attorneys delegate work to serve clients as effectively as possible.

Because so much of the documenting of a music career runs through his office, the lawyer often serves as a clearing house for business advice. Attorneys constantly work with other professionals such as accountants and managers. Since this team of advisors more or less orbits the attorney's office, the attorney consistently is in touch with all aspects of an artist's career, probably more so than any other professional. Often, in evaluating prospects and making business decisions, the client looks to the attorney for the big picture.

Finding an Attorney

One of the things you want to know about a prospective attorney is whether that person is a *music* attorney. For instance, the probate lawyer who helped settle your uncle's estate probably knows little, if anything, about the music business. However much you may like and trust this lawyer, you're better off finding someone with an understanding of the business.

This doesn't necessarily mean that you should deal exclusively with lawyers who have many years of experience in the industry. Even though the veteran may have had the opportunity to develop contacts and a keen grasp of major issues, the less-experienced lawyer may be able to handle the job quite competently. In recent years, the field of music law has seen many

excellent seminars, books, journals, law school classes, and continuing education courses. Through study and personal dedication, a lawyer may
acquire an excellent grasp of the issues.

What's important is that the attorney seriously concentrate on music
law; most problems arise when attorneys stray from their ordinary practices
into fields they haven't studied. Realistically, it doesn't require the services of
a heavyweight industry lawyer to draft your form studio agreement or register your songs for copyright. The time you'll require that highly experienced
person in your corner is when you're negotiating a deal where a long-term
commitment or a lot of money is on the table. When the stakes are high, you
want to be represented by someone who's been down that road before.

Perhaps *the* major issue with your attorney (and for all professionals) is
trust. If you don't think the attorney respects you as an artist but, rather, that
he sees you as a fee, find a different lawyer. If you simply fail to relate to your
lawyer and find it hard to have enough confidence in him, then he shouldn't
be representing you. In many ways, trust is more important than anything else.

Over the long haul, a less experienced music attorney who'll go
through a wall to do right by you is more valuable than a big shot who treats
you like another cow in the herd. You'll respect this person's advice more,
because you know it's personal, not generic. As corny as it may sound, a
major part of an attorney's effectiveness derives from the capacity to understand where you're coming from. After all, if someone doesn't quite comprehend your personal goals and objectives, that person's ability to help you
achieve them is compromised. Conversely, you'll feel comfortable that the
lawyer who identifies with your cause will be effective in championing it.

Another issue that can arise is conflict of interest. For instance, if an
artist is negotiating with a record label and the attorney's firm does work for
that label, there's a conflict. Hypothetically, at least, you can't be certain that
your lawyer is holding your interests paramount (as required) or compromis-
ing them because in the long run you're a less significant client than the label.

The way to deal with conflicts, to begin with, is to find out whether they
exist. You should specifically request that your lawyer disclose any conflicts.[102] If there is none, so much the better; but if there is, how do you
resolve it? One way is to flat-out assume you can't trust anyone in a conflict
situation, in which case you find another lawyer, at least for the situation in
which the conflict arises. Or, you can decide that you trust your lawyer so
much that you'd like to have him represent you, even after disclosure of the
conflict. If you really feel good about your attorney, this might be the way to
go. It's strictly a personal decision.

When to Get a Lawyer

While there's no rule of thumb here, we will say this: Of the three major
specialists (attorneys, managers, and agents), the last one that most artists

feel a need for is an agent, and the first one the artist may want to hire will be an attorney. Legal issues can crop up very early in a career, before a manager or an agent is involved. This is especially prevalent in young band situations, where members feel the need to make a partnership agreement.

Most lawyers charge by the hour, and much of the work they perform can be completed on a project basis (for instance, copyright registration for a batch of songs). Not so for the work of managers and agents; they charge a percentage of the client's income. Consequently, they usually have little interest in a new client who isn't yet in the position to generate much revenue.

If you think you might require the services of an attorney, use your common sense. Talk to other musicians who've been through a similar situation and find out what they recommend. Should you have any doubt, at least chat with a lawyer; a competent one will be able tell you whether you currently need professional services or can wait awhile.

MANAGERS

One of the great sources of confusion for artists is the role of a manager. Vaguely, everyone knows that a manager provides career guidance and nearly all major artists (producers, songwriters, performers, recording artists) have one. But more specifically, it's not obvious what duties they perform. Yes, some managers do try to get record deals for their artists by contacting major labels and shopping demos. But, some music attorneys do this, too; does that mean that those artists don't need managers? No. Do managers set up gigs and tours for their clients? Well, some of them do, in a general way, but actually that's the job of agents—their only job.[103] Since agents usually charge 10 percent, it seems silly to pay a manager's fee of 15–25 percent just to book performances.

As well as we can describe it, a manager actually is the big-picture person, the planner who looks ahead in your career. He examines the various moves you can make to move forward, evaluates their merits, makes recommendations. He creates opportunities and courses of action, so that, in addition to your goals, you have a map of how to get there. He acts as a conscience for the artist; he's a sounding board of objective reason for people whose emotions sometimes cloud their common sense. He helps artistic personalities focus on the realities of business, which is something they're often disinclined to do on their own.

Just as important, the bulk of management time is spent handling routine, day-to-day jobs—the things an artist might undertake himself, if he had the time and business acumen. A significant part of what managers have to offer is basic business sense, aggressive marketing, and the availability to devote their efforts exclusively to management. Since, as managers, they don't have to be artists as well, their clients are that much freer to make music.

What Managers Do

Probably the best way to understand what a manager does is to review some examples. Let's start with the "big picture":

- A manager realizes the group's tacky old photo isn't helping its career. After convincing them of the picture's inadequacy, he finds a photographer for a new photograph, hounds everyone in the group to make it to the session, plays a major role planning the poses and "image," makes sure the photographer gets paid on time, and helps choose the final photo(s).
- A producer is offered a job producing a new record for a famous but tempestuous artist. Although the manager advises against it—the artist often ends up in litigation against his record company and his popularity is waning—the producer is starstruck and insists on going ahead. Through hard work and phone calls to key players, the manager locates an equally juicy job producing a different high-profile artist with much less baggage. The producer gladly takes on this project instead, minimizing the chances for a bad career move.
- A manager has helped his client obtain two offers for touring. One is as part of a festival where the artist will appear in multiple venues with similar acts. The other opportunity is to be the tour opener for a long-established, extremely popular artist. The artist argues for the opening slot—it offers the opportunity to be seen by the greatest number of people. While conceding the point, his manager reminds him the crowds will consist principally of old-time fans who will ignore him while waiting for the headliner. Instead, he suggests his client tour with the festival—not only is it a smaller pond but offers more open-minded audiences, which stand a greater chance of becoming fans.
- A band has been playing to increasingly enthusiastic audiences at club shows and has recorded a strong demo, but the members don't know how to approach record labels. Their manager not only initiates the contacts, he also researches which labels are financially healthy, have stable management, and are actively seeking artists in the vein of his client. The manager calls and visits label contacts consistently to maximize the chance that his artist will receive consideration and to "pitch" the artist.

These are but a few examples; in practice managers perform a vast array of such tasks and creative projects, formulating and carrying out ideas to build opportunity and market their clients.

In addition, managers perform many other less momentous, downright unglamorous, but nevertheless important tasks; for example:

- The manager accepts and sorts out bids from companies desiring to license concession merchandise featuring an artist's logo and likeness
- The manager solicits offers for artist endorsements from musical instrument and pro sound companies
- The manager coordinates personal appearances and interviews while the artist is on tour

While enormous insight, creativity, and brilliance are not necessary in these three examples, astute business judgment, sound organization, follow-through, and sensitivity to the client's needs are required to do the job well.

Viewing the artist's career as a business to be run, the personal manager is the chief operations officer, the VP of finance, the marketing director, the head of sales, and the director of long-term planning. A manager does so many different things, it's hard to compress all of his job description into a short section.

Compensation of Managers

The standard of the industry is that managers are compensated on a commission basis. Typically, commissions range from 15 to 25 percent of the *gross* income generated by the client. Consequently, situations arise where a manager can make more money than his client or, at the very least, appear to do so. For instance, if a recording act receives an advance of $100,000, then a manager who takes a 20 percent commission gets $20,000. For starters, he gets to keep his take; that is, the record label looks to the act, not their manager, for recoupment of expenses.

But keep going. If the act is a group with four equal members, consider that the manager is making 20 percent of the *gross*, while each member is making 25 percent of the *net*. Their gross income is immediately reduced to 80 percent (100 percent minus the 20 percent manager's commission). So, even if expenses were *zero* (which they can never be), each member could earn, at most, only as much as the manager ($20,000; that is, one fourth of 80 percent equals 20 percent).

Why do managers customarily receive such high commissions? Because they're taking big risks, especially toward the beginning of an artist's career. The manager invests huge chunks of time and effort in his client instead of, presumably, doing something else more secure. If the investment of this time and effort fails to pay off, it's a total loss. Not only doesn't the manager get paid for the work he does, he's now forgone income he would've earned in a less risky job. The flip side of this way of thinking is that, if the manager does succeed on behalf of his client, he should be well rewarded for prevailing in the face of risk.

The commission, then, is a form of incentive compensation. The manager who doesn't produce for his client earns little or nothing; but if he produces, he receives a big piece of the action. In any event, artists at earlier stages of their careers typically can't afford to compensate a manager on an hourly fee basis; their earnings are insufficient. On the other side of the coin, once an artist is well established, a manager doesn't have to work as hard to keep the career wheel spinning. In this case, the commission often is negotiated to a lower rate, commensurate with the reduced risk involved for the manager.

The Manager as Power Broker

A powerful personal manager makes good use of the reputation and financial might of his major clients, the friendships he's nurtured, the alliances he's formed, and the favors he can trade. All these qualities are built up by years of experience in the music business wars, dealing with influential players. A well-connected manager can walk right through doors that the new artist, or even a less heavy manager, cannot readily get a foot into.

Obviously, the new artist's dream is to have a manager with the clout and access to create breakthroughs in his career. As it turns out, though, it's unusual for a major manager to take on a client who, for example, isn't already signed to a major label. Once again, "the only time a bank will lend you money is when you prove you don't need it." Well, personal management is like banking—the heavy hitter has little use for an artist who badly needs his clout. Instead, he concentrates on maximizing the dollar return for clients whose careers are up and running. Since the manager is on commission, his incentive is to produce more income for himself by stoking the fires for his artists who are already successful.

Does a new artist absolutely need a manager who wields this kind of clout? Fortunately, no; otherwise, breaking in professionally (especially as an artist or producer) would be even more daunting than it is. As a practical matter, many recording artists don't even have a "real" manager until they sign a label deal, then managers come buzzing around to try to get a piece of the action. As with so many other aspects of the music business, you need a sense of humor about the irony of this development.

Manager from the Start

Unlike law, a profession that regulates membership through a state licensing board (the bar), personal management has no educational or apprenticeship requirements.[104] All that one needs to call himself a manager is a client to manage. The manager who enters the business by taking on representation of an artist whose music he loves begins at the opposite end of the spectrum from the established power broker. Often he has little training or experience in running a business of any kind. What he does have is a powerful belief in his client, the time and energy to work hard, and the willingness to learn along the way.

Part of the romance of the music business is that there are very few rules. Whatever works is right, even if no one else does it that way. History tells us that much can be accomplished from a starting point of absolute zero. An effective manager is one who fulfills his client's objectives; it doesn't matter whether he begins with a track record or not. What matters is getting heard by the right people at the right time and making the most of opportunities. Most artists kick start their careers with the help of inexperienced managers, even by self-management. Hard work, persistence, creativity, and planning can get as much done as contacts and influence. As a general rule, though, if your personal manager has less clout, you can expect things to take longer early on.

Over time, a manager will learn the ropes and develop contacts and influence of his own. Having this kind of person on your team from the start is a big plus. You know the loyalty has been mutually earned, and both manager and client will prosper as their careers blossom. Sometimes, however, your may feel your manager has taken you as far as he's personally capable, and it will be time to move to a more established manager.

Not infrequently, jilted managers view themselves as victims who've been thrown overboard just as all the hard work is about to pay off. When money appears on the table, this sense of rejection often leads not just to hard feelings but to lawsuits. Although the intricacies of management contracts are not within the scope of this chapter, be aware that a former manager may be in a position to lay claim to a chunk of your earnings for years. It's wise to consult an attorney before committing yourself to any management contract.

Finding a Manager

Suppose you've been self-managing and have developed your career to the point where you believe you can attract a personal manager. A good starting point for finding the right manager is the referral from a trusted source. For example, if you have a band whose members are actively networking, seek recommendations from other bands, studio owners, producers, A&R reps, and so on. Your lawyer or accountant may be able to point you in the right direction. In addition, sourcebooks and guides published by trade magazines and industry organizations list managers, often mentioning some of their clients. By being resourceful, you should be able to identify some prospective managers. Then you have to approach them.

The same marketing skills you've developed promoting your career apply to selling yourself to prospective managers. You need to be able to convince them that you have that "something" that can sustain a music career and produce income. This belief can spring from various sources:

- Your career is already up and running, at least to some degree
- Other people in the industry (such as producers and record labels) have expressed interest in you

- The manager hears something special and marketable in your music and talent
- The manager relates to you personally and thinks you are special, bound for success
- Some combination of the above

Managers are businesspeople, but they're subjective individuals, too. Most refuse to take on an act they can't relate to. This is more than a matter of taste—the ability to produce is seriously compromised if a manager just doesn't understand a client as a musician or a person. Be open and sincere in presenting yourself to a prospective manager. Industry veteran manager Bill Aucoin (who's managed the acts Kiss and Billy Idol, among others), views the manager-client relationship this way:

> Simply stated, it's a family. In my opinion, an act should get a manager as early in their career as they can. Artists tend to live in the moment. They need someone with the vision to project where their talent can take them. It's a journey they take together . . . The right manager can make all the difference for an act. When the trust is there, there's no limit to what can be accomplished . . . and if it isn't, then it's a waste of time for everybody.

In the long run, working with a manager you like and trust, who feels the same way about you, is more important than the manager's clout and industry reputation. Staying with Bill Aucoin's family model, the artist–personal manager relationship is a business *marriage*; the touchy-feely things matter a lot. For the marriage to work, the manager must trust and respect your judgment, too.

Be wary of someone who promises to do things for you and says "leave everything to me." Remember, your personal manager is part of your team, and no one on a team is beyond accountability. Trust is just as important in choosing a manager as it is in choosing an attorney. After all, this person is going to bat for your career. You want to feel confident the manager's on your side. This can mean the difference between advancing and stalling your career.

Be aware that many potential ethical dilemmas and conflicts of interest lurk behind the scenes in the management game. For instance, a manager experiencing personal cash flow problems may be tempted to overwork the client or recommend deals that sacrifice long-term benefits for bigger up-front payments. In the short term, these provide good results for the manager's bank account, but down the road, they're bad for the client. This is another example of why trust is so important, but still, the wise client stays apprised of what's going on in his own career.

AGENTS

While the jobs of manager and attorney are far-reaching, the job of an agent is much more limited in its scope. Basically, an agent's job is to book performances, which includes concerts, television, and movies, so "limited" doesn't mean insignificant. The agent's fees are payable only on the income so produced, meaning that that the agent receives no portion of recording or writing royalties. By contrast, a manager's commission is based on virtually all sources of income produced by the client.

Many artists act as their own agents until their careers are fairly far along. Usually, an artist will have found an attorney and manager before he feels the need for an agent. When it's time for a full-time agent, the standard fee is 10 percent. This is governed not only by custom, but also by union contracts in most states. Agents earn their commissions by securing paid work for their clients. As with managers, it is important that there be a strong understanding between agent and client. An agent who doesn't relate to the artist's music will not be nearly as effective as one who senses how that artist fits into the marketplace.

The same guidelines for choosing a manager apply to choosing an agent. That said, the agent isn't much of a day-to-day presence in the client's life. Most of the agent's dealings are with the manager, not the artist. So, it's also important for the manager to have confidence in the agent and vice versa. Commonly, the manager is the individual who brings the agent onto the management team.

Agencies come in all sizes. Several of the biggies that book comedians, actors, and movie directors also handle musicians, while other, much smaller agencies may specialize not only in musicians, but also in particular genres of music. There is no formula as to which agent is the right one for you. It might be comforting to have an agent who handles many acts in your genre; on the other hand, you may feel better served by an agency where you are the only act in your genre—provided you believe in the agent who'll be doing your work.

As in management, clout matters. Major players are able to capitalize on long-standing, mutually profitable relationships to help their clients. For example, a large agency with clout might be able to obtain film or concert work for a developing act, which would be inaccessible to a smaller agency. Does this mean that, in choosing an agency, the bigger the better? Not necessarily. At a big agency, you may feel that, as one act among many, you're not as important as the firm's more established clients and will not receive the same level of attention. Quite possibly, a smaller agency will devote much greater time, energy, and commitment to your career. In the long run, this may prove to be of greater benefit.

Accountants

Accountants[105] play no role in an artist's career development, and they have little to do with generating income. However, what they do is important—they help the artist identify his sources of earnings and instruct him on how to hang onto them.

As a musician, you have a small business. Money comes in from various sources (royalties, appearances, concessions, etc.), and money gets paid out in the form of expenses (including taxes and fees for managers, attorneys, and agents). You and your manager are operating on the fly; that is, when expenses are payable, you pay them with the money you have on hand. No particular matching is done to see whether the dollars you use to pay expenses were generated by the activities that gave rise to them. The job of an accountant is to match, allocate, and report your profit and loss; ensure compliance with tax laws; and identify profitable and unprofitable enterprises, to aid in decision making.

To illustrate, here are a few examples of what CPAs do:

- You spent a lot of money making your last record, and you think that building a home studio might help save money. Your accountant can help you analyze whether this is a cost-effective move in the long run.
- You've heard about saving your earnings in a profit-sharing plan, but you don't understand what it is or whether you qualify. Your CPA does.
- It seems your manager is living awfully high lately. Your accountant can audit your books to find out whether you're being overcharged.

Some CPAs specialize in representing musicians, just as some attorneys do. Familiarity with the field is important, and if possible, you should try to find a music-business CPA. However, it's less imperative here than in law—the accountant is not making deals the way the attorney is.

The most important things to look for in an accountant are competency, a sense of duty, and an understanding of your particular needs. For once, you need not be concerned with whether this person likes your music, knows anything at all about music, or believes in your career. However, it's still important for you to feel this is a person you can trust and that you communicate easily with one another.

The CPA will be working with your manager, your lawyer, and you. Though he's not an inside member of the management team, his input does have a big effect. He will advise against unnecessary expenses, projects with low rates of return on your money, and enterprises he considers too risky. He will calculate, and then hound you to make, regular tax payments (and you'll be glad he did). If he seems focused on numbers more than you enjoy, be glad—that's what you're paying him to do. Accountants charge hourly rates for their services (stay away from accountants who want to charge a percentage of your earnings). Sometimes CPAs calculate their fees on a flat-rate basis; for instance, "I'll charge you $5,000 to prepare your state and federal tax returns."

You'll find your accountant through word-of-mouth and on recommendations from your attorney and manager. Since they'll have to work with the CPA and presumably have some knowledge of who the good ones are, such recommendations are valuable. As always, try to avoid conflict-of-interest situations. For instance, if the CPA also represents your manager, you'd be right to wonder if he'd be eager to report that your manager was hoarding your money in his own interest-bearing accounts or charging off his betting habits as "business expenses."

PUBLICISTS

Publicists sometimes are referred to as "public relations firms." The job of publicists is to obtain media exposure for their clients. Publicists have connections with newspapers, television, radio, magazines, and other outlets in which stories and news about clients can appear. This free advertising isn't really free; you have to pay your publicist. However, depending on where you are in your career, the money spent may be well worth it. As mentioned in the previous chapter, buzz does great things for a career.

When you manage your own career, you are your own publicist. Putting together your press kit, Web site, and bio, doing fanzine interviews, and arranging an appearance on a local cable TV show are all examples of the kind of publicity developing artists routinely handle themselves. Often, your personal manager takes over these duties when he assumes his job.

At some point, though, your manager may feel that he's running up against a brick wall, trying to obtain, for example, a feature article in a major publication or an appearance on a nationally broadcast television show. The publicist has valuable contacts and the reputation for feeding interesting stories to these media. Perhaps he can accomplish what your manager can't; at least, he can make it happen faster.

Sometimes the job of the publicist isn't to create buzz but to orchestrate damage control when a client is caught in an embarrassing situation or an unfavorable light. The well-worded, timely issued press release has been known to reduce a potential public relations disaster to an insignificant blip or even create sympathy by putting positive "spin" on the situation. Experienced publicists know all about spin and can help maintain or even boost career momentum from seemingly minor ingredients.

Publicists are adjunct members of the management team. They work under the supervision of your personal manager and can be of valuable service. Most of the time, though, they are role players—advisors you need now and again but not in day-to-day affairs.

BUSINESS MANAGERS

If you're fortunate enough to become a substantial earner and to accumulate assets, your lawyer or CPA may recommend you seek the services of a business manager. A business manager is someone who helps you hang on to and invest the earnings from your career. The services of such a person are not specific to music. This person could just as easily be working for any other high earner, such as a TV actor or professional ballplayer. An effective business manager can make the most of your assets and help you achieve financial security.

Unfortunately, there have been some recent cases in which business managers lost substantial sums of money of their high-profile clients, through massive negligence, gross incompetence, and occasionally through outright embezzlement. The entertainer is particularly at risk for this kind of loss, being inexperienced and unschooled in business (which, ironically, is one of the reasons to engage a business manager in the first place). In addition, since music careers are often of shorter duration than other careers, the musician is far too busy earning money while possible to adequately supervise the business affairs (again, probably one of the motivating factors to hire a business manager).

Business managers sometimes start out as accountants themselves; others begin in real estate, financial advising, stock brokerage, insurance, and law. As with personal managers, no special qualification or background is required. Sometimes the attorney or CPA becomes the de facto business manager for a client. The danger here is lack of independent examination— the person who's responsible for oversight is the one whose activities are being overseen. If possible, avoid this situation.

Unlike personal managers, attorneys, and agents, a business manager is not a necessity. Many people correctly feel they can handle and invest their own earnings with the help of their CPAs and lawyers. This is not to say that business managers routinely do a poor job. On the contrary, there are many fine ones whose day-to-day competence doesn't make the newspapers the way the corruption or incompetence of "bad apples" does. Needless to say, the trustworthiness, reputation for straight dealing and business acumen, and absence of conflict of interest are prime factors in choosing a business manager. Still, your own scrutiny, and that of your lawyer and accountant, also should oversee these activities.

V

CHANGES IN THE MUSIC BUSINESS

CHAPTER 14

THE MUSIC INDUSTRY IN TRANSITION—THE FUTURE IS NOW

Very few businesses are static, and the music business is no exception. Increasingly, the business itself is *about* change, because popular music is perceived, at least, to be on the cutting edge of culture. At the end of the 1990s, the major forces at work affecting the industry (in no particular order) are:

- The impact of technology on the way music is made, transmitted, perceived, bought, and sold
- The consolidation of power within the music industry, most notably, major record labels and commercial radio stations
- The fragmenting of markets for popular music
- Changes in demographics and spending patterns
- Changes in the concert industry (discussed in the chapter on touring)
- Emerging creative careers in the music business

Each of these forces has identifiable effects on today's music industry, as well as ramifications for the future.

Although no one, in or out of the music business, can predict the future with certainty, we feel that strong trends are well underway and will continue to be a factor for years to come. The trends do not exist in a vacuum; some of them are intimately related to each other. By discussing these ongoing changes and tendencies, we hope to better prepare today's musician for the true environment of the industry.

TECHNOLOGY AND PIRACY

Some years back, when the analog audiocassette became a viable, inexpensive medium, the major labels and industry trade groups such as the RIAA[106] were up in arms about the potential for piracy—that is, the unauthorized copying (and selling) of records, with loss of revenue for both the labels and the artists. Their danger to the industry having been overrated, cassettes are still with us. Now the perceived threat to the well-being of labels and artists is digital technology.

Digital technology currently is used by the industry to make records, but that isn't what annoys the RIAA. The reasons for their bother are these:

- Flawless reproduction of an original source signal is already with us. Modern "CD burners," in essence, turn every commercially available CD into a master recording. There is no generational or other quality loss in digital duplication—every copy is indistinguishable from the original. Piracy (also called "bootlegging") is easy to accomplish in the digital domain.
- The Internet permits unfettered transmission of recorded music and downloading (via MP3 files) by every person who has a hard drive and CD burner. Technology to send, receive, and download music cheaply, quickly, and easily isn't perfect (MP3s offer not-quite-CD-quality sound)—but it's good enough for most consumers.

The combination of these two factors is seen as a threat to the revenue stream of the record companies, and to artists, whose royalties are paid out of that revenue stream. Already in a panic about declining sales, the music industry has maintained lawsuits against file-sharing services and individuals who heavily use them.[107]

THE INTERNET AND MP3 DOWNLOADS— RECENT DEVELOPMENTS

Almost everyone has heard of MP3s—compressed digital music files which are transferable via the Internet.[108] At the time the first edition of this book was published a company called MP3.com maintained a Web site (MP3.com), which contained recorded music to download—both free samples and complete albums for sale. Acts posted their music for free, and the company boldly stated its intentions to "bypass the middleman" and put major labels out of business.

In 2000, we predicted that MP3.com would be acquired by a major label, and we were right. Ultimately, even with major label support, the company never became profitable. It went out of business as a free site in December 2003. The record industry became far more upset over Napster, a

Web site (and company) which essentially enabled unlimited free downloading of copyrighted material. Napster was closed down after a lawsuit, and now is a pay download site owned by major BMG.

Other peer-to-peer (PTP) file-sharing sites have sprung up, but the record industry has lost its lawsuits against them. Undaunted, the RIAA litigated against some individual downloaders in hopes of having a deterrent effect.[109] According to the labels, most "free" Internet music is theft—it undermines the very existence of a music industry by taking money out of the pockets of labels and artists. Ultimately, they say, this harms fans also, because it operates as a disincentive to produce music.

Since the emergence of MP3s and wide-scale Internet file-sharing (including illegal file-sharing), the music industry has been working to combat the perceived threat with its own technology, the Secure Digital Music Initiative (SDMI). SDMI is a format for digitally storing music designed to prevent unauthorized reproduction of recorded material (such as CDs). Most observers (including the authors of this book) believe that such digital rights management (DRM) is technologically futile—it's just too easy for potential pirates either to hack DRM programs, or to re-digitize music into MP3 files.

THE INTERNET AND OTHER TRENDS IN THE TWENTY-FIRST CENTURY

In the first edition, we identified four major trends:

1. that online transmission of digital music was not a passing fad, and that major changes would take place irrespective of DRM technology;
2. that MP3 (and like formats) would change the way popular music is bought and sold;
3. that major record labels will survive and continue to be the major sellers of pop music, but the way they do business will change; and
4. that career path opportunities for artists will not change as dramatically as some artists and Internet proponents believe.

On points one through three, our prognostications proved completely correct—at least for the immediate future. The jury is still out on point number four, and we have further comments to offer regarding career paths.

The outcome of the "MP3 wars" could not have happened any other way. The history of popular music is in large part technology-driven, and some handwriting is always on the wall. For example, in the early days of the twentieth century, sheet music publishers sued piano roll makers for copyright infringement.[110]

Later, when radio became a major force, ASCAP[111] got in a major fight with broadcasters over performance royalties. This disagreement led the broadcasters to establish their own performing rights society, Broadcast Music, Inc. (BMI). Technology just keeps moving forward, and law and business practices either adapt or fall behind. In no event can the genie be persuaded to go back in the bottle. Consumers want the convenience, speed, and flexibility of Internet transmission of digitally recorded music—they are already getting those things, and they will get even more in the future.

As noted earlier, in the first edition we predicted that the corporation MP3.com would be purchased by a major label and that scenario played out (though the company's original operations folded). This attempt to "beat 'em and join 'em" at the same time is just one example of the music industry's inconsistent approach to the issues surrounding the online transfer of MP3 files.

Consumer Popularity of Digital Music and File Sharing

It's fair to say that five years is half of a generation, and in some cases more, in pop music. Trends rapidly come and go. To most listeners, vinyl records are an artifact from an earlier era, like wood-burning stoves. Teenagers no longer recall cassettes as a dominant medium. Many young people listen primarily to MP3 files[112] that they have been downloaded from the Internet without paying for them. Since this method of obtaining music has always been part of their world, they don't consider it to be theft—in this view, music is just out there on the Net for the taking.

Naturally, artists and record labels have been alarmed by the "free" view of music. Napster, the first free file-sharing service, was shut down after a successful lawsuit, but others have taken its place. In 2003 and 2004, the RIAA filed suits against individuals in the hopes that others would be encouraged to refrain from using free file-sharing for fear of legal reprisal. As noted earlier, these efforts may have succeeded to a degree, but unless the industry changes the way consumers *think*, the problem of enforcement is just too large to inhibit large-scale downloading,

Proponents of unfettered downloading argue that this practice actually *increases* music sales (of CDs and pay downloads). They reason that the Internet vastly enhances the exposure, hence the market. They concede that yes, some people steal music they would otherwise have to buy, but maintain that sales lost this way are minute compared to the extra revenues generated because so many more people willingly pay for music they would not have heard otherwise. Here's the model: music fan Bob downloads a song or two of the Newbies without paying. Bob likes what he hears, so he supports the Newbies by purchasing the whole album.

Though this must be true sometimes, what if Bob likes just two tracks and isn't willing to buy the entire album to acquire them? The alleged net sales gain isn't backed up by any sales figures. We *don't know* whether Bob buys the album, or downloads the rest of it without paying. Moreover, fan interest in general seems to be moving away from albums and towards individual tracks.[113] There are logistical problems with the "free music leads to purchases" model—for instance, listeners too young to have developed the habit of buying CDs at "brick and mortar" stores probably don't possess the credit card necessary to purchase music at an online fee site.

THE MUSIC INDUSTRY'S AVERSION TO FILE SHARING

The industry's most obvious objection to file sharing is that it creates the opportunity for consumers to obtain music the major labels produce without paying for it. If a person walked out of a CD store with an armload of CDs and bypassed the cash register, this action would constitute theft. Why not when he downloads?

"Internet freedom" advocates claim that major labels have been overcharging consumers for years, and that consumers will gladly pay reasonable prices for good music. These claims sound overly idealistic to our ears. Adults who download entire albums rather than buy them, do so because "everyone else does" and because they don't expect to get caught—kind of like cheating on one's tax return. Youngsters whose sense of right and wrong is less well developed, and who have grown up with the Internet as a fact of life—well, most of them don't give it a second thought.

Whether an adult or child downloads free, the music industry sees a problem. Though the labels concede the Internet is a great tool to widely and efficiently promote their product, they want to keep the same per-unit profit profile while growing the market, not trade off growth in total units distributed against revenues lost to downloading.

Moreover, labels claim that diminution of their profit incentive results in less music for fans. To us, this logic breaks down because making "professional sounding" master recordings in today's world is no longer dauntingly high-priced. Not even distribution of recordings needs to remain the province of majors. That function, too, can be accomplished online at low cost, without the extensive, costly "brick-and-mortar" network required to distribute "hard" product (CDs, cassettes, and vinyl).

DECLINE OF THE LABEL AND DEATH OF THE RECORD STORE?

At the height of MP3.com's hubris, executives predicted their company would drive the major labels out of business by "eliminating the middleman." Artists would bring their music directly to the public, thereby cutting labels out of the loop. Though MP3.com itself failed, the fear the company (and sites like Napster) instilled in labels continues to haunt them.

The primary fear is not of their product's being pirated, bootlegged, or stolen, but rather, rendered entirely irrelevant. Production and distribution technology that allows bands, singers, and instrumentalists cheaply and efficiently to produce, promote, advertise, market and distribute their music without resort to the traditional model would (at the very least) severely impact labels, if not doom them entirely. Presently, labels are surviving (though not thriving), but bricks and mortar record stores have suffered badly in recent years.[114]

Besides trying to quell competition by impairing the genie's emergence from the bottle (for example, suing Napster and individual downloaders, pursuing DRM schemes, lobbying Congress to pass laws to limit Internet radio), the music industry has also grudgingly conceded that it needs to change to survive. Among these changes are:

- CD price reductions[115]
- Agreements to enter into the "per song" download market using online retail sites such as Apple's iTunes
- Encouraging direct music sales from their own websites
- Augmenting declining or stagnant traditional sales by tapping into new revenue sources such as "partnering" with artists or non-music products

Certainly, labels have little to gain by relying on a model that was becoming outmoded by mid-1999, when affordable home computer "CD burners" began to proliferate and Napster became a force. Since then, traditional specialty retail outlets for hard product (CDs) have suffered (Wherehouse, Tower, and Sam Goody have closed many locations and considered shutting down entirely), while "big box" discount stores like Costco and Wal-Mart have largely supplanted the "record store" in the mainstream pop CD market.

The ability to obtain recorded music online directly from a label (or an artist) poses a problem for record stores. Clearly, chains catering to mainstream pop are an endangered species, though many observers believe that "hands-on" stores will always survive in some form because human beings love to browse and impulse buy in retail outlets. Moreover, they say, record stores potentially provide a service, in the knowledge of the sales staff, and this is not readily obtainable online.[116]

For brick and mortar record stores to continue to exist, we believe, they'll need to offer a combination of expertise, hard product that's *not* mainstream, and instantaneous downloading of a wide variety of material. In addition, they probably will need to offer for sale other products such as MP3 players, audio and photo supplies, and other high-tech consumer goods, both to augment income and to bring traffic into the stores. Hardware and software technology already permit consumers to obtain music by paying, downloading, and burning a CD, all within a few minutes.

Record stores may soon carry most of their titles this way, rather than through physical inventory.

Will Major Labels Continue to Hold Most of the Cards?

In the first edition of this book, we predicted that "major labels will survive and continue to be the major sellers of pop music, but the way they do business will change." We stand by this prediction—as long as major labels continue to dominate access to new music for the majority of consumers. Right now, the end of this control is not in sight.

It's true that from 2000 to 2003, CD sales declined significantly. Labels blame downloaders ("pirates"); musical idealists blame the labels themselves for putting out so much cookie-cutter, unworthy product that consumers are disgusted; cultural historians view the decline as part of a down cycle following a long upswing of prosperity. No study has proved whether any of these factors is more important than the others, or even whether the assertions are true at all. Intuitively, they all make some sense.

The first part of the twenty-first century is not the first time record sales have fallen. In the early years of the Great Depression (1930–1935), sales dropped far more precipitously—by some estimates, more than 70 percent. The record industry blamed competition from radio, the first technology-enabled form of "free music." Business-cycle advocates theorized, "incomes are down, people have lost jobs, what do you expect?" Cultural historians explained that then-new film "talkies" lured music fans away—just as web-surfing, video games, and other forms of entertainment today compete with music for consumers' entertainment time and dollars. Still, the industry recovered and thrived.

Radio is still where the majority of consumers learn about new music. Today, radios in cars and at work (where most listening takes place) continue to be tuned to conventional FM (and to a much lesser extent, AM) broadcast stations. When alternate forms of broadcast music are easily and cheaply available to break the lock of access currently enjoyed by major labels, their dominance over popular music might suffer. In the long run, they could decline into insignificance, but for now, it's still their show.

Despite the recent downturn, 2003 CD sales of majors were not as bad as had been predicted. If the industry is contracting, the rate of contraction has slowed. Consumers continue to demand some new music in their lives. Significantly, they get exposed to it via mainstream outlets that are entirely the province of major labels: FM radio, music videos, major-media print advertising, large-venue tours. Smaller competitors aren't *serious* competitors. They simply cannot afford the cost of access.

Some observers predict that the Internet will level the playing field, but for now it's still tilted in favor of those with the big bucks. If you've been online, you know there are millions and millions of Web sites and that despite the ingenuity of search engines, finding what you're looking for is not always easy or even feasible. Now consider an online market with no labels, but millions of artists. It would be near-impossible for any one artist become known to large numbers of people. This is where labels come in. With their clout and money, they can direct consumers to the music they're selling—through Internet advertising as well as through the traditional media of radio airplay, print and broadcast advertising, and tour sponsorship.

Because of the vastness of cyberspace, the importance of the ability to direct the consumer to the product is not diminished by the Internet; it is magnified. For this reason, we not only believe that major labels will not be "buried" but that their importance in the marketplace will not diminish. Who the big players are will change, as some companies are more nimble in adapting to emerging markets, but this was always true.

Clearly, the labels will have to adapt to consumer preferences for online sales, but in the past, they've always responded to changing technologies by providing for those preferences—be it the change to vinyl LPs from 78 rpm records, the growth of cassettes, or the dominance of CDs. Remember, the labels were up in arms about the bootlegging possibilities of cassettes long before they manufactured prerecorded cassettes. Not only did they survive this perceived threat, they managed to have their most profitable years even while the cassette refused to go away.

HOW MUCH WILL CAREER PATHS CHANGE?

We've run into a number of artists, usually do-it-yourselfers with no clear plans, who say, "Well, my CD's almost finished. Once it starts selling heavily on CDBaby.com, I'll make some money, then I can quit my day job and do music full time." With all due respect, they're kidding themselves. The Internet is a great tool to help attain many goals, but don't expect the Internet, by itself, to propel you to stardom.

Turn on your car radio, or go to one of the music video channels on your TV; you'll hear thirty or forty current songs in heavy rotation. In most areas, your radio receives perhaps five or six stations that play current pop music; the typical cable TV hookup gets no more than two or three video music stations. Many of these stations overlap, playing the same songs and artists. Presently, the vast majority of people hear about new records through these media, commercial pop radio and music television, which major labels dominate.

Now, consider the world of the Internet. Compared to radio or TV, it has an infinite number of channels; you're not limited to a half-dozen choices. So, surfing from one band Web site to another, your chances of hearing music you're willing to buy are pretty slim. There's no filtering effect at all, no discretion exercised by any A&R department. Everything's out there, from utterly inept beginners (the largest category) to the pros.

"But," you may say, "what about CD Baby?"[117] Doesn't it bring in consumers to listen to my band?" Well, yes, but . . . That site contains a very large number of acts (over 50,000), so each act has plenty of competition. This much choice is actually daunting. It's like walking into a record store with 50,000 albums by artists you've never heard of—where do you start? Plus, in order to try out the music, the listener must be pro-active and go to the music, it doesn't just come to the listener.

By contrast, when at home on the couch, watching TV, or driving in a car, listening to the radio, this person is passive and reactive. The stations relieve listeners of the burden of choosing. Granted, fewer choices are available, but most listeners don't want that many choices. If they did, they'd be much more active in choosing the varied music that is already available in record stores.

On CD Baby and similar sites, many acts compete with each other for the Net browser's attention. With no other marketing help, the chance that your act will be listened to by large numbers of music fans is infinitesimally small. Now, consider marketing help: If the site listing your CD has a banner ad for your group or some other device to send people to check out your music (for instance, a prominent recommendations list or a button that directs people: "Hot new music, click here"), then you're cooking. But, where's the money going to come from to provide this extra marketing muscle? The average unsigned act doesn't have it, that's for sure.

On the higher-profile "independent music" sites, there's no filtering of quality or marketability such as the major labels do to select acts that are "radio-friendly." Such sites potentially provide large numbers of listeners, *but only for all of their acts taken together.* For any one act, the number of listeners is small—unless some other means (for instance, radio airplay, magazine advertising, or Internet advertising) increases it. There's a huge difference between listeners thinking they have a choice of thirty or forty new records every few months and tens of thousands.

We feel that the presence of independent music sites,[118] or personal Web sites, does not change the game that much for artists. Yes, the Net can be a valuable tool. And, the further along you are in your career, the more valuable it may prove to be. However, a new act does itself a disservice to believe that a CD listed on CD Baby, by itself, is sufficient to promote a career to a full-time level. To sell in the numbers needed, the act should continue performing live, seeking airplay, and perhaps enlisting the help of a major or independent label.

Consolidation of Power in the Record Industry

At no time in the business could more than ten labels arguably be called the "majors"; for most of the 1990s, there were six or seven (depending on how you counted). Periodically, and as recently as the 1970s, several majors combined in mergers and consolidations (for instance, the creation of Warner-Elektra-Asylum, WEA). In the past, typically, one or two new companies would start up and join the ranks of majors within a few years after each round of consolidations.

Most observers feel that this cycle has ended. It appears that, in the foreseeable future, fewer and larger majors will dominate the label scene. In late 1998 and early 1999, the then biggest-ever consolidation was consummated, as Universal Music Group (UMG) purchased Polygram for $10.4 billion, a fine chunk of change by any standards. As a direct result, labels on which many of the most beloved and successful artists had appeared—A&M, Geffen, Motown, Mercury, and Island—pretty much vanished. During the corporate restructuring, many employees lost jobs and many acts were cut from rosters. Time-Warner sold Warner Music to a private group led by Edgar Bronfman, Jr., who formerly headed up the parent company that acquired Universal. As of this writing, there are five majors: Sony, BMG, Universal, Warner, and EMI. In June 2004, European antitrust regulators approved a Sony-BMG merger. Should American authorities follow suit, as most observers expect, then the number of majors will drop to four. The new Sony-BMG entity will control more than 25 percent of market share.

Several factors point to this shift away from the cycle of consolidation, emergence of new majors, and then reconsolidation. First, the more "Fortune 500" the business becomes, the more the labels respond like other multinationals. They want the biggest chunk of market share they can get and are used to paying out big bucks to maintain or enlarge it. In this environment, it's harder for smaller players to become majors. Second, the industry has become more of a high risk-high return environment, much like that of movies. The start-up costs for a new act—recording, production, promotion, videos, and so on—are much higher than they used to be. Bruce Flohr, former vice-president of A&R for RCA, told us, "whenever I make a recommendation to sign a new act, I'm committing about a million dollars of the company's money."

Ironically, the corporate culture itself is one reason for the increasing costs of new acts, because it requires investments to have a visible, short-range payoff. Companies now feel that nurturing acts for two or three albums until they break is not responsive to the demands of shareholders. With so much riding on a first album, even more money is spent to help it break. The majors not only have the most formidable resources to play this game, but in so playing it, they define the rules for everyone. Once again, sheer financial muscle is a distinct advantage.

As an artist, you may wonder if it matters whether you sign with a label that is one of five (soon to be four) majors, rather than one of eight. It does. Those numbers are indicative of the complete victory of the bottom-line corporate mentality at the remaining majors; this change has profound, real effects. To begin with, labels today are more likely to be run by money people—accountants and lawyers—than by music people. In past years, label heads were music enthusiasts, willing to take chances on new talent because of a sixth sense that an act had market appeal. They combined profit motive with a sharing of the artistic vision.[119]

Most of today's executives have no such acumen. Now, it's more probable that a truly creative or cutting-edged act will be passed over as too risky, in favor of more generic artists. Moreover, in terms of spending company money, these executives are inclined to go with the surest bets they can. So, they're more likely to bid for the services of proven stars than to try to create new stars, which leaves fewer resources for signing and developing new talent.

Still, major labels can't survive indefinitely with only proven acts, because some of these will lose popularity, die, retire, or go out of vogue. There will always be room for new acts, but what will the opportunities be for a given artist? As mentioned earlier, there is an increased sense of urgency within majors for new signings to produce profits quickly. One effect of this is the pressure to have instant hit records.[120] Today, an artist whose first album doesn't sell well enough will rarely get a second or third chance.

The perceived need to produce instant, cash-flow-producing hits results in the marketing of what techno artist Moby refers to as "lowest common denominator music that works on the radio but doesn't generate any loyalty."[121] Instead of being encouraged to develop a long-term sense of identification with *artists*, the audience is urged to consume *songs* on a one-by-one basis. This leads to a succession of what are disparagingly (and accurately) referred to as "one-hit wonders." Sure enough, this trend accelerated in the late 1990s. Artists become as disposable as the music—hardly a promising sign for those seeking an actual career, much less artistic and creative fulfillment.

Because the majors have a near-absolute lock on commercial radio and music television, they control most of what consumers are exposed to and, therefore, buy. The majors manipulate what is desired, then they satisfy that desire—effectively controlling both demand and supply. As a result, less choice is left for consumers than in a more open market, and there is less choice for artists who wish to sell music. According to techno artist Moby: "You have to fit the mold, and radio defines that mold. Right now, if you're not a teen pop star, an R&B artist, a hip-hop artist, a generic alternative-rock band, or a female singer/songwriter, you might as well not even think about making records."

Because he doesn't fit into these prefabricated formats, Moby clearly has an ax to grind, but his point is well-taken.

There's an alternate point of view to this fatalistic characterization: In the 1990s and beyond, consumers are mistrustful of major conglomerates and try to find ways to satisfy their individual needs outside the corporate lock step. The explosive popularity of Internet commerce, with its growing acceptance as a place offering greater choice, is the most obvious manifestation of this wing spreading.

A historical analogy backs up the notion that the market will begin to open up: comparing FM radio to the Internet. In the early 1960s, AM radio was largely tepid and highly formatted. Save for a few classical music and educational stations, FM barely existed. Within a few years, FM stations proliferated and prospered, mostly by offering much more adventurous programming. Ultimately, this led to the growth of the industry as a whole. The majors benefited the most, as they jumped in and co-opted the market. Nevertheless, during the period of expansion, a far greater diversity of artists got a chance to be exposed to audiences.[122]

In addition to the Internet, the other factor that can play a part in providing greater opportunities for artists and more choice for consumers is the independent label. The increasing consolidation of the majors creates opportunity for indies in several ways:

- Because major labels are a bureaucratic, high-cost industry with a long reaction time, indies have an advantage in bringing new and diverse music to the market
- Because indies are largely headed by music people rather than money people, they're better at spotting trends and reacting to tastes
- Major-label music will (or largely already has) become so generic, that the indies will be where music fans turn
- Compelling artists dropped by major labels for not having an immediate hit single may find a home at indies

Despite mergers and other economic forces that have brought us fewer, larger companies and increased the prevalence of a short-term, bottom-line mentality, artists will still find opportunity in the record business. Even though the major-label environment offers less diverse opportunity for artists than in years past, the indies should fill a consumer need and sometimes provide a talent pipeline to the majors. Some observers even predict a consumer revolt is in the offing, which would result in a mammoth shift of power away from major label dominance, but we believe this is the wishful thinking of passionate individuals.

Concentration of Power in Commercial Radio

Power in the world of radio is concentrated in two ways:

1. Commercial pop radio has grown to dominate the world of breaking new albums as never before, largely through financial tie-ins with major labels.
2. Conglomerates now own many stations. Ten conglomerates collect nearly two thirds of the revenues of the commercial radio business in the United States.

These developments are interrelated. As radio stations are controlled by fewer owners,[123] they acquire greater power to make or break records in most markets.

Wherever this kind of concentration occurs, it means that the business leaders are money people, not music people. Furthermore, the fewer players there are in a market, the more homogenized it becomes, due to less competition to challenge the status quo. In many areas (major metropolitan markets, not small towns), the *same company* owns all but one or two radio stations. So, there's no competition between stations to present adventurous programming of new artists.

In an interview with *Music Connection* magazine,[124] music executive Michael Rosenblatt stated that the industry should find another way (in addition to radio) to market music to the public:

> Because radio doesn't give [expletive] about music. All they care about is getting more money for their Levi ads. In fact, if they could do all weather and get a higher Q rating with the eighteen- to thirty-four-year-old demographic, they would change over tomorrow. It makes no sense being beholden to this other industry to break our music when they don't care about it. We have to figure out a way to get to our consumer without it, and then we'll all be very happy.

So far, no one in the record industry has figured out how to do this; "drive time" radio and "workplace" radio are still where most people hear new records. In addition, the major labels are more than a little hypocritical about marketing alternatives. Labels are still fighting digital transmission formats, while Internet proponents view them as alternative means of getting the word out.

Virtual Radio

The best way to understand what's called "virtual radio" is to understand its opposite, which we call "real radio." In real radio,

- Stations in the different cities are owned by separate companies
- Within a geographical market, the stations are separately owned
- Station program directors and disc jockeys have discretion to play or not play records based on their own hunches, tastes, and reading the fans' desires

FM radio was very much like this in the late 1960s and early 1970s. The result was a noticeable increase in the diversity of popular music played on the radio, hence increased opportunities for artists who might have been shunned just a few years earlier.

By contrast, these are the attributes of virtual radio:

- Stations in different cities are owned by the same set of conglomerates
- Often, within a geographical market, most of the stations are owned by just one or two companies
- No one at the local stations has discretion in deciding what records to play, and local disc jockeys and program directors are eliminated

In the virtual radio format, the actual music broadcasts originate in the corporate headquarters of a conglomerate. The disc jockeys and their shows are recorded there, then the recordings are transmitted to the various stations around the country designated for the particular music format. For instance, listeners in Albuquerque, Dallas, Atlanta, Seattle, Los Angeles, Minneapolis, Pittsburgh, Denver, Cleveland, New York, Phoenix, Chicago, Boston, and other cities would hear the identical show, not just the same music but the same disc jockeys.

Virtual radio is beginning to catch on in a big way. Most industry observers feel it will dominate radio in a few years. This kind of centralization isn't done to increase consumer choice or to make the shows more interesting. In fact, it has quite the opposite effects. First and foremost, it's done to save costs. Instead of having disc jockeys and a program director at each station, each format has just one set that can serve perhaps two dozen stations around the country. In addition, virtual radio increases the conglomerates' clout in selling ad time—they can deliver on the national level.

Virtual radio and the concentration of power that creates it are unpopular in many quarters. Advocates of artistic and broadcasting diversity and of local control of radio outlets led a drive to allow more FM stations in major radio markets. A petition was filed[125] with the Federal Communications Commission (FCC) to authorize the creation of more of these low-power FM (LPFM) stations and in early 2000, the FCC authorized LPFM for "noncommercial educational broadcasting only."

Not unexpectedly, the corporate radio chains, led by the National Association of Broadcasters (NAB), were against the proposed change. They argued that new stations would crowd the FM band, causing interference that would prove detrimental to their own broadcast efforts and to the public's enjoyment of radio. LPFM proponents viewed this reaction as disingenuous and self-serving. They asserted that low-power FM stations would serve neighborhoods in metropolitan areas without creating interference with adjacent high-power signals—and would bring the benefits of low-cost market entry, local control, and diversity of ownership and content.

In the end, the NAB and other constituents of the broadcast industry lobby won the significant battle: the FCC, though it did generally grant the petition in favor of LPFM, limited the scope of LPFM to exclude commercial use. Under the Federal Communications Act, the airwaves (being finite) are deemed a public resource. This is why the radio industry is so heavily regulated, with license requirements and so on. Supposedly, the mission of the FCC is to protect the public interest, but with stations selling for many millions of dollars, it appears that private interests are the ones being protected.

Niche Marketing

In metropolitan San Diego, California, where the authors live, the seventeen pop music FM radio stations that cater to the drive time and workplace listener are listed below:

Nine Owned by Clear Channel Communications:[126]
1. 101.5 classic rock
2. 93.3 contemporary hit radio
3. 105.3 rock
4. 94.1 ("my 94.1") adult contemporary
5. 91.1 ("91X") alternative rock
6. 90.3 ("Z90") rhythmic contemporary hit radio
7. 92.5 ("magic 92.5") jammin' oldies
8. 95.7 ("U.S. 95.7") contemporary country
9. 99.3 ("KOOL 99") oldies

Two owned by Infinity Broadcasting[127]
1. 103.7 classic hits
2. 96.5 adult contemporary

Three owned by Jefferson-Pilot Communications[127]
1. 94.9 modern rock
2. 97.3 contemporary country
3. 98.1 smooth jazz

This leaves two others: 100.7 ("Star 100"), owned by Midwest Television, Inc., which plays contemporary hit radio; plus one locally-based independent station, 102.1 ("SETS 102"), which programs in the adult album alternative (AAA) format.

Of these sixteen stations, four (101.5, 92.5, 99.3, and 103.7) play virtually no current music. Of the remaining twelve, there is substantial programming overlap between:

93.3 and 90.3 (contemporary hit radio);
91.1, 105.3 and 94.9 (rock);
95.7 and 97.3 (contemporary country);
101.5, 99.3 and 103.7 (oldies); and
96.5 and 100.7 (adult contemporary)

Intuitively and through experience, everyone knows you stand a good chance of hearing the same records repeatedly as you switch stations.

Further limiting what San Diego listeners get to hear, even stations that play substantially new music also have noncurrent music in constant rotation. For instance, the hard-rock station 105.3 plays some of the same tunes and artists as the "classic rock" stations 101.5 and 103.7, and "oldies" station 99.3.

The vast majority of the music on San Diego radio is programmed by the chains' national and regional program directors[129]—folks without any connection to the community. Their connections are to the major record labels, which, via a web of "independent promoters," pay their parent companies for access to radio.[130] The chances for a local act (or, for that matter, any act not hooked up with a major label) to get a song placed into regular rotation are effectively zero.

Ten of the seventeen stations are owned by a single company: Texas-based Clear Channel Communications. Therefore, nearly 60 percent of the pop-music radio market in the San Diego area is in the hands of one owner, which "competes" mostly with itself. This results in niche marketing, which is categorized more by the target market demographic than by any other factor, least of all the notion of presenting new, diverse music. When you listen to the commercials on these stations, the market-driven nature of the formats is achingly apparent, broken down primarily into age and sex, but also income and other factors.[131]

The tendency toward the familiar and generic is reinforced by market research conducted by the stations. To find new songs to play that most easily connect with the target audience, research firms hired by the broadcasters phone households to find persons who fit their demographic (for instance, women age twenty-five to thirty-four). Once such a person is identified, a researcher plays eight seconds each of test songs to see how well each one goes over.

With this kind of research, cutting-edge, unfamiliar, and more adventurous records lose out in favor of ones with the stock, formulaic sounds—voices, melodies, chord changes, and rhythms people are used to hearing on the radio. Naturally, the results of tests conducted in this manner indicate people want more of the same—so, they get it. Eight seconds isn't much time for a music fan to warm up to a new sound. Remember, radio stations make money not by playing music but by selling advertising time.[132] They are paid by advertisers to deliver a demographic—the largest number they can get of members of the group to whom the ads are marketed.

ALTERNATIVES TO COMMERCIAL RADIO

In addition to LPFM, whose future is iffy, are two main alternatives to commercial pop radio. One is college radio. In certain markets it is actually a presence, but in most cities it isn't. The reasons for this are the small number and low power of college radio stations (resulting in a low coverage area) or that, in many areas college radio is available mainly on cable. Cable radio just isn't a force with most consumers. They prefer the mobility and freedom of old-fashioned, through-the-air radio, especially because so much radio listening is done either in cars or on boom boxes or personal headphone radios.

The other alternative to commercial radio is broadcasting over the Internet—so-called Webcasting. Unlike traditional radio, Webcasts are not licensed or regulated in any way by the FCC, because there's no problem with availability of space on the electromagnetic spectrum. No matter how many Webcast sites are created, the Internet always can accommodate more without diminishing or interfering with the existing sites. Somewhat speciously, the NAB uses the feasibility and existence of Web-based broadcasts as a rationale for opposing LPFM.

The reason why the broadcast industry likes the present system is that there are a finite number of radio outlets available in a given market, which allows control of markets. Although Webcasting hypothetically provides an alternative, at present it isn't a very viable one because:

- Sound quality isn't nearly as good as FM radio.
- It isn't as convenient or mobile. That is, to listen to Webcasts, most people have to sit in front of their PCs. "Changing stations" back and forth is time consuming.
- Current cell-phone technology (and high cost) effectively preclude use of mobile Webcast reception for most Internet users.

The present barriers are primarily technological. It is unclear whether portable, affordable Webcast receivers are feasible within the near future, or at all. Moreover, the necessity of using part of the electromagnetic broadcast spectrum may create limits such as already exist under the current, FCC-regulated realm of radio.[133]

FRAGMENTED MARKETS

In the "old" record industry, the most successful label presidents, A&R heads, and producers were said to have "good ears." They could listen to an act or a recording and predict that audiences would react positively. There wasn't much market research—good ears were strictly an intuitive phenomenon. Of course, in the attempt to turn a quick buck, there were plenty of sound-alike or clone acts, but niche marketing hadn't reached its present state of sophistication. As the radio experience shows, the marketing of music has increasingly led to a pigeonholing of the target market and the music that they'll be willing to buy.

It isn't apparent when you go into a record store, but in most cases a new act must be neatly classifiable to have a chance of being picked up by a major label. Earlier in this chapter, we quoted an artist named Moby who identified the five genres into which he feels an act must fit to "even think about making records." The categories he identifies may be different from the categories of five years ago, or five years from now, but the basic observation is correct. The manner in which music can be sold determines which music will be released. If this seems backward, you're thinking too much like an artist and not enough like a businessperson.

For a moment, imagine that the commercial radio stations are separate stores in which these specific genres of music are sold, just as shoe stores sell shoes or tire stores sell tires.[134] If a group, or its record, doesn't fit the market demographic format, then it doesn't "belong" on one of the stations selling new music. Go one step further: If the record can't get airplay, it can't be sold. If it can't be sold, major labels aren't interested, no matter how brilliant the artist. Despite formatting, sometimes an act that doesn't fit any current format not only has its music released on a major label but attains substantial airplay and sales—the Dave Matthews Band comes to mind. Still, their story is an exception.

Read the trade magazine interviews. Major label heads and A&R reps nearly always say that they're looking for high-quality acts with great songs, originality, vision, and staying power. Nevertheless, the vast majority of acts they sign are fairly formulaic ones that they hope can get airplay on pop radio—and most of those are gone after no more than two albums. Why this discrepancy? There is no single answer, but a big part is that the executives are under enormous pressure to run the label like a business rather than a fan club. Marketing determines the product, whereas as recently as fifteen or twenty years ago, the reverse was true. The trends we've been discussing only add fuel to the fire.

Some observers believe that the way the labels do business creates a closed system. In this view, niche marketing so controls the expectations of consumers that more adventurous, artist-based music would fail in the market anyway. This chicken-and-egg proposition is very intriguing, but it's absurd to think that any major label would embark on a full-scale effort to break the mold. The risks are just too great. Remember that only 4–5 percent of all major label releases so much as break even. No label executive wants to take a chance that the figure will drop even lower—the head that rolls may be his.

If you're an original artist whose music doesn't readily fit into one of the current niches, should you just as well forget about a career? Fortunately, no. First of all, you just might be able to convince a major label to get behind you anyway. As mentioned earlier, the Dave Matthews Band managed to do so, and everyone involved prospered. Second, you *might* be able to change your approach—without making any major compromises—to better fit in to the market picture. If this is unacceptable, you can go DIY or with an independent label. If your music is ahead of the curve, the mass market may catch up in a few years.

We spoke to some artists and songwriters whose music had been acoustically based but had recently began adding hip-hop beats to their songs. They tell us that they do so in response to what they believe radio, record companies, and publishers are looking for. If you think this constitutes selling out, try to understand it from the vantage point of the artist as businessperson. Such decisions are based not on artistic considerations but on the much more down-to-earth ones of money and survival. You can't be sure what you would do in their shoes. Whether these choices obtain the desired result is another question, which can be answered only on a case-by-case basis.

DEMOGRAPHICS AND SPENDING TRENDS

Roughly stated, the record business's version of demographics is as follows:

- The peak years for record-buying are ages fifteen to twenty-four. After this, people have other distractions such as jobs and family.
- From ages twenty-five to thirty four, consumers' interest in new music, and spending on it, gradually diminishes, until by age thirty-five they hardly figure in the market.
- Men and women in the prime music demographic usually like different genres. For instance, men age fifteen to nineteen are the major consumers of rap and hard rock, while women age fifteen to nineteen like dance music and light pop.
- After age thirty-five, people still buy some music but basically just old favorite artists.

This thinking is fairly ingrained in the industry, and as pointed out earlier, demographic markets that are ignored will seem to drop out. So, the thirty-five-and-above crowd does spend less on music than they used to, but is it fair to conclude they just don't care anymore?

The concert market suggests that the answer is no. The older demographic attends concerts in large numbers, so it can't be said they're no longer interested in music. Moreover, it hardly seems plausible that people of, say, the age range of forty to fifty-five have no money to spend on music.

Consider that they're in their peak earning years, buy luxury cars, take expensive vacations, and purchase many other costly consumer goodies.[135]

To an artist, the industry's demographic bias means that if you wish to have a career in the business, you really owe it to yourself to figure out who's going to buy your music and anticipate where the trends are going. Sometimes, the answers are self-evident. For instance, if you're in a young band playing for young kids, you know who your market is. But if, for example, you and your fans are older, you might have to think like an A&R person in order to sell yourself to a record label. Consider other, more established artists whose music bears some similarity to yours and think about which stations in your area play their songs, how those acts promote themselves, and so on.

Thinking like this isn't rocket science, just solid common sense—and it can make a big difference to your career. The label executives and managers we interviewed told us they're favorably impressed by artists who give thought to their career paths. They're looking for partners, not pawns. Industry professionals want to work with a pro-active artist who's as much in charge of his career as he is of his art.

FULL CIRCLE: THE RE-EMERGING LIVE PERFORMER

For most of this book, we've spoken of the music business and the record business as pretty much the same thing. In dollar figures, the record business (and major concert business, which is hooked into it) does in fact dominate the music industry. Though they were always interdependent, the record business grew so fast and so big that most people have come to think of "the record business" as "the music industry."

But for artists, this was not always the case. Up until at least the Swing years of the late 1930s (and more significantly, the rock and roll avalanche of the mid-1950s), selling records was not the major source of income for artists. To be sure, recordings (at least the ones that sold well) were a welcome source of added revenue, but in the main, artists supported themselves not with record royalties, but by personal appearances.

Recordings were, in effect, advertisements for live shows. Up-and-coming stars looked forward to making their breakthrough at the hip nightclub, the famous ballroom, the classy theater, and the prestigious concert hall. Even today, top artists like Barbra Streisand can play two weeks in Las Vegas and earn far more than by selling records. Look at the direction that the record business is headed—with its emphasis on:

- records rather than artists
- hits rather than art
- singles rather than albums
- image rather than substance

- visuals rather than music
- sonic production effects rather than songs

The above list begs the question: Why stake your career on the short-term business judgments of musically ignorant corporate "suits" in a conference room? Going a step further, some observers maintain that the record business as we know it is headed for extinction—and soon. We feel their judgment is premature.

Nevertheless, we also believe artists would do well to look to the pre-rock and roll model of how the music business operated. Artists should be pro-active in building careers that can be maintained without the necessity of major label backing. Today's technology facilitates recording, promotion, and distribution of music, but the one thing that cannot be replaced by computers is the live, mistakes-and-all, human performance. We urge serious, career-minded musicians to look to this "troubadour model" not merely as a way of sustaining viability in an evolving marketplace, but also of maintaining contact with their own reasons for originally seeking a creative career in music.

EMERGING CAREERS

The advent of new technology has expanded the boundaries of the music business and all the entertainment field. In the course of researching and writing this book, we've come across new careers that are outside the traditional ones discussed earlier, offering opportunities that didn't exist just a few years ago. Just as well, since in popular music, there's almost no call for some traditional industry jobs of just a generation ago (notably arrangers and conductors), and according to some musicians, demand for session players is declining.

Some of the emerging fields are so new that, even though they're growing rapidly, there still aren't many participants yet. Most participants have both keyboard skills and computer skills. Further requirements may include composing, producing, and engineering. The growth trend appears to be long term. Here are some examples of new careers:

- *Web site designer with music.* Web sites are multimedia extravaganzas. Especially for larger commercial sites, the budgets are there for music to lend pizzazz to the site.
- *Interactive music provider.* Video games (actually computer games), for instance those marketed by major league sports, contain music to add to the game experience. Storytelling and educational CD-ROMs also have musical accompaniment.
- *Background music creator.* Background music for businesses, including things like the jingles customers listen to while they're on hold, is growing, as business becomes more media savvy.

• *Multimedia musician.* Convention displays and advertising are examples of the musician working together with, say, a graphic designer or copywriter to create presentations to support sales of products and services.

These examples are just a few of the long-term possibilities for which there's already an increasing demand.

The advent of advanced computers and software reduced traditional jobs in some fields, while creating others in the same field. For instance, computers now enable decidedly inartistic individuals to perform some work that formerly required commercial artists; however, there is great demand for trained artists who also can use the sophisticated software to manipulate and create images.

Computer technology affects music in similar fashion. If the newer careers have a common thread, it's that most of the jobs require the musician to think beyond music itself to the larger purposes of the projects involved.[136]

For instance, it isn't just the music that's being sold, it's a CD-ROM with images, text, and music. In the long run, computers may create more opportunities for enterprising people than previous forces in the music business. Here's a word of advice from Tristan des Pres, who writes music for Sony Interactive, a major game maker:

> My musical training is in composition, and I have a lot of hands-on training which led to a deep knowledge of computers. These made me an ideal candidate for this kind of work. Now I'm at a point where I'm consistently being pursued by various game companies and corporate recruiters [to take other jobs]. My advice is, be aware of new technology, combine the creativity of a musician with the tools offered by computers.

Tristan managed to combine two of his passions into marketable skills. Despite some industry trends that seem to narrow or limit opportunity, there are encouraging ones which point to growth.

NOTES

1. A "phonorecord" is whatever medium is used to store a song. Vinyl records, cassette tapes, and compact discs are all examples. So are wax cylinders and piano rolls of earlier years.
2. Distribution includes online distribution such as fee-per-song downloading on Apple's iTunes.
3. As of this writing, new bills are being introduced at the rate of two or three each year, primarily due to panic in the record industry and the relentless efforts of the its lobbyists.
4. The sole exception is the Warner group of labels (formerly of Time Warner), which was "taken private" in 2003 by Edgar Bronfman, Jr., former head of the Seagram's liquor empire. Still, it's run like a multinational corporation.
5. Despite highly publicized illegal downloading and piracy, CD sales are still robust. Total unit sales in 2003 dropped around 3 percent (not nearly so badly as had been predicted), after double-digit declines since 2000.
6. This type of distribution may be changing; see chapter 14, "Changes in the Music Business."
7. For more on this, see "Who's the Boss," later in this chapter, for a discussion of options.
8. Please refer again to "Who's the Boss."
9. Even producers with a reputation for frugality sometimes exceed the initial budget. In which case, the company (kicking and screaming) usually kicks in enough money to finish the project. Whether this is treated as the company's money or another advance (i.e., the artist's money) depends on the bargaining clout of the act.

10. In plain language, mixing is the process of combining the many (24 and up) raw tracks of isolated instruments and vocals into a balanced and seamless whole, with the volume of each "voice" at a correct level relative to the others, having the right stereo image, reverb, and other sonic gloss.

11. Master tapes are the tapes that record the actual performances, on (usually) 24 or more tracks. (Today, many masters are recorded directly to hard drives, not to tapes.) The final stereo version is mixed onto a mixdown tape (or hard drive file). Also, any original recording from which duplicates are made may be referred to as a "master."

12. A new artist who has some bargaining power or great savvy might be able to negotiate for fewer options. This uncommon scenario could result from a bidding war between labels or unusual goodwill between an artist and a label. But the royalty rates for proven acts almost always exceed those of baby acts.

13. Although this can be a sore spot for established artists as well.

14. This is particularly true since 2000. Since then, the industry has contracted, offices have been closed, employees laid off, etc.

15. Occasionally, this cuts the other way—the first to market fails to win acceptance but paves the way for later acts.

16. In such case, an artist usually can get out from under the contract without further ado, but now the act's lost time, lost opportunity, and has been released by the company that signed it—hardly the formula for a running start to re-establish a career.

17. Or an "imprint" or sublabel of a major label.

18. However, in the rap, hip-hop, and dance music genres, the producer may (see chapter 11, "Producer or Engineer").

19. A few indies outgrow this status. Their situation will be discussed later in this chapter.

20. With skilled engineers and producers, some "cheap" gear and studios can achieve results rivaling big studios. But, for the most part, the indie rock sound is simple and minimalist.

21. Alternative rock and hip-hop have become mainstream and now have a strong commercial radio presence. However, the edges have been smoothed out to minimize the abrasive, cutting-edge flavor; "it's all pop now," says one executive.

22. For example, indyMusic.com, IndiSonic.com, musicianassist.com, and evor.com.

23. Zines contain artist interviews, concert reviews, underground comics, gross-out humor, CD/tape reviews, miscellaneous rantings, and advertisements for shows, local band recordings, tattoo parlors, record stores, and the like.

24. "Quite simply, another company finances your production and distributes your products, for either a profit split or a sales commission. It's especially beneficial if the indie uses the saved money to properly promote the release, or if the distribution company can get your product into places you couldn't get into on your own," says indie label head Eric Goodis.

25. This is discussed in greater depth in chapter 14.

26. Presently, the latter is a very big "if."

27. Recording quality will improve with an experienced engineer, of course, but the price goes up. Relatively speaking, it's still cheaper than it's ever been.

28. Viewed in perspective, this is also a reflection of just how much business is out there.

29. Another "ominous trend" was file-sharing—free downloading from Web sites such as Napster (which is no longer free). No one knows for certain whether such downloading hurts CD sales, but the music industry clearly believes it does.

30. This is discussed in chapter 4.

31. In the days when the vinyl record was the prevailing medium, commercial recordings were called "records." The term prevails even though CDs and (decreasingly) cassettes now dominate.

32. Sometimes records that ignore the market sell spectacularly, but this is the exception, not the rule.

33. This can lead to the lament, "They're a great live band, but their records aren't very good."

34. It also makes it not genuinely live.

35. If tracks are recorded with great separation, the singer can redo his part later. See footnote 34.

36. The same basic philosophy goes into mixing and mastering.

37. For hip-hop, it IS the sound. For solo artists, it guarantees total control.

38. In the April 26, 1999, issue.

39. This number of annual releases in 2003 was estimated to be in excess of 33,000.

40. Indie distributors reach deeply into independent record stores.

41. In some cases, of course, there's no choice—the artist is unable to get a deal with a major or independent label anyway.

42. See chapter 14, "The Music Industry in Transition."

43. Just as the self-contained groups of the 1960s (beginning with the Beatles) didn't require as much outside songwriting help. See the next-to-last section of this chapter, "The Songwriter–Band Member."

44. See also chapter 14, "The Music Industry in Transition," for a discussion of emerging careers.

45. The *image* being marketed, however, is that of the singer. The producer is often transparent and anonymous, but a few of today's top production teams have attained star status themselves.

46. As noted in earlier chapters, in dance pop, rap, and hip-hop, where samples and loops have become the norm, the input of actual players is often diminished or non-existent.

47. Still, plenty of male artists get hair transplants, dental caps, and more.

48. June 7, 1999, issue. We changed the contact information for the management company.

49. Handsome but modestly talented male country singers commonly are referred to in the industry as "hat acts."

50. Rather than by capturing live performances of musicians, which was the origin of recording.

51. The exception here would be the artist who's also a brilliant (and objective) producer, but there are very few of these.

52. A solo artist who also is a staff writer might be considered an employee but that would depend heavily on the specific contractual arrangement.

53. Sometimes postgroup careers flourish, but such cases are the exception.

54. Yes, we know Fleetwood Mac made their most artistically and commercially successful albums when various members were romantically involved or breaking up. In their unique case, the group members managed to channel very intense personal disappointment into a spirit of cooperation. This isn't recommended for your band.

55. Or, for example, a group may form a corporation in which each of four members owns 25 percent of the stock shares. Full discussion of the legal distinctions between corporations and partnerships is beyond the scope of this book.

56. In 1999, the Associated Press quoted Carl Gardner, an original member of the Coasters, complaining about the unauthorized name appropriation by "knockoff" groups: "These guys are making like they're the real Coasters. They're in their twenties and thirties, and I'm seventy years old." Gardner supports a strengthening of trademark law.

57. In overall concept, service marks are comparable to copyright. In practice, they have their own special set of rules.

58. With the possible exception of publishing, as noted in the previous section "Group Leaders."

59. Everyone in this account shall remain nameless.

60. Distinctions between "classical" and "popular" music have been accentuated in the twentieth century. In the era of the great composers, what we now call classical music *was* the popular music.

61. While albums still are released, increasingly they are collections of singles rather than coherent artistic statements. The reasons for this are disputed and a discussion is beyond the scope of this book.

62. Credits for session musicians almost never appeared prior to 1973. In that year, under pressure from the musicians' union, this changed; credits now are required.

63. This occurred in the late 1970s and early 1980s.

64. One author of this book in fact had a producer switch on his bass.

65. And for much other work, such as major label recording sessions and live network television.

66. That the market for union studio musicians is not growing does not help their bargaining position. This point will be covered in more depth in "Changes in the Session Scene," two sections ahead.

67. This can lead to copyright infringement problems. In the early days of sampling, users sometimes "stole" samples without crediting or paying the copyright holder. Now, permission and payment are the norm. See chapter 1.

68. Although, by and large, this is not true in the country capital, Nashville.

69. Or hard drive; as earlier noted, many original masters entirely bypass tape as a medium.

70. Some directors have been known to write scripts and act in their films, but it's the exception, not the rule. Similarly, and as noted earlier, producers sometimes write music and play on recordings, particularly in the dance, hip-hop, and rap genres.

71. A small number of major artists have learned to produce themselves, but it's rare to see an album credit with the artist as sole producer, if only because second opinions are so important.

72. Some examples are rap, grunge, and heavy metal. Of course, as the genre with which he's identified cools down, the "my sound" producer generally does, too.

73. Not surprisingly, this group of producers includes many producer-engineers.

74. For self-evident reasons, this issue isn't as relevant in producer-driven pop.

75. The artist signs an agreement not only to pay the producer, but to authorize the label to pay that producer directly, out of the artist's royalties.

76. He almost always consents; but reread the comments of Laurent Besançon in the body of the paragraph.

77. A similar role is played in a live concert setting; the person who mikes the stage and runs the mixing board is called the "sound man," a job not within the scope of this book.

78. Examples of outboard gear are reverberation chamber emulators (reverbs), digital delays, and other signal-processing units to enhance and alter recorded sounds. In the case of direct-to-hard-drive recording, digital plug-ins are employed in place of outboard gear. Plug-ins allow signal processing in the computer, obviating the need for outboard gear.

79. Or hard drive, if tape isn't used as the initial tracking medium.
80. With digital recording, this mixing board often appears on a computer screen and is manipulated by a mouse.
81. This process is followed even where plug-ins are used.
82. Various versions can be made. For instance, there might be a rough mix with backing vocals and one without.
83. Equalization is the balance of bass, treble, and midrange of an instrument or voice.
84. Mastering, the final preparation of a recording for commercial duplication, also is an engineering function. As it is more technical than creative and a smaller part of the process, mastering is not within the scope of discussion here.
85. In some cases, they can cut their rates even further because their studios are located in their homes, so they don't have as much overhead as studios that pay rent.
86. In Los Angeles, a major music center, zoning regulations prohibit businesses in residential areas. By getting the zoning authorities involved, commercial studios were able to severely curtail home studio operations.
87. Exception: If you're lucky enough to stick around in the business for a really long time, the self-selection process results in your shows being attended primarily by die-hard fans for whom you can do no wrong. They'll love you for just showing up. Still, that's no reason to make less of an effort than you made in earlier days.
88. It's been said that writing about music is like dancing to architecture.
89. This is equally true for bios posted on Internet sites.
90. If, for example, you are a recording engineer, here's a place you can save money.
91. Web site photos may be color. However, hard copies you send out should conform to the B&W standard.
92. Some acts post on their Web sites partial MP3s of an entire album's worth of songs (ten, for example). If you're using the site as a promotional tool, we recommend sticking with three songs you judge to be the most accessible.
93. For that matter, so should everything in your promo package.
94. Include your Web site and e-mail information as applicable.
95. This rule of thumb applies to Web sites too.
96. For the importance of delivering the goods live, see "Performance," the first section in this chapter.
97. See "Smoke and Mirrors," the preceding section.
98. May 9, 1999.
99. Interchangeably referred to as "attorneys."
100. Also known as "personal managers."
101. In politics, this opportunity is called "access."

102. Most larger firms have a computer program and database to reveal conflicts.

103. In many states, booking shows requires an employment agent's license, which most managers don't have.

104. In California, you have to be licensed by the Department of Motor Vehicles to sell cars, but anyone can claim to be a music manager and go after business. Go figure.

105. Also referred to here as "CPAs" (certified public accountants). Although noncertified accountants exist in some states, stick with CPAs. They've completed rigorous educational, testing, and apprenticeship requirements.

106. Recording Industry Association of America.

107. The deterrent effects of these actions are highly debated; moreover, some observers argue that the extra sales generated from exposure gained by downloading more than compensate for piracy losses.

108. Other programs exist, but presently MP3 is the most prominent.

109. CD sales in the fourth quarter of 2003 were actually higher than in the corresponding period of 2002. This was the first gain in a long time, and the industry claims that the anti-downloading suits were the reason. No one really knows—maybe it's because consumers liked 2003's product better than 2002's.

110. The case went to the U.S. Supreme Court, where in 1908 the publishers lost (*White-Smith Music Pub. Co. v. Apollo Co.*). Not to worry, they must have had a good lobbyist: the Copyright Act of 1909 explicitly created "mechanical" rights to, in essence, reverse the case.

111. The first and for a while, the only performing rights society (see chapter 2.)

112. Either on their computers or on portable MP3 players.

113. Discussed in articles like "Death of the Album," USA *Today*, December 5, 2003.

114. For instance, Wherehouse filed for Chapter 11 bankruptcy protection in 2003 and closed over 120 stores. Tower Records, another large chain, considered filing Chapter 11 bankruptcy proceedings in 2001, then put itself up for sale in 2003. There were no takers and, in early 2004, Tower filed.

115. As reported in the *New York Times* (Sept. 4, 2003), Universal Music Group, the world's largest record company, cut wholesale CD prices to $9.09 from $12.02, with corresponding reductions in retail prices.

116. At least in "real time."

117. CD Baby is the most prominent site of its type. By referring to it generically, we also refer to similar sites.

118. For example, independent music purveyor Cornerband.com partners with Kazaa, one of the prominent "PTP download" sites which the RIAA has been unable to shut down via legal action.

119. They weren't saints. Music lovers or not, some of them robbed their acts blind.
120. Many observers feel this trend is killing off the album format in favor of singles. Ironically, the recent emphasis on singles is often partly blamed for poor sales performance by the majors.
121. As quoted in the *Chicago Tribune* (June 7, 1999).
122. Radio is discussed in the next sections of this chapter.
123. Recall that, due to broadcast spectrum limitations, the Federal Communications Commission can license a relatively small, fixed number of stations in a given geographic market. Radio isn't like the newspaper business, where you always can start another paper, no questions asked.
124. June 7, 1999, issue.
125. The petition was called RM-9242.
126. Of San Antonio, Texas.
127. Part of New York–based Viacom, which owns CBS, MTV, Showtime, Country Music Television, Comedy Central, Nickelodeon, VH1, BET, Blockbuster Video, etc.
128. Headquartered in North Carolina.
129. 102.1 is the only arguable exception.
130. This structure is employed to avoid paying stations directly to play records without revealing the "spin" was paid for by the company, which is illegal "payola." For more on this system, see Eric Boehlart's March 14, 2001 *Salon* article, "Pay for Play".
131. While San Diego is our example, its radio market is typical.
132. In the March 3, 2003 issue of *Fortune*, Clear Channnel CEO Lowry Mays stated: "If anyone said we were in the radio business, it wouldn't be someone from our company…We're not in the business of providing news and information. We're not in the business of providing well-researched music. We're simply in the business of selling our customers products."
133. So far, the NAB has managed to get Congress to pass legislation which requires Webcasting royalties that are too expensive for start-ups, effectively precluding competition.
134. More accurately, radio stations sell ad time. The music they play is the "advertising" to keep people tuned in.
135. As an aside, we think the industry is overlooking a potential gold mine.
136. In some ways, what goes around comes around, because advertising jingles and film scoring have always required this sensitivity.

INDEX

accountants, 219n105
advice from, 186, 187
  compatibility of, 186
  compensation of, 186
  competency of, 186
  conflict-of-interest, 187
  duties of, 173, 185–187
  finding, 187
  specialization of, 186
  taxes, 186
ADA, 73
adaptability, 170–171
administration deal, 22
advances, 31–32, 40
Aerosmith, 120
AFM. See American Federation of Musicians
agents
  cheating by, v
  compensation of, 185
  duties of, 173, 184–185
album oriented rock (AOR), 129
"all rights reserved," 10
Allen, Andy, 73
alternative music, 43–44, 53, 214n21
alternative rock, 43–44, 46, 51–52
A&M, 200
American Federation of Musicians (AFM),
  138–139, 217n65
Andreone, Leah, 105, 110–111, 113
Anka, Paul, 100
AOR. See album oriented rock
A&R representatives, 30, 37, 39, 40, 107
Arlen, Harold, 92
arrangers, vii
art, v. business, 64
artistic control, 61–62
artwork, and layout, 68–69
ASCAP, 19, 20, 21, 23, 25, 193, 219n111
Aucoin, Bill, 184

baby-act, 35, 87, 214n12
back catalog, 16
background music creator, 211
band names. See also group acts
  importance of, 123–124
  ownership of, 123–124, 174

Batteau, David, 93–94
The Beach Boys, 127
The Beatles, 92, 100–101, 117, 118
Berlin, Irving, 91
Berry, Chuck, 117
Besençon, Laurent, 149–150
Beyoncé, 129
"biography" (bio), 162–163
Blondie, 123
BMG, 193, 200
BMI. See Broadcast Music, Inc.
bootlegging. See piracy
breakage, 175
breakeven point, 33
British Invasion, 60
broadcast industry, vi
Broadcast Music, Inc. (BMI), 19, 20, 21,
  23, 25, 194
Brown, James, 128
budget, 34, 213n9
business managers, 173, 187–188
Butler, Jonathan, 93
"buzz," 167–168, 174
The Byrds, 117, 127

cable radio, 207
career, v, 160
  emerging, 211–212
  objectives, 62
  paths, vii–viii, 198–199
Cargo Records, 54
CD Baby, 199, 219n117
CDbaby.com, 70, 198
Chicago, 125
choice, 65, 67–68. See also do-it-yourself
classic rock, 60
Clear Channel Communications, 85, 205, 206,
  220n126
The Coasters, 123
college radio, 207
commercial radio
  alternatives to, 207
  centralization of, 204
  concentration of power in, 202–203,
    220n123

conglomerates in, 203
   demographics, 206–207, 208
   fragmented markets on, 207–209
   major label connections to, 206,
     220n130
   motives of, 206–207, 220n132
   niche marketing on, 205–207, 208
   overlapping programming, 205–206
   "real," 203–204
   typical market of, 205–206
   "virtual," 203–205
   commercially satisfactory, 35, 214n13
   compulsory license, 5, 13, 17, 18, 25
   compulsory rate, 18
   concert business, vi
   conductors, vii
   conflict of interest, 178
Constitution, U.S., 4, 13
contracts, 174–175
Cooke, Sam, 100
copublishing, 22–23, 25
copyright, vi, 3–4, 13
   administration, 16, 25
   "all rights reserved," 10
   assignment, 16–17
   benefit of, 13
   current law, 12–13, 17, 18, 19, 20–21,
     23–24, 25
   duration of, 11
   eligibility, 6
   infringement, 5, 6, 8, 9, 11–12, 16, 193,
     217n67
   intellectual property, 3–4
   "made for hire," 10–11
   nature of, 4
   notice, 9–10, 12, 13
   official date of, 8
   origins of, 4
   ownership of, 5, 10–11, 16
   "poor man's," 12, 13
   registration of, 4, 6, 7, 8–9, 16
   renewal, 11
   rights of, 7
   as symbol ©, 9, 12, 13
   U.S. Office of, 8–9, 12, 13, 18
Cornerband.com, 219n118
Costco, 196
CPAs. *See* accountants
Creedence Clearwater Revival, 123
Crespo, Jimmy, 120, 133, 137, 140

Dave Matthews Band, 75, 127, 129, 208, 209
deal points, 35
DeBlasio, Ron, 114–115
demo, 100, 165–166, 218n92. *See also*
   do-it-yourself
demo shopping, 177
demographics, 191, 206, 208, 209–210
des Pres, Josquin, 135
des Pres, Tristan, 212
DiFranco, Ani, 63, 64, 71, 73, 74, 75, 113

Digital Millennium Copyright Act (DMCA),
   24, 213n3
digital music, 194–195
digital recording, 57–59
digital rights management (DRM), 193
direct distribution, 70–71. *See also*
   do-it-yourself
direct license, 18
direct sales, 72
disc jockeys (DJs), vii
distribution, 17, 18, 30, 37–38, 40, 45,
   69–70, 74–75, 213n2. *See also*
   do-it-yourself
DIY. *See* do-it-yourself
DJ. *See* disc jockeys
DMCA. *See* Digital Millennium
   Copyright Act
do-it-yourself (DIY), 29, 57–75, 113, 165
   advantages of, 58
   art v. business in, 64
   artistic control in, 61–62, 73
   artwork/layout for, 68–69
   budgeting, 65, 67, 68
   career plan for, 198
   challenges in, 65
   choice of material in, 65
   choosing engineer for, 66–67
   choosing producer for, 67–68
   choosing studio for, 66–67
   cost of, 58, 215n27
   decision making in, 64–65
   demographics in, 71
   distribution for, 69–71, 74–75
   geographics in, 71
   lining up talent for, 65
   majors v., 73–75
   manufacturing for, 68
   market factors in, 71–72
   perception of, 63
   performance and, 72
   profit in, 63
   promotion and, 72, 74–75, 79
   punk revolution and, 60–61
   reasons to, 59–60
   recording, 64–69
   royalties and, 73
   samples/loops in, 69
   statistics in, 71
   stepping stone of, 75
   studio v. live for, 66
   tradeoffs for, 73–74
   trends toward, 59–60, 215n29
   vanity of, 62–63
Dolan, Mary, 78, 105, 109, 112
downloading, 24
The Drifters, 123
DRM. *See* digital rights management
Dylan, Bob, 91

The **E** *Street Band*, 127
The Eagles, 92, 128

Elfman, Danny, 102
EMI, 200
engineers. *See also* do-it-yourself
  apprentice, 153
  assistant, 153, 154
  choosing, 66–67
  compensation of, 153–154, 218n85
  definition of, 150, 217n77, 218n84
  equipment of, 150–151, 155, 217n77
  home studio, 154, 218n86
  independence of, 153
  mixing, 151–153
  musical background of, 155
  ProTools, 152
  synchronization, 151
  tracking, 150–151
  training of, 154–155
evor.com, 214n22
exclusive rights, 4, 5, 13, 17, 19

fair use, 5, 13
Fairness in Music Licensing Act, 20–21
fanzines, 49, 50, 61, 74, 214n23
Federal Communications Commission
  (FCC), 204–205
Felder, Don, 92
50 Cent, 129
file sharing, 24, 25, 192, 194–195, 215n29,
  219n107
first use, 17, 18
Fishkin, Paul, 50, 53, 54, 59, 117
fixed, tangible form, 7, 13
flat fees, 23, 25
Fleetwood Mac, 124, 128, 216n54
Flohr, Bruce, 61, 200
Folk Alliance, 113
foreign licensing, 23, 25
foreign rights, 23
free goods, 17

Geffen, 200
Generation X, 43
"getting dropped," 32, 213n8
Gibson, Rod, 81–82, 83
Goodis, Eric, 54–55, 215n24
The Greyboy Allstars, 61, 62
Greyboy Records, 61
group acts, 117–129
  advantages of, 117
  band name importance for, 123–124,
    216n56
  compatibility within, 117–119, 216n54
  day to day life of, 128
  decline of, 128–129
  disadvantages of, 117
  image/appearance of, 126–127
  income sources for, 128
  leaders of, 119–121
  moneys divided within, 122, 125–126,
    128
  musical chemistry within, 117–119

partnership agreements within, 121–123,
    179, 216n55
  personal chemistry within, 117–119
  pigeonholing of, 126–127
  pressures on, 119
  responsibilities of, 121
  roles within, 120–121, 128
  star among, 126–127
  training for, 127–128
  unique sound for, 127
group dynamics, 101, 106
Guitar World, 64
Guns and Roses, 127

Harburg, E.Y., 92
Harrison, Nigel, 123
Harry Fox Agency, Inc., 19
headliner, 82
Heart, 127
Henley, Don, 92
hit song, 92–93
Holder, Mitch, 131–132, 133, 138, 139,
  140, 141, 142
Holly, Buddy, 117
hook, 92–93
Hootie and the Blowfish, 75

Idol, Billy, 184
income, 23
independent music sites, 199, 219n118
independent radio, 49–50, 215n30
independent record labels, 29, 38, 43–55.
  See also do-it-yourself (DIY)
  advantages of, 47–48
  expectations of, 53
  future of, 55
  high-water mark of, 52
  incentive toward, 54
  joint release with, 52
  majors' effect on, 53–54
  mind set of, 50–52
  operation of, 52–53
  opportunities of, 202
  philosophy of, 47–48
  promotion by, 49–50
  rise of, 45–46, 59, 60
  staff duties of, 46–47
  trend spotting in, 202
  trends toward, 47–48, 59–60, 215n29
  underground network, 48–49, 61, 64
indie. *See* independent record labels
indie rock, 43, 48
IndiSonic.com, 214n22
indyMusic.com, 214n22
Infante, Frank, 123
Infinity Broadcasting, 205, 220n127
infringement of copyright, 5, 6, 8, 9, 11–12,
  217n67
in-house, 29, 39
in-kind marketing expenses, 38
in-stores, 74

intellectual property, 3–4
interactive music provider, 211
Internet, 13, 24, 26, 38, 48, 49, 50, 61,
    70–71, 74, 87, 192–199, 202–203, 207,
    218n89, 220n133
Island, 200
iTunes, 196

Jefferson Airplane (Starship), 123
Jefferson-Pilot Communications, 205, 220n128
John, Elton, 92, 128
Johnson, Deborah Liv, 72, 73, 75, 79,
    110, 113
joint release, 52

Kaye, Carol, 132, 134
Kazaa, 219n118
Kiss, 184

lawyers
    access through, 177
    business advice from, 177
    compatibility with, 178
    competency of, 177–178
    conflict of interest with, 178
    contracts, 174–175
    copyright services, 176
    demo shopping, 177, 218n101
    duties of, 173, 174–177
    finding, 177–178
    immigration services, 176
    intellectual property, 176
    lawsuits, 175
    negotiation, 176
    non legal functions of, 176–177, 187
    specialization among, 176
    trademark services, 176
    trust and, 178
    when to hire, 178–179
Led Zeppelin, 128
Lennon, John, 92, 118
Lewis, Jerry Lee, 117
license, 16
    compulsory, 5, 13, 17, 18, 25
    direct, 18
    fee, 19, 21, 24, 25
    foreign, 23, 25
literary work, 7
live performer, rebirth of, 210–211
low-fi, 43, 44–45, 46, 214n20
low-power FM (LPFM), 204–205, 207
Lynyrd Skynyrd, 81

"**m**ade for hire," 10–11
major record labels, 29–41. *See also*
    do-it-yourself
    adaptability of, 198
    advantages of, 54–55, 74
    artistic control with, 61–62
    bottom-line mentality of, 201
    changes to, 55, 191

commercial radio connections to, 206,
    220n130
    competition with, 197
    consolidation of power in, 191, 200–202
    decline of, 195–197, 211
    demographics, 209–210
    departments in, 46
    do-it-yourself v., 73–75
    future of, 197–198, 210–211
    "getting dropped" from, 32
    investment in new acts of, 200
    joint release with, 52
    manipulation by, 201
    mind set of, 50–56
    new partnership model of, 39, 41
    number of, 200
    obligations of, 37, 214n16
    options, 35, 40
    organization of, 29–30
    risk aversion of, 208
    shortcomings of, 31
    signing with, 31–32, 149–150
managers, 179, 219n103
    access of, 182
    artistic sense of, 184
    big-picture view of, 179, 180–181
    business sense of, 179, 184
    changing, 183
    cheating by, v
    clout of, 179
    commissions, 181–182
    compensation of, 181–182
    conflicts of interest, 183, 184
    contract with, 183
    duties of, 22, 79–80, 81, 83, 106, 113, 173,
        180–181, 187
    effectiveness of, 183
    family model of, 179
    finding, 183–184
    incentives to, 181–182
    irony of, 182
    marketing, 179
    outgrowing, 183
    power of, 182
    referrals for, 183
    relating to, 184
    reputation of, 179
    requirements to be, 182, 218n104
    respect of, 179
    selling yourself to, 183–184
    training of, 182–183
    trust of, 179
Manilow, Barry, 102
manufacture and distribution, 17, 18, 25,
    68–69, 213n2
market factors, 71–72. *See also* do-it-yourself
market research, 206
marketing, 30, 37–38, 39, 40, 64, 71, 107,
    160
master tapes, 35, 214n11
mastering, 35, 218n84

Mathias, John, 148, 154
Mattox, John, 120
Mays, Lowry, 220n132
McCartney, Paul, 92, 118
McGuinn, Roger, 117
mechanical rights, 19
"mechanical rights organization," 19
mechanical royalties, 5, 17–19, 23–24,
    25, 115
Mercury, 200
MIDI. See musical instrument
    digital interface
Midwest Television, Inc., 205
Mitchell, Joni, 91, 128
mixing, 34, 151–153, 214n10
Moby, 201, 208
Motown, 200
MP3 files, 194
MP3.com, 192, 195
multimedia musician, 212
multinational conglomerates, 29, 39, 213n4
multitracking, 66
Music Connection, 73, 108, 203
music contractor, 138
music industry, vi
    changes to, 191–212
    contraction of, vi, 197–198
    future of, 197–198
music publishing business, vi
musical instrument digital interface
    (MIDI), 141
musical works, 6, 13
musicianasst.com, 214n22

Najor, Zachary, 61, 62
Napster, 192–193, 194, 195, 196
National Association of Broadcasters
    (NAB), 204– 205, 207
The Neptunes, 102
networking, 169–170
new partnership model, 39, 41
Nirvana, 55

online transmission, 12–13
opening act, 82
originality, 6
overcommercialization, 83
overdubbing, 66

payola, 37–38
peer-to-peer (PTP), 24, 193, 219n118
performance
    advertising and, 160
    royalties, 19–21, 23, 24, 25, 80, 115
performing rights organizations, 19,
    20, 23, 25
Perkins, Carl, 100
Phish, 129
phonorecords, 5, 13, 17, 25, 213n1
Pink Floyd, 128
piracy, 24, 39, 192, 193, 197

The Platters, 123
plugging, 15
Polygram, 200
"poor man's copyright," 12, 13
Porter, Cole, 91
press kit, 166–167
pressing and distribution deal, 52, 215n24
"producer switch," 135–136
producers, 112–113. See also do-it-yourself
    advances for, 148–149
    arrangers and, 147
    artist as, 146–147
    choosing, 67–68
    compensation of, 148–149, 217n75
    deals for, 149–150
    definition of, 143–146
    engineering background of, 146, 217n73
    history of, 144
    musicality of, 145, 147
    "points" for, 148, 149
    producer-driven pop and, 146–147
    psychologist, 147–148
    responsibilities of, 144
    song doctor, 147
    technology and, 144, 146
production manager, 81
professional help
    accountants, 173, 185–187, 219n105
    agents, 173, 184–185
    business managers, 173, 187–188
    lawyers, 173–179
    managers, 173, 179–184
    publicists, 173, 187
    solo artist and, 113
professionalism, 161–162
promotion, 30, 37–38, 49–50, 72, 74–75, 79,
    81, 161, 162–163
promotion (promo) package, 162–166, 169
ProTools, 152
PTP. See peer-to-peer
public domain, 4
publicists, 173, 187
publisher, 15–16, 94–96
publisher's share, 16, 20, 25
publishing, 15–26. See also royalties
    contract, 15, 18, 94
    copublishing, 22–23, 25
    defined, 25
    mechanics of, 16–17
    rights, 23–24, 94, 95, 98, 99, 100, 149
    self, 21–22, 25
    subpublishing, 23, 25
punk revolution, 60–61
pure profit sharing, 54

radio, 207. See also commercial radio;
    independent radio
"radio-friendly," 34
Raitt, Bonnie, 93
The Record Plant, 154
record sales, 197

record stores, 195–197, 219n114
recording
    budget, 34, 213n9
    control of, 35
    process of, 34–35
    timing of, 36–37
    tracking, 34
recording industry, vi, 200–202
Recording Industry Association of America
    (RIAA), 192, 193, 194, 219n106,
    219n118
recoupment, 31–32, 40, 80, 149
registration, 4, 6, 7, 13, 15
    advisability of, 11–12
    fee, 8, 11
    form PA, 8
    form SR, 8
    how to, 8–9
    requirements, 8–9
reputation
    adaptability and, 170–171
    attitude and, 159
    audience response building, 160–161
    "biography" (bio) and, 162–163
    "buzz" and, 167–168
    competence and, 168–169
    courtesy and, 169
    demo and, 165–166, 218n92
    familiarity and, 168–169
    importance of, 159–160
    networking and, 169–170
    overproduction and, 166
    performance building, 160–162
    personality and, 168–169
    press kit and, 166–167
    professionalism and, 161–162
    promotion package and, 162–163, 169,
        218n93
    publicity photos for, 163–164
responsibility and, 169
résumé and, 162
    stagecraft and, 161–162
résumé, 162
RIAA. See Recording Industry Association
    of America
Richard, Little, 100, 117
Righteous Babe Records, 63, 71, 75
rights
    changes in, 23–24
    copyright, 6
    exclusive, 4, 5, 13, 17, 19
    foreign, 23
    publishing, 23–24, 94, 95, 98, 99, 100, 149
    synchronization, 23, 25, 115
road manager, 81
The Rolling Stones, 127, 128
Rosenblatt, Michael, 203
royalties, 3–4. See also do-it-yourself
    changes to, 20–21
    do-it-yourself and, 73
    equation for, 32

limits on, 20–21, 35
    mechanical, 5, 17–19, 23, 54, 115
    performance, 19–21, 23, 24, 25, 80 115
    publishing, vi, 6, 7, 15, 16, 21–25, 54, 94,
        95, 101, 149, 192, 217n75
    real and imagined, 32–33, 73
    recoupment, 31–32, 80, 94, 95
    reductions of, 32–33
    right to receive, 8
Rudolph, Barry, 155

Sam Goody, 196
sampling. See also do-it-yourself
    royalty, 19–20
    technology, 6, 69, 92, 111, 141–142,
        216n46, 217n67
Scheff, Jason, 125
Seattle sound, 51
Secure Digital Music Initiative (SDMI),
    193
self producing, 33–34, 67
self publishing, 21–22, 25, 62–63
selling yourself, 96–97
service mark, 124, 216n57
SESAC, 19, 20, 21, 23, 25
session musician, 131–142
    adaptability of, 136
    attitude of, 136–138
    breaking in as, 139–140
    career longevity of, 137–138
    changes for, 140–142
    compensation for, 138–139
    contract for, 138
    credit for, 131, 134, 217n62
    definition of, 131
    music notation reading for, 132–133
    passion of, 132
    rate of pay for, 138–139
    royalties for, 139, 217n66
    scale for, 138–139
    Special Payment Fund for, 137–138
    specialization of, 133–134, 137–138
    tools of, 134–135
    union for, 138–139
    versatility of, 133–134
    work ethic, 136–137
session musicians
    competition among, 137
    demand for, 142
    MIDI and, 141–142
    "producer switch" and, 135–136
    sampling and, 141–142
SFX Entertainment, 85–87
sheet music, 23, 25
signing
    advance for, 31–32
    deal points, 35
    options, 35, 40
    realities of, 33–34
Simon, Paul, 91
singer-songwriter, 99–100

solo artist, 103–115
    age and, 108–109
    choice to become, 104–105
    day in life of, 113–115
    demands of, 114–115
    image of, 106
    income of, 115
    look of, 107–108
    presentation of, 109–110
    producer of, 112–113
    production/engineering for, 111
    professional help for, 113
    team behind, 103–104
    training for, 110–111
songwriter, 91–102
    band member and, 100–102
    becoming a, 96–97
    business of, 97–98
    conflicts for, 95–96
    contract for, 95
    decline of, 97
    independent, 98–99
    opportunities for, 102
    process for, 93–94
    singer-, 99–100
    skills of, 92–94
    staff, 94–96
    types of, 91–92
Sonny Bono Term Extension Act, 11, 21
Sony, 200
Sony Interactive, 212
sound recordings, 6, 8, 13
Special Payments Fund, 139
spending trends, 209–210
Spevak, Brian, 48, 50, 51, 52, 54
sponsorship
    advantages of, 82
    disadvantages of, 83
Springsteen, Bruce, 127
stagecraft, 161–162
statutory rate, 17, 18, 25
Steely Dan, 127
Sting, 91
"stolen" song, 11–12
Streisand, Barbra, 210
studio, 66. See also do-it-yourself
subpublishing, 23, 25
synchronization rights, 23, 25, 115

talent scout, 30
Talking Heads, 123
Taupin, Bernie, 92
technology
    changes brought on by, 191, 211–212
    low cost, 45–46
    piracy and, 192
    publishing rights changing with new,
        23–24
    sampling, 6, 69, 92, 111, 141–142,
        216n46, 217n67
Thorpe, 167, 168

ticket prices, 85
Time-Warner, 200
Top 40, vi
tour accountant, 81
touring season, 80
tours, 77–88. See also SFX Entertainment
    accountant for, 81
    changes to, 191
    club or coffeehouse, 78–79
    cost of, 80
    headliner, 82
    history of, 77
    importance of, 88
    industry of, 85–87
    longevity through, 87–88
    major venue, 80–81
    objectives of, 78, 79
    opening act, 82
    pay for, 78
    production manager for, 81
    realities of, 83
    reasons for, 81–82
    rewards of, 84
    road crews for, 79–80
    road manager for, 81
    season for, 80
    sponsorship for, 82–83
    support on, 79
    theater or mid-level, 79–80
    ticket prices for, 85
    types of, 77–78
Tower Records, 196, 219n114
tracking, 34
trademarks, 3
"troubadour model," 211
Twain, Shania, 129
Tyler, Steven, 120

underground network, 48–49, 50, 52,
    64, 78, 214n22
Universal Music Group (UMG), 200

Vans Warped Tour, 82–83
voice problems, 111

Wal-Mart, 196
Warner Music, 200
Web site designer, 211
Web sites, 169, 218n95
Webcast, 107, 220n133
webcaster, 24
Wherehouse, 196, 219n114
Wikso, Ron, 137, 140
Williams, Pepper, 105, 110
writer's share, 16, 20, 25

Young Dubliners, 120
"your publishing," 21–22

zines. See fanzines

CANBY PUBLIC LIBRARY
292 N. HOLLY
CANBY, OR 97013

Books from Allworth Press

Allworth Press is an imprint of Allworth Communications, Inc. Selected titles are listed below.

Making It in the Music Business: The Business and Legal Guide for Songwriters and Performers, Third Edition
by Lee Wilson (paperback, 6 × 9, 256 pages, $19.95)

Making and Marketing Music: The Musician's Guide to Financing, Distributing, and Promoting Albums, Second Edition
by Jodi Summers (paperback, 6 × 9, 240 pages, $19.95)

Career Solutions for Creative People: How to Balance Artistic Goals with Career Security
by Dr. Ronda Ormont (paperback, 6 × 9, 320 pages, $19.95)

Gigging: A Practical Guide for Musicians
by Patricia Shih (paperback, 6 × 9, 256 pages, $19.95)

The Quotable Musician: From Bach to Tupac
by Sheila E. Anderson (hardcover, 7½ × 7½, 224 pages, $19.95)

The Secrets of Songwriting: Leading Songwriters Reveal How to Find Inspiration and Success
by Susan Tucker (paperback, 6 × 9, 256 pages, $19.95)

The Art of Writing Great Lyrics
by Pamela Phillips Oland (paperback, 6 × 9, 272 pages, $18.95)

How to Pitch and Promote Your Songs, Third Edition
by Fred Koller (paperback, 6 × 9, 208 pages, $19.95)

The Songwriter's and Musician's Guide to Nashville, Third Edition
by Sherry Bond (paperback, 6 × 9, 256 pages, $19.95)

Moving Up in the Music Business
by Jodi Summers (paperback, 6 × 9, 224 pages, $18.95)

Profiting from Your Music and Sound Project Studio
by Jeffrey Fisher (paperback, 6 × 9, 288 pages, $18.95)

Rock Star 101: A Rock Star's Guide to Survival and Success in the Music Business
by Marc Ferrari (paperback, 5½ × 8½, 176 pages, $14.95)

Please write to request our free catalog. To order by credit card, call 1-800-491-2808 or send a check or money order to Allworth Press, 10 East 23rd Street, Suite 510, New York, NY 10010. Include $5 for shipping and handling for the first book ordered and $1 for each additional book. Ten dollars plus $1 for each additional book if ordering from Canada. New York State residents must add sales tax.

To see our complete catalog on the World Wide Web, or to order online, you can find us at *www.allworth.com*.